SHIV SENA WOMEN

For my niece, Ishika,
'Tumi ushaar shonar bindu ...'

ATREYEE SEN

Shiv Sena Women
Violence and Communalism
in a Bombay Slum

INDIANA UNIVERSITY PRESS
BLOOMINGTON AND INDIANAPOLIS

This book is a publication of

Indiana University Press
601 North Morton Street
Bloomington, Indiana 47404-3797 USA

http://iupress.indiana.edu

Telephone orders   800-842-6796
Fax orders   812-855-7931
Orders by e-mail   iuporder@indiana.edu

First published in the United Kingdom by C. Hurst & Co. (Publishers) Ltd.

© 2007 by Atreyee Sen

Printed in India

Cataloging information is available from the Library of Congress.

ISBN 978-0-253-34962-0 (cl.); 978-0-253-21941-1 (pbk.)

1 2 3 4 5 12 11 10 09 08 07

CONTENTS

ACKNOWLEDGEMENTS

This long research journey has been enriched by people who shaped my thoughts and, at times, changed the course of my life. I am privileged to acknowledge their contributions along the way.

Foremost, I thank the Felix Foundation for offering me a three-year scholarship to pursue a PhD at the School of Oriental and African Studies (SOAS), University of London. This book is a revised version of my doctoral dissertation. I am also deeply grateful to several other funding bodies – the Central Research Fund (University of London), Professional Classes Aid Council, Gilchrist Educational Trust, Ernest Cassell Educational Trust, Newby Trust, Northbrook Society, Leche Trust, the British Academy and the Charles Wallace India Trust – for offering me research, maintenance and travel grants.

I am indebted to devoted friends and family members without whose presence in my life this monograph would not have been completed: my paternal and maternal grandparents, for magical memories; my parents, for keeping my nest; an incredible sister, for fighting my battles along with her own; my niece, Ishika, for being a humorous pal; Lizzie and Pablo, for never taking me seriously; Andrew, for being delightful and obnoxious; Krishna and Gopa, for support and shelter; Urvi and Bappa, for food and frivolity; Rubina and Vasudha, for cheering me on; Shumona, for holding my hand through the years; the Osellas, for being my surrogate family in East Sussex; fellow PhD students, especially Keiko, Alyson, Deboshruti, James and Helen, who shared their isolation and ideas with me; Shahpar, for a long history of conversations; several friends from my school, university and professional life in Calcutta, Delhi and London, for unconditional love; Nilanjan, *je ne sais quoi*, a travel mate, a motivating companion and so much more.

In my field, I wish to thank Bobby and Shibba for their warm hospitality; the activists, academics and journalists, especially Sainath, Vaibhav and Phadke, for their guidance; the members of various NGOs, the police officials and firemen who took time off to give me valuable advice; all the members of the Tata Institute of Social Sciences, the Nirmala Niketan Institute of Social Work, the Centre for Education and Documentation, the Centre for Study of Society and Secularism, the Rashtriya Swayamsevak Sangh Library and the

Universities of Bombay and Pune, who helped me along the way. Every day and in every way, I am immensely grateful to the Shiv Sena women (and several Rashtriya Swayamsevak Sangh members), without whose cooperation this book would not have materialised. I have changed their names and fictionalised some of their electoral constituencies to protect their identities.

I am indebted to various faculty and administrative members at the University of Sussex (where I held a post-doctoral fellowship, and later a lectureship in Anthropology) who relentlessly displayed their faith in me. There are some people I would like to thank in particular: Professor Barbara Einhorn, my mentor, for being optimistic about the potential in my research; Professors James Fairhead and Jane Cowan for their guidance; Geert de Neve for fun; Jon Mitchell for friendship; Filippo Osella, Nigel Eltringham, David Pratten, Alex Aisher and Jock Stirrat for coffee, cigarettes and conversation; and the entire faculty of the Department of Anthropology for creating an energetic, vibrant and dynamic scholarly ambience. Simply running into them in the corridors or cafés at the university gave impetus to my research!

I greatly appreciate the contribution made by various other academics who inspired and encouraged me for many years: Dr Prasanta Ray, Presidency College (Calcutta), for instilling the love of cultural anthropology in me; Dr R.K. Jain, Dr Dipankar Gupta and Dr Avijit Pathak, Jawaharlal Nehru University (New Delhi), for encouraging me to undertake a PhD; Dr Rudrangshu Mukherjee, for his wonderful affection; Professor J.D.Y. Peel (SOAS), for watching over me; all the members of the SOAS Anthropology department for their constant support; Dr Mukulika Banerjee (University College London), for helping me understand the concept of 'counter-victimology' within gender studies; and last but not the least, Dr David Mosse, for thorough doctoral supervision and serenity in the face of my mood swings.

The book is the product of a series of debates and dialogues with its publisher, Michael Dwyer, and its committed copy-editor, Jonathan Hoare. I have presented papers on the whole and parts of this book at conferences, seminars and workshops at SOAS, London School of Economics and Political Science (LSE), University of Reading, University of Sussex, University of Cambridge, Association for Asian Scholars Annual Meeting at Chicago (2005) and the American Anthropological Association (AAA) in Washington (2005). Discussions around these sessions were a learning experience for me. I also organised an international workshop with Dr David Pratten, University of Oxford, called 'Global Vigilantes'. This workshop, sponsored by the British Academy (in the UK) and the Wenner-Gren Foundation (in the US), further informed my research trajectories.

My reading and writing on the subject of gender and conflict, and dealing with the complexity of the issue, left me tired and overwhelmed. The presence and memories of songs, sights, poetry and people (not mentioned here), which made this research journey so much more bearable, deserve a place here.

AS
University of Sussex, 2007

1
INTRODUCTION

He must have foreseen the difficulties that lay ahead for him; he would have to convince the red men to accept him as one of their own. He set out upon the long adventure. He lived for more than two years on the prairie, sometimes sheltered by adobe walls and sometimes in the open. He rose before dawn, went to bed at sundown and came to dream in a language that was not of his fathers. He conditioned his palate to harsh flavours, he covered himself with strange clothing, he forgot his friends and the city, he came to think in the fashion that the logic of his mind rejected. During the first few months of his new education, he secretly took notes; later he tore the notes up—perhaps to avoid drawing attention upon himself, perhaps because he no longer needed them. One morning, without saying a word to anyone, he left.

In the city he was homesick for those evenings on the prairie when, long ago, he had been homesick for the city. (Borges, 1999: 334–5)

To carry out ethnographic research on right-wing women in contemporary India is, perhaps, a long adventure, especially when the region is marked by various sagas of separatism and communal conflict. Throughout history the past has been appropriated and manipulated to justify present discord. Land and places are infused with different and contested forms of cultural memory that have been actively constructed, transmitted and re-interpreted through the generations (Appadurai, 1981b). In the last decade alone the clash between Hindus and Muslims has reached such a height that sustained brutalisation of the enemy has been openly sanctioned within warring communities. On this map of communal violence Hindu fundamentalism etched its own mark by giving rise to a cluster of organisations that fostered national and, most often, local political, social and religious insecurities for many years. One such organisation was the Shiv Sena (Shivaji's Army), a regional political party named after a martial Hindu king. For several decades the Shiv Sena exerted the cultural superiority of the native Hindu people in the state of Maharashtra in western India, thereby demanding for themselves economic and political power (Gupta, 1982; Katzenstein, 1979). In the late 1980s the Sena developed nationalistic aspirations and decided to move 'from region to religion'. The party turned towards Hindutva, a violent pan-Indian move-ment which fervently upholds the religious and political supremacy of the Hindu community (Katzenstein *et al.*, 1998).

Through the early 1990s the women's wing of the Shiv Sena, the Mahila Aghadi (lit. Women's Front), played a conspicuous role in sustaining com-munal tensions in Maharashtra's capital, Mumbai. Although the wing was developed as a support network within a manifestly 'male' movement, the Aghadi emerged as an autonomous task force with its own agenda of deliver-ing 'social justice'. The overt participation of Sena women in orchestrating the 1992–3 Hindu–Muslim communal riots in Mumbai provided the initial impetus for this exploratory exercise in gender and urban violence. This book uncovers the complex relationship between poor women and the 'extremist' Shiv Sena movement and highlights the 'potential' in communal conflict to offer limited power and autonomy to underprivileged women and children. It is based on intensive fieldwork in the slums of Mumbai where low-income, working-class women have allied themselves with this violent, ethno-nation-alist organisation. It tells their stories.

This book suggests the Mahila Aghadi cautiously manipulated a nationalist discourse to address more localised gender interests. Drawing its primary membership from the expansive slums of Mumbai where, despite their strong political affiliations, poor-women cadres continued to face the consequences of migration, urban displacement and industrialisation, it was a united and efficiently organised group involved in collective action. Although the Sena women's wing emerged as a 'sub-group' through ideological and political patronage, it became popular by contesting restrictive decrees on women imposed by patriarchal slum communities in particular, and fundamentalist movements in general. By participating in an essentially masculine performa-tive arena such as riots and attendant nationalistic activities, poor women overtly displayed loyalty to a nationalist cause but covertly wrested important social spaces and economic leverage within the exclusivist ethos of a com-mercial city. Determined to contest women's vulnerability and seclusion, the Aghadi developed mobilisational strategies and coordinated women's actions *without* threatening the integrity of the party. As a consequence, although the wing spawned various women's militant squads, their violence remained am-plified as 'religious valour'.

This study further shows how children of right-wing slum families became the recipients of militant ideologies and, by organising armed violence to overcome vulnerabilities within a life of poverty, 'fitted' comfortably into the party mechanism. As valiant mothers, most women authorised this agenda for the next generation by encouraging their families to be at 'permanent war', a state which, if attained, could fully legitimise urban 'woman-and-child' soldiering.

Research here also identifies a number of vexed socio-political realities that determine the dynamism of right-wing movements in non-Western societies. Women and children usually support nationalist struggles from the periphery, but at crucial points of communal tension they can actively participate in violence to coalesce as social groups and assert their presence within a movement. Hence, this book also illustrates the ways in which poor women and their children observe and experience the social and emotional value of working collectively, albeit within the context of a violent struggle. Furthermore, it underlines the experience of collective action as the most potent catalyst in reorganising male discursive practices. As a result, 'warrior' Sena women become the primary retainers and perpetrators of a fierce nationalistic discourse, acquiring negotiated social and economic spaces either by default or as reward.

The analysis offered here peripherally critiques policy-making by development specialists, which remains non-interventionist, incomprehensible and inaccessible to its recipients. Along the way, it also points out a few failures of academic feminism and feminist activism in India. It raises questions within the shared discourse of gender and conflict, contests deterministic theories about violence and fundamentalist principles, and also suggests how the secular NGO movement may rethink its primary objectives. In sum, this book shows how an anti-feminist militant women's group emerges not only as a satellite of a male-dominated nationalistic movement (to which it undoubtedly owes its origins) but also as a product of complex patterns of displacement affecting the lives of poor urban women and children.

This ethnographic study, however, is neither a venture to undermine the efforts of activists/feminists to collectivise impoverished women, nor an attempt to sanction group violence as an alternative form of 'poor women's rebellion'. While working in the Sena-dominated areas I witnessed the marginalisation of the 'bad', violent and non-conformist poor by local NGOs. My research therefore highlights the grievances of the Sena slum women to address, partly, the frustration of feminist activists. Despite her own pro-choice position, Ginsburg (1993) studied the actions of women anti-abortion activists; similarly, even though I stand against violent nationalisms in all their real and symbolic manifestations, I share Ginsburg's concerns about circumventing the worldviews of 'women we don't like'. I remain optimistic that 'tales from the other side'—that is, why underprivileged women choose to be part of a nationalist discourse—will enable NGO workers to bridge years of rivalry between secular and religio-nationalist women.

In analysing their action, the contradictory relationships between the Sena women and various forms of collective violence are explored here. While some active members of the Aghadi displayed an overt militant identity, there were other slum women who engaged in violence in more devious ways. There were still others who participated reluctantly in political conflicts, lest they lose the social and economic support of the Aghadi in their everyday lives. Consequently, in describing the events and experiences surrounding the lives of these women, their active *and* permissive agency in perpetrating violence are both acknowledged and highlighted. Permissive agency concerns the support networks developed by slum women that range from cooking and cleaning for men and women who played a more prominent, public role in violence to reinvigorating male rioters by providing emotional support. Active agency, meanwhile, is primarily concerned with public displays of aggression, most of which centre around women's direct, destructive roles against persons and property.

RISE OF THE SHIV SENA: WOMEN'S VISIBILITY/INVISIBILITY

The reasons for the rise of the Shiv Sena are debatable, but there is little doubt over the events that preceded the party's emergence as a political power. Maharashtra had been a national, 'secular' Congress party stronghold since India's independence in 1947. However, over several decades the Congress government faced various social and political challenges, and the party became increasingly destabilised by internal feuds over policy debates. It also faced the onslaught of various fanatical secessionist social movements. The lower castes became hostile towards Brahmanical Hinduism and an energetic peasant struggle heightened rural-urban divides (Katzenstein *et al.*, 1998). Furthermore, a fragile economy produced high levels of unemployment (Lele, 1981), especially after the Mumbai textile strike (Bakshi, 1984; Pinto and Fernandes, 1996; van Wersch, 1984). In this context the Shiv Sena emerged (in the 1960s) as a small 'grass-roots' cultural organisation under the patronage of select Congress leaders. The fledgling group offered to oust specific communist leaders who opposed Congress trade-unionism, but instead of openly declaring their affiliation with the Congress party, Sena members claimed that they willingly attacked Left leaders who spurned culture, tradition and idol worship (Katzenstein *et al.*, 1998). Once it had grown in power and popularity, the Sena stepped out of the shadows of Congress ministers to contribute to the multiple disruptive elements that undermined Congress dominance in the state (Banerjee, 2000). As Poornima, a septuagenarian former Sena cadre put it while reflecting on 'those' days:

'Pawar*saab* [a Congress minister] said "c'mon, c'mon" when we were breaking the Left stronghold in the trade unions. The secessionists said: "Yes, yes. You and we have the same anti-outsider agenda." But when we became powerful, everyone said: "Beat these damn Sena people." '

The organisation strategically exploited the societal, economic and discursive transitions described above to find its way into the political fray (Eckert, 2003). The party was officially launched in 1966 in Mumbai under the leadership of Balasaheb Thackeray, the Sena's charismatic supreme leader and philosopher, who began his career as a cartoonist in an English daily and went on to become the champion of 'cultural populism' in the state (Heuze, 1995: 216). Consequently he emerged as the most controversial and influential figure in Mumbai's political and cultural landscape. After his party had won several municipal elections and had established itself in the minds and lives of the Marathi-speaking population,[1] he called himself 'the remote-control of the Maharashtra chief minister'. The party finally allied itself with the Bharatiya Janata Party (BJP), a pan-Indian Hindu fundamentalist organisation, to form the state government in 1995. Although the Sena was removed from state power in 1999, Thackeray continued to regulate and restrict social, economic and political activities effectively in Mumbai.

Ever since its inception as an ethno-centric cultural organisation, the Shiv Sena has been accused of orchestrating communal riots not just in Mumbai but all over the state. Even though it was the Sena men who grabbed headlines with their violent and murderous activities, the women played an instrumental role in creating and sustaining communal tension, orchestrating direct or indirect attacks on migrants and Muslims, well in keeping with the group's larger aims as an ethno-nationalist movement. As a consequence, over the decades— from the 1960s on—the once submissive Sena women emerged as 'sentinels' of the streets of Mumbai, usually patrolling borders with Muslim slums.

The Sena's affinity for organised violence peaked during the 1992–3 Mumbai riots. In December 1992 Hindu fundamentalists in northern India destroyed the Babri Masjid in the temple town of Ayodhya.[2] The Shiv Sena, allegedly in alliance with the city police, clamped down on the Muslim population in Mumbai, because the latter had 'dared' to hold public protests against majoritarian oppression. First in December 1992, then much more intensely the following month, the city witnessed large-scale death, destruc-

---

1 Marathi, spoken by Maharashtrians, constitutes a strong linguistic identity.
2 Hindu nationalists claimed the Babri Masjid was laid on the foundation of a Hindu temple marking the birthplace of Lord Ram. The destruction of the mosque and its effect are discussed further below and in Chapter 2.

tion and unfettered violence. Furthermore, the riots saw 'the unprecedented feminisation of violence' (Sarkar and Butalia, 1996: 6) in which the Shiv Sena women's front organised attacks on Muslim ghettoes. As a result, the Mahila Aghadi became prominent and the Sena women developed a reputation as notorious women 'gangsters'.

Literature tracing the role of women during the rise of the Sena movement is sparse, even though they constituted a considerable section of the party membership. However, Thackeray's cartoon journal *Marmik* (Morality), launched in 1960, offers some indication. Some of the issues mocked women emulating elements of 'Western culture' by carrying caricatures of women smoking or in 'shocking' outfits. These caricatures partially defined the position of 'ideal, Hindu, Marathi' women within the Sena movement: they must reject Western influences and adhere to 'conventional' forms of dress and behaviour. In contrast, the party's daily newspaper, *Saamna* (Challenge), which was launched in 1989, well after the birth of the Sena women's wing in 1985, contained few writings articulating the concerns of women. Even the party's propaganda campaigns and political pamphlets did not highlight women's activities. However, a few of Thackeray's vituperative speeches, beginning with 'battered women, go ahead and snarl at men now', were published in the party mouthpiece. Thackeray's aggression added to his popularity as a ruthless dispenser of justice, a leader without hollow political sermons. According to one senior Sena woman: 'Our [women's] great grievances would've remained discussed only at home, if Balaji didn't speak them aloud on the mike. He's like God to us.'

Women did deify Thackeray, but only to an extent. They asserted that blind faith in a single leader was not their sole motivation for joining the movement. They identified social, political, economic and historical reasons for women's mobilisation into a pro-mob organisation. It is this journey, one neglected by the Sena, that is highlighted in this book.

According to feminist scholars, social movements in Maharashtra are marked by women's invisibility, even though they often played a supportive, militant role. For example, in the anti-price-rise movement, which began during the 'droughts and inflation' phase in 1970s Maharashtra, women took to the streets in large numbers (Gandhi, 1996; Mitter, 1991). According to Gandhi, 'while it lasted it was an immensely popular movement with large numbers of enthusiastic and militant women taking to the streets, *gherao*-ing (surrounding) ministers and lobbying in the Maharashtra State Legislative Assembly' (1996: 153). The period between 1975 and 1980 is what Dattar (1995) describes as 're-reading Marx', when women associated with the Left movement were moved to take up gender issues within large workers' organisations. According to Omvedt, women 'surprised their male counterparts with their militancy' (1980: 9). The 1980s is described as the beginning of the anti-rape struggle in Maharashtra, a movement sparked by sexual violence on lower-class and tribal women (Agnes, 1996; Agnes *et al.*, 1996; Dattar, 1995). Then the 1990s saw a consolidation of all forms of women's struggles, including those within peasant movements in Maharashtra (Dattar, 1995).

Scholars have asked pointed questions about how and why women's voices within these movements remained weak, even though they played an assertive public role. Kishwar (1999), debating whether peasant struggles in Maharashtra can even be called 'women's movements', commented that gender issues remain submerged within these social movements due to the political machinations of male leaders. Reflecting on social action and women in India, Dietrich (1992) points out that women are only involved in the sustenance of an ideology and not in its production, putting them in a secondary position within any movement. In several of their writings on social movements Dattar (1999) and Poonacha (1999) expressed their disappointment in the anti-price-rise movement, feeling women could have used it as a platform to overcome their secondary roles and develop their own forms of political expression. However, like other social movements in Maharashtra where women occupied a subordinate position, the Sena women also remained subdued within a movement which was not overtly battling for gender justice.

Several feminist scholars and activists attempted to put women from different social movements on to the same platform. Initially they seemed to assume homogeneity of women's experiences across cultural barriers. However, there were resistances to these assumptions from lower-caste women. For example, in the case of 'untouchable' Dalit women, being Dalit overrode all other identities. Eventually a partial acknowledgment of cultural variability in women's aspirations began to emerge. Academics and activists were prepared to recognise women's conjoined militancy with men against oppressive class and caste structures, but they were unprepared to witness women carrying out sustained and organised violence against minority religious communities. Activists recoiled from playing an interventionist role in the lives of aggressive, Hindu fundamentalist women, with whom academics and activists experienced ideological clashes. Thus for a long time women's affiliation with the aggressive Sena movement was carefully overlooked. However, over the years the Aghadi's membership grew and in 1999–2000 the number of Shiv Sainik women in Mumbai was approximately 6,000. (There were no official censuses within the Aghadi since the line between direct female recruitment and women sympathisers remained blurred.) The Sena women finally drew attention to themselves after they displayed organised militancy during the

Mumbai riots (1992–3). During an interview, Bhave, a prominent social ac-
tivist/academic in Mumbai, said:'I was shaken, I was shaken when I watched
the Shiv Sena women go on the rampage.'The few studies that peered into
the worlds of Sena women revealed that they had developed solidarity across
class and caste boundaries which feminists had aspired for (Agnes, 1996;
Banerjee, 1996). Yet the enemy was identified as the Muslim Other, and
not patriarchy.

From the point of view of the Sena women, they were 'different' from
all other women who took part in social movements in Maharashtra. They
conceded that they received little intervention from outside (activists, aid
agencies) and minimal recognition from within (the party). Yet they still remained an island of imaginative ideas and constructive activities from the
beginning of the Sena movement. While rediscovering their lives, this book
shows how generations of Sena 'fundamentalist' women reconstructed their
own histories, identities and actions to challenge notions of the mechanical
inclusion of women in social movements.

SOME ANALYTICAL APPROACHES AND SENA WOMEN

Ethnographic studies on fundamentalism suggest that religio-political discourses derive their credibility from a system of power that subjugates wom-
en. Women are turned into inanimate symbols or carriers of cultural and
domestic dignity, and the bodies of women become battlegrounds for communal contests. Studies on women and communalism reveal how most poor
women become victims of rape, molestation, genital mutilation and other
forms of sexual assault, which are a celebration of victory during physical
clashes (Das, 1995; Kishwar and Vanita, 1984; Thapan, 1998; Uberoi, 1996).
The role of women as peacemakers and voices of opposition to conflict is also
emphasised. Further, the passivity of underprivileged women in the face of
victimhood is highlighted by scholars dealing with fundamentalism in South
Asia (see Bunch, 1992; Davies, 1994; Jain, 1992; Kumar, 1993; Mani, 1998;
Omvedt, 1995; Qadeer and Hasan, 1987; Rajan, 1993; Schuler, 1992; Sharma,
1997; Tharu, 1993) and also at the global level (see Kandiyoti, 1991b; Moghadam, 1994; Parker *et al.*, 1992; Yuval-Davis and Anthias, 1992). Building on
this range of previous work, this work highlights the more complex forms
of women's initiatives that emerge from the interplay between women and
local religious identities. It shows how women contest their repression and
confinement, incorporating an aggressive gender politics within changing
climates of hate and hostility.

There *are* women's groups who are known to take up martial roles for a
cause. In India, for example, female militancy was sanctioned during the days

of the anti-colonial struggle when women joined nationalist underground movements and private armies (Sarkar, 1992). More recently, small 'terrorist' organisations like the People's War Group in the state of Andhra Pradesh, left-wing Naxalite movements in the states of Uttar Pradesh and Bihar and the Liberation Tigers of Tamil Eelam (LTTE) in Sri Lanka have trained and mobilised women for armed conflict. Women were introduced to guerrilla warfare primarily because there was a crisis in manpower (all the men having being arrested or killed by the state [Cunningham, 2003]), as also because women were less suspected of terrorism (which, for example, allowed an LTTE woman suicide-bomber to approach an Indian prime minister easily and assassinate him [Hellmann-Rajanayagam, 1994]). In another example the Dalit Panther movement in the state of Bihar trained its women to use guns against attacks by local high-caste landlords (Murugkar, 1991); also the women's wing of the Rashtriya Swayamsevak Sangh (RSS) (National Volunteers Corps), another pan-Indian Hindu fundamentalist organisation, was motivated to train women in the use of sticks and swords not only so that they could protect themselves from sexual assault, but also because building stronger bodies would enable Hindu women to bear more children. The growth of the Hindu fundamentalist movement around the Babri Masjid mosque–temple debate marked the entry of women into the Hindu 'nationalist' project (Bacchetta, 2002). Apart from RSS cadres, women from several caste and class groups actively took part in the violence prior to and following the destruction of the mosque (Sarkar, 1996, 2001; Sarkar and Butalia, 1996). Concerns over these phenomena have produced a small body of literature exploring the dynamics between women's aggression and religion and politics in South Asia. Sarkar and Butalia comment: 'It took us courage to explore the theme of women and the Hindu right. Because for the first time in our history, so many women participated so prominently on the side of the [far] right' (Sarkar and Butalia, 1996: 3). However, instead of critiquing women's involvement in violence from a secular or feminist point of view, the present study looks at the Sena women's unique perception of the course of the Hindu fundamentalist rhetoric and discusses their strategies to make their violent public role indispensable within the movement.

Women can, of course, take the initiative to contest social dictates without resorting to militancy. A collective protest in public can also become a potent form of resistance. For example, the Islamisation programme in Pakistan is generally believed to have diverted women away from the public sphere and kept them confined within the home, as housewives and mothers. Nevertheless, some scholars have shown how sections of poor women in rural Pakistan have come together to establish egalitarian economic and social relationships without contesting the laws of Islam (Gardezi, 1990; Mumtaz, 1991; Rouse, 1986; Shaheed and Mumtaz, 1990). Also, in Sri Lanka women formed an organisation called the Mother's Front to resist the government's programme of randomly arresting their sons for alleged anti-state activities (de Alwis, 1998; Jayawardena and de Alwis, 1996). In Bangladesh rural women persuaded their local communities to oppose *purdah* (veiling) for the inconvenience it caused women travelling long distances for employment purposes (Gardner, 1995). And in India women within the Hindu right movement glorified their position as devoted mothers and wives, at the same time mobilising themselves beyond their homes (Bacchetta, 1993; Basu, 1998; Mazumdar, 1995; Sarkar, 1991, 1996, 1998). The Sena women also indulged in various forms of non-violent activism. Paradoxically, their public action to resist religious decrees needed the gloss of religious legitimacy.

In various ways, not immediately apparent or noticeable in the public domain, women critique their subordination and resist controls over them through songs, personal reminiscences, sabotage and cheating (Jeffery and Jeffery, 1998; Shaheed, 1994). In *Weapons of the Weak* (1985) Scott takes up a similar subject, looking at ordinary, everyday peasant resistance. He argues that 'dominant' values do not really penetrate into the poorer classes. Hegemonic ideas are always contentious and are continually being resisted. Conformity is calculated, not blind, and beneath the surface of symbolic and ritual compliance there is an undercurrent of ideological resistance. While describing the overt mechanisms of physical repression, he contends that the need to make a living is the most compelling reason for resistance to be covert. In this context some scholars have successfully revealed that women *are* capable of more subtle forms of resistance and have argued for a need to explore the distinctive ways in which women act, the different people over whom they exercise agency and the agendas that orient their actions (Sangari, 1996).

This study weaves together these various strands of thought (and resists certain assumptions in them) to explore a local variation of the interplay between women's agency, violent action and communalism, a form of communalism which is fostered by everyday social relations and patriarchal structures. This interplay creates conditions in which women resort to direct violence, political activism *and* covert strategies to resist the dominance of a masculinist discourse. During the period of fieldwork for this study, several riot situations or other circumstances of group violence occurred in which the Sena women in the slums played a very active role. Women claimed they did not act in fear or as victims, nor did they view themselves as peacemakers. Rather, they insisted that their involvement in violence be seen in terms of how it helped them achieve a degree of power in the public domain and restructure the gender dynamics in marginalised urban slums. This feeling of power came primarily from gaining independent physical space, freedom of mobility, self-protection from sexual offenders and also through the subjugation of an 'enemy'. Thus the use of collective violence was an alternative way for women to cope with the existential uncertainties of a life in poverty.

The women in this study were born into a world in which certain statuses and ways of being already existed. They were defined in various ways and through discursive norms before they emerged as Shiv Sena women. Bourdieu (1990) talks of *habitus*, the central feature of which is the *implicit* learning of practices, rules and behaviours that are never *explicitly* stated, talked about or taught. This includes the way people inhabit their bodies, gender differences, dispositions of social class and certain forms of knowledge. People embody and therefore reproduce and perpetuate the world into which they are born—norms, ways of acting etc.—through practice and a type of unconscious reiteration. However, although the world is already constituted, it is never complete or constituted entirely (Merleau-Ponty, 1964). Instead there is, according to Sartre, 'a small movement [human freedom] which makes out of a totally conditioned social being a person who does not give back the totality of what he has received from his conditioning' (1969: 64).

Specifically in relation to gender, Butler looks at how 'systems of power produce the subjects they subsequently come to represent' (1990: 15). But as soon as Butler establishes her point—that gender roles are socially and culturally produced—she emphasises their instability and therefore the *possibility* of their transformation and redefinition. So for every time a woman (or man for that matter) reproduces the norms and discursive practices that defined her parents and that are supposed to define her as a person (e.g. as passive or violent), there is a small potential for marginal transformation. Hence human beings are all (to some extent) agents in their own creation, and they all have some small choice in the matter, which means they do not give back completely the cultural and existential burden bestowed upon them.

It is important to study the militant Hindutva women from this standpoint of the transformative potential in agency in order to recognise alternative motivations for women's action within a fundamentalist movement. Such studies could contribute to understanding and perhaps even countering some of the trajectories and dynamics of contemporary communalism. For example, the Shiv Sena men assumed women to be passive recipients of male dictates and saw 'saving Hindu religion' as the main purpose for their joining a fundamentalist movement. The Sena women, however, participated in this conservative religio-nationalist movement to experience greater 'freedom' from limiting patriarchal values. Consequently, this study aims to counter some of the static cultural identities attributed to women in fundamentalist movements.

The agenda of the women's fronts of fundamentalist groups like the Sena Mahila Aghadi is probably defined by the unique mingling of diverse women and their varied ideas and interests. The sources of women's actions could be traced back to their immediate, religious and political aspirations, to their strategies and need for creating support bases and to their attempts at inventing tradition, engineering symbolism and recruiting cadres through political mobilisation. What made the Sena women unique was the pursuit of a multi-point personal and political agenda *behind* their violence. Their agenda (declared privately in interviews) had more to do with asserting visibility as women than any real commitment to Hindu fundamentalism. Some of their pursuits even departed markedly from the objectives of Hindu fundamentalism, but they designed strategies to work their way around it. Can women develop a contradictory relationship with fundamentalist movements? This question is central to the present study which, since it tries to show what sorts of agents women can be despite their subordination, contributes to countering victimologies of women, especially in the context of religious violence.

THE FIELDWORK

Borges movingly traces the emotional trajectory of an ethnographer who disrupts his own life to mingle with the lives of others. In the process he becomes familiar with the unfamiliar and discovers a sense of belonging where he has never belonged. After returning to his 'own life' the ethnographer loses his 'normal' perception of time and becomes 'homesick' for a space that was never to be his home. Similarly, during research for this study I 'adopted' the metropolitan city of Bombay (renamed Mumbai in 1995 by the Shiv Sena).

Compared to the anti-Sikh riots in Delhi that followed the assassination of Prime Minister Indira Gandhi in which the official death toll was 2,723 (though the Carnage Justice Committee [CJC] put it at 4,000), the Mumbai riots were of a much lower intensity. However, even though they saw the mass destruction of property and an official death toll of between 800 and 1,000,[3] the Mumbai riots were marked by the fact that they brought to the fore the women's wing of the Shiv Sena, who were conspicuous in their role of aiding and abetting the violence. Throughout the period of fieldwork the

---

[3] According to the Sri Krishna Commission Report on the Mumbai Riots of 1992–3, which was eventually published on 16 February 1998.

Aghadi consistently repeated that it gained visibility through its active or understated involvement in the Mumbai riots, which hence became a turning point in the lives of its cadres.

Research was centred in Nirmal Nagar, a slum region in Mumbai and a highly 'strategic' location for its residents. Adjacent to the important Bandra (E) highway, it also had two local rail stations nearby and the Bandra national rail terminus. With a canal on one side, the area could also be accessed by small boats. These channels of transportation were referred to as 'getaway routes' by the slum dwellers. It was therefore easy to understand why the area was better known as the heartland of crime in Mumbai. Nirmal Nagar was a lucrative source of illegal income and was eyed by most political parties a source of additional funds. However, this Hindu-dominated locale was always a Shiv Sena stronghold. According to the Sri Krishna Commission Report on the Mumbai riots, which came down heavily on the residents of Nirmal Nagar, the community-wise distribution of the population was 60 per cent Hindus, 30 per cent Muslims and 10 per cent members of other religious communities such as Buddhists and Parsis (1998: 23). The Muslims lived along the border of the slums in a residential area now called Hoshiarpur. There used to be some Muslim homes within the main area of Nirmal Nagar, but they were burned down during the riots, forcing the residents either to flee or to move into Hoshiarpur.

Communal trouble started in Nirmal Nagar on 6 December 1992, the day the Babri Masjid was destroyed. According to a resident Sena woman, it began 'after a Ganesha idol in the local temple was broken and its decapitated head was found rolling in the corner of the temple complex.' A local Sena leader, notorious for his inflammatory and communal sentiments, did not waste time in blaming the Muslim community and promptly declared 'war'. This led to several clashes over a prolonged period of time between Sena people (both men and women) and men from neighbouring Muslim homes.

Most women in Nirmal Nagar were hard-core Sena loyalists. Some of them played an active role during these riots and remained in the area despite threats of Muslim retaliation. However, the bordering area of Hoshiarpur continued to live in fear of the Sena women because the latter had developed their own line of attack to keep 'vigil' in the area. Some Muslim men, who received treatment for trauma in local hospitals, complained of prolonged violence-related disorders. The Muslims were demoralised because the Sena women continued to humiliate them, often burning, looting and destroying their property, even though the riots were long over. Recalling George Orwell's metaphor of a 'mental atmosphere', the communal tension in the area was a palpable reality in the lives of the residents.

Chaturwadi, the area of Nirmal Nagar in which I worked, consisted of forty to fifty closely-knit shacks, with unauthorised extensions. Several 'original' owners (the first group of migrants who had reclaimed the land and built the shacks) had returned to their villages, handing them on to the next generation of friends and relatives from their ancestral region. The Shiv Sainiks[4] living there formed semi-extended families, which consisted of a family's core members along with friends or adopted-'by-word' siblings. Some of the shacks had 'BPL' (Below Poverty Line) written on the door by government agencies and NGOs. Yet there would be a colour television blaring in one corner and the lady of the shack would welcome guests with bottles of cold water from her double-door, frost-free refrigerator. Some of the assets were stolen, some acquired illegally and some were gifts from rich employers. Over time it became obvious that the residents of Nirmal Nagar were employed in a range of legal and illegal jobs. For example, Babu Rao, a male Sena cadre, was a peon at an office during the day and smuggled car parts at night. Sharda, a female Sena cadre, sold dry fruits during the day and marijuana at night. While some residents ran local shops (like tailoring and grocery outlets), others shuttled from the heart of the city to its outskirts in search of livelihoods. The women, even if they were employed outside the home, performed most of the household chores.

In Chaturwadi, the local Shiv Sena Mahila Aghadi leader was Kamla. In the evenings she visited the *shakha* (the party office in the colony), which served not only as a cell for redressing grievances, but also as a centre for recreation, solidarity and planning. Evening gatherings included idle banter, mimicry and the exchange of jokes, some of which were about Muslims and circumcision. During the day Kamla went around doing what she described as 'real' social service work, which included threatening or assaulting 'deviant' people irrespective of their religious loyalties. For example, on receiving a complaint that a local shopkeeper was clogging drains by throwing plastic bags into them, Kamla and her Aghadi task force tossed the erring shopkeeper into the sewer and kept him there until he cleared the mess. This study primarily focuses on the various aspects of such aggressive behaviour displayed by the Sena women living in this slum colony and how the motivation for and practice of women's violence affected the male exercise of power and authority.

This aggression among women was always a cause for concern for NGOs operating in the area and also a 'nuisance' for some of the police personnel. There was constant speculation and search for an answer: why are the women being violent? Are women no longer nurturers? The Assistant Commissioner

---

4 Members of the Sena (*sainik* = warrior).

of Police (ACP) in Nirmal Nagar, while putting forward his own arguments, laid out case files to prove the women in the slums were 'especially' harsh and criminal. For example, in one case a mother stopped her son from fleeing after he had assaulted another slum-dweller with whom he was locked in a land dispute. She ordered her son to kill the half-dead man and finish the job. 'How a woman? Why a woman?' These were still the questions. Given that some of the colony members came from the eastern belt of Maharashtra where Shivaji, the iconic Hindu leader who fought against the Mughals, was raised and from where he selected his chief army recruits, some of whom were women who consequently had a martial history, the ACP argued that 'violence ran in their blood'. He appeared to be satisfied with his own understanding of the situation.

METHODOLOGY

As anthropologists we try, I think, to recapitulate our experiences of primary disorientation and of trying to find our feet in a place where our common sense assumptions about the world take us exactly nowhere.... But the 'setting' eventually becomes populated with people you grow to know, sometimes to love, sometimes to dislike, almost always to respect. The grey house down the street becomes not just any grey house; it was Tanoue-san's home, where I might be invited for tea, if I happened by at the right time. (Kondo, 1990: 7)

Mumbai, its slums and the Sena families also became familiar and comprehensible in the process of doing research. Before setting out I had a planned structure for my work, but from the day I stepped off the train at Dadar station in Mumbai and my bag snapped open to spill my specially-tailored, saffron-coloured Hindutva *salwar kameezes* onto the platform, I knew nothing would be under my control. And things never were.

I started with meeting academics, journalists, police officials, NGO workers, hospital attendants and Sena sympathisers to acquire a sense of the city, the riots, its communal structure and thus make myself familiar with the operations of the Shiv Sena. I met them in restaurants, their homes, on train platforms, in psychiatric wards, in their offices, on the road, on the beach and recorded our conversations at random. Attempts to approach the Sena through Bal Thackeray, the party supremo, proved futile. After prolonged negotiations with his secretaries I managed to organise a brief telephone interview, but he dismissed me as a 'Bengali researcher rat, who would collect data in one way and write something else about the Sena'.

After much grilling by senior Aghadi leaders (and a Sena-appointed detective), who were finally convinced that I had come 'all the way from England' to listen to the voices of the Sena women, I was allowed to attend their meetings. At this stage I forsook my recorder because it inevitably made the women conscious and distracted and hindered them from speaking freely. A few questionnaires revealed the women were cautiously parroting party lines on paper. After the meetings some of the women who could read English started to check my notes and took offence at a few of my critical comments.

I became a common face at the meetings and befriending Kamla, an infamous Aghadi leader in Nirmal Nagar, I was surprised by and grateful for the frequent invites to her family home (built on illegally acquired land) in Chaturwadi. On my first visit to her home some stark images caught my eye: her daughter-in-law rubbing her son's hair into a soapy lather, drops of which formed spots on the bubbles of scum that floated in the open sewer next to her house; the gloom on the walls (and in their lives) broken by bright, saffron-robed photographs of Thackeray throughout the house. Only then did I realise that the real process of participant observation had begun, the memories of which are now inscribed on the pages of this book.

I rented a room near Nirmal Nagar, where I would stash away my field notes or hide when I got into trouble (with the Sena men for 'instigating' women or turning down their sexual advances, for asking unwarranted questions etc.). I went everywhere with the women. I sat in on their demonstrations, walked in their protest marches, watched their social service activities; I talked, ate, drank, played mischief, smoked surreptitiously and took part in their recreational activities. The women introduced me to a world they thought was theirs and over which they had the right to rule. But they only caught glimpses of my world; they thought they knew everything about it anyway. I went with the women when they took to the streets and stood watching when they burnt effigies of Abu Azmi, a Muslim corporator of the Samta Party (the new name for the Muslim League) who recorded 'anti-India' statements. I watched Sena women corporators attack and strip two Muslim women corporators in the House of Parliament, and then, having eaten ice-cream with the Sena women on the beach, went home and helped during dinner, played with Kamla's grandson, told her son how to manage his dishonest accounts, and at the end of the day curled up in bed to write my notes. Now I loved them, now I hated them. Now I was an insider, now an outsider, but always an observer.

I suffered several paradoxes and grave ethical dilemmas, which continue to haunt my writing. I felt my work came at a price: that of betraying the victims of violence with whom it is far easier to sympathise.[5] While living

---

[5] The plight of the riot victims and the reshaping of Muslim identities after the

in the Sena-dominated slums the Aghadi monitored my movements, and my initial attempts to interact with Muslim households were met with hostility. I discontinued working closely with Muslims lest I lose the confidence of my women informants. Thus I represent just one side of the demands for justice, revenge, forgiveness, freedom and relief. I worked with the perpetrators who wanted to convince the anthropologist, and through her the world outside, of the passion, the necessity, the benefits, the normalisation and the immediacy of violence. As an anthropologist, a friend and a listener I had the responsibility of taking stories from their narrow existential reality to a wider world. Through their construction of me as a sympathiser and an agent of the *bhari duniya*, the whole world, did they also construct an image of the world that would support their aggression? I always felt too guilty to ask what they expected in return for my year-long stint amongst them. The Conclusion of this book includes a brief discussion of the issues of ethics and security that arose during the fieldwork in the hope of emotionally equipping future anthropologists working with criminalised groups.

Writing about people's experiences of violence has been difficult, but *presenting* descriptions of violence has been tougher. Trying to maintain the strong divide between writing violence and voyeurism is a problem several scholars investigating cultures of violence have faced. Rodgers, in analysing his experiences of working with urban gangs in Nicaragua, writes: 'Certainly, it is true that the subject of violence is such that inevitably any participatory research-based investigation lends itself somewhat to sensationalism, especially when one has actively partaken in violence' (2001: 18). As a participant observer I have tried, in accounts, to retain the authenticity of violent episodes, even though I was deeply conscious of their disturbing nature and their potential to offend the sensibilities of a reader. Kondo (1990), studying how selfhood is constructed in a Japanese industrial and familial setting, argues that the liveliness and complexity of everyday life cannot be encompassed by theoretical models which rely on organisational structures, 'typical' households and referential meanings. 'And to examine that complexity and richness in its specificity leads towards a strategy that expands notions of what can count as theory, where experience and evocation can *become theory*, where the binary between the "empirical" and the "theoretical" is displaced and loses its force' (1990: 8). In my research I have tried to move away from critical and theoretical perspectives on conflict, towards a more aesthetic apprecia-

rise of Hindu nationalism has been eloquently highlighted in the works of several scholars. See Brass, 2003; Engineer, 2004; Padgaonkar, 1993; Panikkar, 2002; Sardesai, 1995; K. Sharma, 1995.

tion of the everyday realities, the circumstances and the violence in the lives of Sena slum women.

It has also been difficult to forget the women and children I feared and adored. In the city, invoking Borges, I became homesick for those evenings in the slums on the fringes when, long ago, I was homesick for the city. Shortly after I came away, a woman I worked with very closely was shot dead. A massive fire in Chaturwadi slums burned down several shacks and killed eight children; maybe I had played with them. A fellow anthropologist put things in perspective: 'When you are in the field, you are a part of things out there. When you return, the field carries on without you.'

2

URBAN ALIENATION AND THE BIRTH OF
WOMEN'S 'GANGS'

Tarabai (probably aged 70; she guesses she was born in 'the year of the bad storms' in her father's village in western Maharashtra): 'What can I say about my life? Our village was very small, called Kurul. My husband and I, we married at the age of sixteen and after that stayed there for twenty years. I was fair and could sing. My husband's family didn't want me because I couldn't bring enough dowry. But my husband liked me very much. He persuaded his elder brothers to let him marry me. Well [sigh], such love does not always last. We used to all live together. My husband's two elder brothers, their wives, their children and us. I thought I'd be lucky without in-laws. But my older sister-in-law was a tyrant. We didn't work in the fields. We'd cook and clean and wash and take care of the cattle, we prepared cow dung, strung *bidis* [slim leaf cigarettes]. But my husband was under a lot of pressure because apparently income was low and I didn't bring enough money as dowry into the house. This went on for a long time. I had two children, both healthy boys you know, even that didn't stop my husband's family from taunting me. There were a few men from our village who'd come into the city to work. My husband felt he should also go with them and check out whether there was work in the cotton mills. He came back and said that he'd try. He packed his bags and left. I was standing at the door, trying to hide my tears by biting into the edge of my sari, but he just left. Just like that. All the people in the village said it was my fault. If only my father was a rich man.

'I didn't know how to read or write. So the only news I got of my husband was when men from our village would come home. Then he came home one day. He had cotton stuck to even his loincloth. It took me days to wash it off. But he did bring some cash, which his elder brothers took from him. I was happy that he was back. One night he bit my ear and said that people in the city show their love this way. Then he said he had to go again. This time I insisted that I go with him. What is all this ear-biting business? He agreed, even though his brothers were angry.

'Then I came to Bombay for the first time. What noise, what people, no trees. My husband took me to a room in this house. There were lots of people staying there. I thought this was his room. But then one night we were just getting close, when there was loud knocking on the door. We grabbed our clothes and my hus-

19

band opened the door. There was a man and a woman standing outside. They said they'd rented the room from that night and that we had to leave. We were out on the streets in the middle of the night. My husband took me where he actually stayed. It was a boy's dorm kind of thing. Dirty, smelly, only men. Apparently the men worked in shifts throughout the night. So someone or other was awake. How could I stay there? He said we could sleep on the floor. I thought dawn would never come. I felt that was a shameful night.

'I came back to the village. My brothers-in-law were waiting to pounce on me, which they did. Then a few weeks later my husband said he'd found a room in a labourer's slum and I could go there. I didn't want to return to the city. I asked the men in the village whether the room was really his and they said it was. So I went again. The slum was dirty, there was no place to do my toilet in the morning. We had to hang our butts over railway tracks, cover our faces and do it in the open. Our children had to do it near the drains. But I still felt happy to be with my husband. I was young then. At that time I heard about the Shiv Sena for the first time. Everyone said they were "helping" Marathi men get jobs and were trying to keep non-Marathi speakers at bay. I didn't pay any attention at first but it sounded interesting.

'But I did miss my village. Once my brother-in-law sent us news that they'd dug a well on our land and asked whether we would come for its inauguration. My husband didn't get a break. So I went with my children. I was so happy to see my sisters-in-law. They were family after all. You know when there are so many steel vessels in one house, they're bound to make a noise. All women have fights. But despite being in different circumstances, all women have to be like water. Just flowing into and filling up different moulds.

'I stayed in the village for a long time, till I started to worry again about whether my husband would be able to digest hotel food for long. I couldn't forget that bite on my ear [giggles]. But I always remembered that he was surrounded by friends and relatives, I knew he'd be taken care of. I always thanked *ganpati bappa* [Lord Ganesh]. After a while I came back. I had my youngest child, Raju.

'My husband's mill closed down. When we told our family members we wanted to return, they forbade us because apparently the land wasn't producing enough to feed so many mouths. They didn't even want to see Raju or bless him. So we thought we'd try and look for other work in the city. My husband kept hoping the mill would open. He didn't support the strike that much. He didn't think the mill management would actually not listen to their demands and begin selling off the mills. It was our bread and butter. The labourers had meetings every day. People said the Shiv Sena was also trying to dissolve the strike. They felt that Datta Samant [the trade union leader who led the strike] was a bad man. I only knew there was less and less food in the house.

'Then there was this woman in the slum who said she knew a man who'd get me some jobs. I went to him. He said I could pick up syringes from hospital waste and make money. I shuddered. But I said "Yes". Then I met this woman who said she knew a woman who did this work and that her hands were always soaked in blood from the pricks. I told the man I couldn't do it. He was very angry and said, "So what can you do?" And I thought, I know how to make *bidis*. He seemed pleased and gave me a job making *bidis*.

'During the day I went to this long corridor between houses at the edge of the slum and made *bidis*. He gave us 7 to 10 rupees at the end of the day. I used to sing and work like I did in the village. The man would always come out to listen. Then one day he said he'd give me a radio if I sang for him at night in his house. I refused. The next day he asked me to leave because he said I wasn't working hard enough. That night I went to his house to "sing". I never got the radio. Also I never cried so much while "singing". It's getting dark. Have some tea.' [Tarabai gets up and goes into her shack, lights her stove and sits next to it.]

AS: 'And then?' [Turning to Sudhabai sitting next to me.]

Sudhabai [scowling]: 'Then? What "then"? "Then" everyone's story becomes the same. We were all women who couldn't get back to the village, and trying to get some money, and trying to survive. "Then" news travelled from one woman to another that the Shiv Sena was doing good work. By that time my husband had turned to organised crime. We had to eat. The Shiv Sena gave him a lot of backing. They said they'd organise the Marathi slum women to fight for their rights as well. And "then" we started to go to the *shakha*. That's the answer to your "then".

'At that time the *shakha pramukh* [the Shiv Sena branch officer] used to come to our house often. My brother would pay him a part of his loot. He turned to me and said: "Why don't you women also get together and go fight for money?" So I thought the news that was going around was true. These Sena people did want to help poor slum-dwellers. Some of us women got together first. First we talked about our common problems, then we found out who the men were who were employing us or harassing us. Some women had to enrol into the Sena office. Others like me, whose husband was an active Sena member, were known by everyone in any case. Also everyone thought the most violent people were Sena members. So when we went to all these men employers we just had to look at them. By that time there was a fire burning in our eyes. Men just turned to ashes.

'Once I slapped this man who was trying to pinch my bottom in a lane. He was flabbergasted. By the time he recovered from the shock and tried to rush at me, the warrior women from other shanties came out with their rolling pins. After many, many years at last it was our turn to "sing" and also to make these men dance to our tunes. We were finally a women's gang. All this didn't happen overnight. It took a long time for women to get together. But the fact that they did, the fact that they kept working their way around all the obstacles to meet in the *shakha* or anywhere else, this showed how much women wanted to do what they did. We didn't join the Sena just to shout for the Marathis. Women's individual strength was already there. How can we disregard the fact that it was the Sena that brought us together and we discovered how powerful collective strength can be?'

'Where did people's morality go when we were sleeping with employers just to get food? When we forcefully tried to get our due by using violence, suddenly people were lecturing us about women and morality.' (Ramatai [70], in support of her retired 'warrior' friends)

Ramatai was one of the first female cadres of the Shiv Sena; she now lives in a tin shack in a Mumbai slum. Migration into Mumbai as 'father's cook and cleaner destroyed my chances of marriage and motherhood', she laments. Another woman, Sudhatai, spent her life working at a calendar factory whose owner called on her every night before payday. After she became an active member of the Shiv Sena the factory owner stopped his regular 'visits'.

This chapter analyses the power of 'marginalised' urban spaces in the creation and dissemination of a culture of female militancy. It shows how lower-class women in the Mumbai slums, by affiliating themselves with an aggressive urban movement, came to violently control a range of physical, material and social spaces, in the process moving away from positions of subordination. Further, it explores the narratives of older slum women and traces the birth of female militancy in the slum areas. These older women, now marginalised from the movement's youth-oriented action-based programmes, physically 'created' the slums (by reclaiming swamps and wasteland), formed meaningful relationships with their environment and invested these locales with a backdrop of resistance.

Urbanisation entails not only the growth and development of a city but also the transformation of existing spaces (Smart and Smart, 1998). In Mumbai the slum became a complex space which redefined and reconceptualised social groupings. Further, the migration and relocation of peoples created new social and kinship networks. This ethnography illustrates how, while sustaining a façade of being structurally muted within such an environment of constant transition, women (over two overlapping generations) tacitly and explicitly resisted naturalising discourses on femininity and 'the home'. Slum women strategically chose to infuse their physical environments with the threat of conflict, as women's presence in (and patrolling of) these contested urban spaces became a source of both real and symbolic power.

During the period of fieldwork, the older Sena women brought forth narratives about their intensely personal encounters with anomie in the slum-life of Mumbai. Groups of slum women were affected by large-scale unemployment arising from the Mumbai Textile Strike in 1982. As textile workers lost their sources of livelihood, the women in their families were compelled for the first time to seek employment in the skilled and unskilled sector, leaving them vulnerable to various forms of economic and sexual exploitation. At this juncture, when working (Marathi, migrant) women were coping with various experiences of alienation, the Sena began to unionise slum women under their bow-and-arrow banner. This gave women an opportunity to air and share their grievances; it also made them realise the possibility of countering exploitation and of 'protecting' their jobs as a group. For example, women labourers could make sure they obtained work all year round by threatening or at times thrashing contractors at construction sites in their locality. In this context women saw how the use of collective violence ensured satisfactory results.

Several scholars have looked at women within resistance movements and their malleable ideologies (e.g. Bacchetta, 2002; Blee, 2002; De Grazia, 1992; Ferber, 2003; Ginsburg, 1993; Peto, 1999; Sarkar, 1998). While attempting to recover women's stories and trying to revise received knowledge about them this book briefly examines the history of the Shiv Sena and its official move from ethnic politics to saffronisation (in 1984). It highlights the Sena women's *own* rationale for supporting the pan-Indian cause of Hindutva, which was related to their growing aspiration to maintain links with rural women, legitimise female militancy in their localities and carve out a visible public role for women. This led to the formation of the Mahila Aghadi, the Sena's women's wing, in 1985. The front became a platform for chalking out strategies that allowed women to gain considerable control over several spheres of their lives—as migrant women, as urban workers and as violent 'warriors'.

The older women's affiliation with a violent, right-wing, political project had a transformatory impact on their daily lives, and the use of force helped them move beyond traditional feminine roles. However, their life histories did not become a string of indiscriminate reflections on critical events. The 'retired' female militants clearly expressed a fervent desire to *justify* the emergence of their combative urban identities: militant activism, participating in violent 'anti-national' activities and transgressing gender boundaries had not turned them into lesser women, they argued. These aged slum women with their peculiar life-histories faced the consequences of migration, displacement, lopsided industrialisation and 'the general ambivalence of identities in global cities' (Southall, 2000: 19). The purpose here is to reveal the 'creative' endeavours of slum women to re-possess scattered spaces within the shifting moral economy of an urban slum. This was how they wanted to project themselves and their circumstances (via the eager anthropologist) to the world 'outside' the slums (*basti key bahar ki duniya*).

The ways in which unstable places often allow people 'to create and defend meaningful collective activities and spaces' (Greenhouse *et al.*, 2002), an argument which has generated several key debates within recent urban studies (e.g. Hansen, 2001; Low, 2003; Smart and Smart, 2004) are also discussed here. The experiences and adaptation skills of slum women offer insights into the complex web of power relations within which gender and urban conflict remains embedded; and the reminiscences of older Sena women show how and why large sections of migrant women took to orchestrated violence and used certain events over the course of their lives in the city slums to co-ordinate militancy. Through all this, myriad perspectives unfold on women, militancy and the politics of urban fear, all of which are inextricably linked to a matrix of unequal gender relations. And while the problems confronted in collecting and interpreting this ethnography will also be indicated—sometimes in broad strokes, at other times in indefinite outlines—women's words have been laboured over to rethink them in less uncompromising and more dynamic terms. Looking back at her life, suddenly preserved in the scrawls and scribbles of an anthropologist's diary, Ramatai urges: 'We were good women in the village. We became bad women in the city. Don't judge me.'

NEGOTIATING URBAN SPACES: DISPLACEMENT, ANGER AND AGGRESSION

Tarabai and Sudhabai, both septuagenarians, made the voyage from their native village to the 'big city', where hopes of commercial success were easily kindled and most certainly extinguished. Their stories show how several rural women journeyed away from certain sorts of stabilities and relationships in exchange for a life in the urban slums. The history of the Sena remains woven into the narratives of these women, telling us how the organisation came to play an influential role among poor women in Mumbai and how, in turn and over time, the personal histories of the older women became ineluctably tied to the political history of the Sena movement.

From its inception the Shiv Sena showed an eagerness to use extreme methods of political action.[1] It began as a 'sons-of-the-soil' movement, making Maharashtrian-centric politics its main platform for initiating all forms of intimidation and violent activity. According to Katzenstein (1979), it made a mark in local politics by asserting the economic interests of Maharashtrians. The Sena claimed that most local jobs, especially in Mumbai, were being usurped by 'outsiders'. This position was followed closely by an ideologi-

[1] Based on *Times of India* reports (available at the newspaper office's library) and *Saamna* edits glorifying such actions.

cal stand against communists. The party later began to champion a national patriotism that claimed their land, honour, women and religion were being seized by 'others' (Katzenstein, 1979; Katzenstein *et al.*, 1998). Sena violence continued unabated, but there were no reports of women openly rioting, although there were cases of their involvement in picketing and demonstrations. This trend towards violent action peaked when Shiv Sainiks wreaked havoc in Mumbai after the demolition of the Babri Masjid in Ayodhya. The riots continued from December 1992 to January 1993 and the city saw the largest mass exodus of Muslims in post-Partition India.[2] Significantly, in what has been described by Sarkar *et al.* (1993) as 'an unprecedented feminisation of violence', large numbers of Sena women and sympathisers overtly and covertly took part in the widespread riots. Most women who had been in the movement over a long period of time claimed that this transformation in their identity, from passivity to aggression, did not take place all at once. It was preceded by a prolonged experience of alienation, precipitated by wider processes of industrialisation, urbanisation and migration. However, many women had felt alone in their experiences, unaware that other migrant women shared a similar plight.

'This is Mumbai, my dear': strikes and unemployment

The first generation of Sena women to relocate from villages in Maharashtra to the slums of Mumbai in the 1970s came with their migrant husbands. Most of the men were employed as permanent or temporary workers in the city's thriving cotton industry. Twelve women, now 'retired' from the party, eloquently related their experiences—and also spoke for their peers, who were either dead or had returned to their native villages—through songs and narratives. One of them occasionally hummed a popular tune from an old Hindi film:

Aye dil hai mushkil jeena yahan,
Zara hatke, zara bachke,
Yeh hai Mumbai meri jaan.

My heart, it's not easy to live here,
Be careful, save yourself,
This is Mumbai, my dear.
[The original version referred to 'Bombay', but the women had obviously 'updated' it to reflect the city's new name]

2 Debates on and analysis of the exodus appeared in *Times of India*, *Indian Express* and *The Hindu* newspapers following the two phases of the Mumbai riots.

With its prosperous textile industry Mumbai was 'traditionally' the cloth-producing centre in India and was referred to during the colonial period as the 'Manchester of the East'. The women journeyed into this Mumbai of the past—harsh, heartless yet 'acting as an urban sponge', absorbing thousands of labourers into its large textile mills and ancillary industries.

According to the reminiscences of these senior Sena women, 'before' (the textile strike in Mumbai) the labourers' slums were permanent but their dwellers were mostly temporary. The shanties would be occupied mainly by workers moving in from the villages, especially by landless labourers during their slack period. After their stint at earning a living in the city most of them would return to their villages, the period of residence ranging from one or two months to ten to twelve years. Poornimatai (60) said: 'We would escort our migrant husbands temporarily, often just to set up a household and return immediately. Or we would stay with them for the period in which they remained in the city, regularly returning to villages during festivals, gatherings, family disputes.' Thus women's residence in the slums was rarely permanent. Even though they took on the hazardous task of reclaiming barren land, carrying bricks, building houses and helping their husbands to settle down, most women would shuttle between the city and the village. Scholars on migratory practices maintain that this is a common feature throughout India because losing ties with their rural roots would often prove undesirable for men, who needed to remain informed about the health and financial status of their families, of land and weather conditions, crop patterns, availability of seasonal labour etc. 'Women would thus return to the villages to fill up the vulnerabilities caused by the absence of men' (Breman, 1996: 71).

While reflecting on the subject of rural-urban migration patterns Tarabai began a song, which roughly translated means:

'O father, hold me to your chest, why send me away; O friends, gather your toys in the courtyard, let me play my last game before I leave as a stranger's wife.'

The poignancy in the words reflected the insecurity of a young bride leaving the valued permanencies of her ancestral home. Yet her song also carried an unmistakable message that women remained far more accustomed to the trials of migratory practices; from childhood they were reminded of their journey away from their natal homes as 'a stranger's wife'. But it was when the Mumbai textile strike caused return channels to their husband's villages to be closed and links with parental homes to be ruptured that the Sena women felt, as Jodhabai (60) said, 'the real trauma of migration, the immense tension of stretching themselves to such extents.'

Growing unrest in the textile industry over several years culminated in January 1982 in the widespread and enduring Mumbai Textile Strike. The background of the strike is too vast to discuss in detail here; suffice to say it should be understood in the context of problems that had been plaguing the industry for two decades and which, according to Bakshi (1984), were primarily economic and technological, but also had a strong labour component. Retrenchment of workers had been carried out for several years; however, when the strike finally occurred, thousands of workers were left unemployed. The mills were closed, the lands were auctioned, the machinery was sold off and the giant mills, with their grand Gothic architecture, lay abandoned throughout the city. Although the workers believed the clash with the management would be resolved, some mills were locked permanently after the first eighteen months of the strike, while others saw a slow shutdown over two decades of failing negotiations between the unions, the mill owners and the state government (D'Monte, 2002). Thousands of people employed in ancillary industries were also rendered jobless.

During the years of conflict between the workers and the management, the Sena was making inroads into the trade unions in Mumbai and offered its support to the Marathi migrant workers. Scholars who have closely studied the Sena movement in Mumbai link both its rise and the cause of the Mumbai riots to the crisis in the Congress party's ability to govern, and also to large-scale unemployment caused by the textile strike (Banerjee, 2000). Yet literature on the strike seems to overlook the significance of this period of unrest in the lives of Sena women. At each turning point in women's experiences of migration, unemployment and urban displacement, the Shiv Sena appear to have intervened to console and comfort them. During conversations over food, drinks and chewing betel nuts the common assertion was that the allure of joining the Sena movement was 'not unjustified'. However, the older women felt bitter that 'in their times' women did not receive adequate recognition within the party. It became apparent that these elderly women, nearing the end of their journey with an urban pseudo-political movement, were pleased that '*chalo, koi to aya hai puchne ke liye auraton ne kya kiya*' (at least someone has come to ask what the women did).

The changing domestic: women, workers and violence

The voices of the older female cadres who survived the strike revealed that the impact on women of the impasse in the textile sector was multiple. First, large sections of women were suddenly forced out on to the streets in search of alternative means of livelihood. Since men were unproductive, women had to bear the sole responsibility of supporting their families. Most of them entered the worlds of street-vending, domestic employment and other forms of unskilled work. Some remained unemployed. Discussing the lives of women workers in the unorganised sector, Omvedt comments, 'the readiness of poor women to do any kind of work to maintain the survival level in the family, this fluidity, makes them the base of cheap labour everywhere, the ultimate "reserve army of labour"' (1993: 70). The stories of slum women showed that they were exposed to urban employment for the first time. Uncomfortable with male supervision at work and also facing sexual harassment, various experiences of exploitation kept them feeling vulnerable and restive. According to Jyotitai (70), a senior cadre, 'Some of us became domestic helpers in other people's homes. The male employers knew we had no choice but to sleep with them, since we had to provide gruel to our men and children at the end of the day. You think our husbands didn't know about it? They just kept quiet and showed their frustration by beating us.' None of the women interviewed for this study were employed as servants, though they faced regular physical abuse at work and at home. They slapped their foreheads as they talked about women 'they knew of' who were compelled to grant favours to employers with sexual perversities. Yet they referred to those women as 'we', overtly expressing their empathy and desire to share their angst with fellow workers in the same plight.

The older women lived in fear of misrepresentation, within and outside the party. Several women, having divulged the 'secrets' of their past, urged me not to represent them as prostitutes, because that was not 'their real profession'. They emphasised that they were 'under pressure' to shed conventional notions of morality, more closely associated with their rural past, and negotiate an emerging urban identity as slum women whose 'beds had moved from the privacy of the home into the public world' (*bistar ghar se bahar aa gaya*). Yet there were no unions or organisations in the slums catering to the specific problems of this 'reserve army' of women in the small enterprises.

At this point, when poor women were desperately seeking support and strength in numbers, the Sena *shakhas* (the party has 224 'branches' spread throughout the city) helped them form unofficial 'unions' in their localities. The older women claimed that by sharing different personal histories they could locate common realms of insecurities in women's lives. The joining of forces helped the women realise that they could wrest certain social and economic benefits if they conspired and acted 'together'. For example, permanent employment in the city was a valued security for women workers. Large sections of Sena women learnt to exclude other jobless women who remained outside the party and hence created endless obstacles for women labourers seeking employment in a Sena-dominated *ilaka* (locality). Groups of Sena women would also march into homes and threaten anyone who employed maids not enrolled in the local *shakha*. One housewife complained: 'We even had to keep our tins of tea and sugar unlocked so the Sena maids could take their "share" at the end of the day. If we didn't, they wouldn't come to work and wouldn't let us employ anyone else. Our hands were tied.' Similarly, the women would smash stalls, dismantle shops and chase out non-Sena fruit-sellers through *bhangchur aur dadagiri* (a favourite expression which literally means 'ransacking and effecting a "big brother offensive"'). Over time women saw the advantages of the public aggression they perpetrated by taking part in these forms of collective action and they also got 'a thrill' (*maza aa gaya*) out of their growing notoriety. 'Our locality, our law' became the motto as they began to control most of the social and economic transactions related to women's employment.

Providing rootedness: women as permanent slum dwellers

The closure of the textile mills had another key impact on women; it led to a change in their status as 'visiting wives'. Most women lost their chance of returning to their native villages and were distressed to find themselves permanent residents in the slums of Mumbai. Sudhabai said they 'had to stay on in the city to provide rootedness to husbands and children, since it was tradition.'

Following 'tradition' women should have remained in seclusion, taking care of the home and hearth, but in these cases they took on the dual responsibility of being the cultural anchor for the family and providing a source of income. Some women complained of depressed husbands, some faced problems of male alcoholism. Jealousy and wife-beating 'in cases of under-employment or unemployment was widespread', remembered Jyotitai. Several women began to control the cash-flow at home, making their spouses hostile. Hence, the dual role of wife and worker and the ensuing domestic strife over imbalance of economic power within the family increased women's need to break the barrier of isolation. While women seemed to be content with the permanent roles as mother and wife, which they were prepared to perform even in difficult circumstances, be it in the village or in the city slums, the senior women contended that the Sena provided a place in which to feel partially comfortable with *other* 'unwanted' urban roles that most women were forced to carry out. 'We hated our new roles as permanent slum-dweller and worker. As Sena members we at least felt protected in the slums and in our work places', said Sudhabai. According to the older women, these conditions led to an increase in the movement's female membership.

New localities: breakdown of kin and caste relations

To migrating village women, various caste and kin considerations were a crucial part of their journey into the city. They guffawed at Hindi films which
showed men and women from villages stepping alone onto the Grand Central Station platforms in Mumbai and the story that usually followed of their
transition from rags to riches. In reality most women would move into the
comfort of clan enclaves where they would be assured of community support through, for example, newspapers, temples and primarily *dabbawalahs*
(food-box delivery services) catering to their specific cuisine, 'so our husbands could be taken care of in our absence', according to Sugribai (70).
The recreational facilities (e.g. singing devotional songs together, i.e. a way
of being together and sharing certain emotions in the face of uncertainty)
and aid in situations of crises (sudden illnesses, childbirth, cash shortages)
provided by extended kin groups also encouraged women to accompany their
husbands into the city.

   After the textile strike the caste-clustering in the *chawls* (clustered housing blocks) and slums around industrial estates crumbled. Several families
had to move to other locations in search of a fresh livelihood. Consequently,
the women went through a process of 'double displacement'—first, they
were uprooted from their villages and second, the support structures offered
within the city's kin-groups disappeared—producing a set of conditions in
which the women's sense of alienation in the new urban life-cycle became
heightened. In the face of instability women would often articulate the need
for 'belonging' and for ready help in a situation of crisis. From the discussions
it often emerged that these circumstances created a compulsion to organise
(and played a part in) increasing women's affinity to the Sena movement.
Within the party the continuing need for support and self-protection merged
localised identities into an overarching 'Marathi' identity. During the initial
phase of their migration women had developed a security system around the
familial and regional divisions of Maharashtra (by living in family or kin enclaves). But within the Sena they felt 'connected'; the feeling of community
that was lost through rural-urban and intra-urban migration was replaced by
'Maharashtrianism'.

   To retain their unity under the Sena banner of militant Maharashtrianism
most women tried to dissolve divisive caste identities as well. One evening I
met with five senior women who could be classified under different Maratha
(non-Brahmin) caste groups (variations of More, Jedhe, Parav, Jadhav, Wagh).
In the village, caste-jealousies revolve around these systems of hierarchy,[3] but

---

[3] According to Lele (1981), who had worked with the above caste configura-

in the urban setting these caste identities remained muted. The older Sena women felt that the lifting of caste veils was something they had experienced earlier; there were occasions in their rural lives when women had to shed their caste/class identities. They narrated stories about certain village festivals, when women from various caste groups could gather and worship the same goddess. Sugribai said: 'Once during a *Marai* (militant goddess Kali) festival we touched the feet of an untouchable woman. She was suddenly possessed by the spirit of the goddess.' This space within caste structures, offered only to women, seemed to make the task of disregarding caste boundaries much easier for them. Indeed, their capacity to set aside some of these social divisions made the unity shared by women stronger than that shared by men. However, there was a practical reason behind this façade of unity. With the weakening of kin enclaves women wanted to transfer dependencies onto the Hindu, Maratha, Sena 'brothers and sisters'. 'Now *they* were there to help us', said Motibai (60). Thus the constant presence of the Shiv Sena during celebrations and crises transformed members of a political organisation into an alternative, insular 'family'. Consequently, the suppression of caste codes, independence from kin enclaves and reliance on political identities did not come from exposure to secular modernity within a global city. Rather, they were more closely associated with a particularistic urban movement and were born out of a desperate bid for survival at the margins of Mumbai.

Anti-outsider agenda: women, economic stress and the urban labour market

When the Sena was officially launched as a political party it had a simple programme: the reservation of jobs and new economic opportunities for Maharashtrians, mainly in the lower echelons of 'white-collar employment' (Katzenstein *et al.*, 1998). The older women claimed they went from door-to-door telling people about the party's programmes and collecting funds. According to the women cadres, 'People thought, if the women were so dedicated and hardworking, the Sena must have some spirit. So much unemployment all around ... people needed to feel they were not alone.'

While there were several socio-economic reasons for the recession in the field of employment, the Sena identified migration from other cultural regions as the main culprit. 'They' (i.e. migrants from other states) were crowding out 'our own' migrants. Given the specific part of the job market the Sena wanted to corner, the 'enemy' was initially identified as 'South

tions, Jadhav was apparently a low agricultural caste, which had declared itself Maratha during a post-Independence census and are thus shunned by other caste groups in parts of rural Maharashtra.

Indians', meaning mostly those from Tamil Nadu. Then the target shifted to non-Maharashtrians in general, the Communists, the *bhaiyas* from Uttar Pradesh, Udipi (South Indian) shopkeepers, *lungi-wallahs* (long, wrap-around garments stereotypically identified with Muslim men), pavement dwellers and then all Muslims—seen as 'anti-India' (Katzenstein *et al.*, 1998). Most recently Christians have become their main adversary. According to Eckert, 'Like many of its brethren movements, the Shiv Sena has swapped target many times. The actual continuity and consistency, however, lay in the militancy of opposition' (2003: 5). In an endlessly shifting urban landscape one of the ways to maintain the internal coherence of a community was to identify and focus on a different group (or groups) whose defining feature may not be the particularity and social specificity of the group itself, but merely its identity as the 'other'.

In this exercise of 'othering' the Sena did not have to *create* new enemies to target. Maharashtrians, like all communities in India, also indulged in the negative labelling of 'other' cultures. These practices were sustained by jokes, tales of hatred and stereotypes that members of a community imbibed from a Bourdieu-esque *habitus*. For example, the Marathis believed that South Indians were given jobs because they 'worked overtime for less pay' and because they also unnecessarily appeased their bosses. The Sena knew well that Marathis would easily identify with the Sena cause if the party put the 'blame' of unemployment and poverty on a community of migrants already mocked and ostracised within the region. So the whole process of 're-discovering oneself as a Marathi' came through a social consciousness built on but not brought about by the Sena. While diluting certain identities like caste, especially among the women, the party sharpened other identities that already existed at the discursive level, as well as at the level of perceptions.

Large sections of women publicly demonstrated against these 'outsiders' grabbing 'their' jobs. While the party's main agenda was that 'outsiders' had no loyalty to the 'Marathi culture', the Sena women gave a more practical interpretation to this cultural nationalism by claiming that the local population, speaking the local language, should have prior claim to employment and housing in the city. They were concerned that the children of 'outsiders' would be assimilated into the local language community and identify themselves with the region in which they now lived. Tarabai, for example, feared: 'If the children of outsiders can speak Marathi and act like Maharashtrians, then the original Maharashtrians would have to face greater competition in the employment sector.'

Most Sena women remained only partially concerned about the 'dilution' of their culture. Culturally alien migrants were (as Tarabai put it) 'like water in milk, they destroy the taste and the thickness'. However, to do their bit for culture policing, the women organised campaigns to blacken signboards in English, or abused non-Maharashtrian businessmen on the streets. Several women appeared to be more agitated specifically about queues at the employment exchange. The myth was that 'all the men in the queues were Maharashtrians'. This raised questions on the notion of the 'local', to which the women gave very specific replies: a local is a Marathi and not a *Bombaywallah* or a *Mumbaikar* (as it is said since the name of the city changed). So here cultural identity (i.e. Marathi) mattered, not the assimilated cultural identity (i.e. *Bombaywallah*) that came with prolonged residence in a city.

The preferences of *Bombaywallah* employers also played a role in agitating some of the Sena women. The older women showed particular hostility towards non-Maharashtrian employers who recruited workers from their own community for easier communication, 'especially these bloody Gujju (Gujarati) *bhaiyas*'. The abusive language used by these senior women, some in their mid-eighties, revealed a conscious decrease in the toleration of culturally alien migrants, a 'natural component of ethnic conflict and migration in India' (Weiner, 1978: 4). These women were generous enough to say: 'You're a good girl, you come and work in Bombay ... but don't bring your whole family and circle of friends along with you! We'll beat them out.' Rural-urban migrants from the same state, however, would not be subjected to the same treatment.

Some of the older women blamed poor management of the mills (most of them run by non-Maharashtrian business houses) as the source of employment woes for husbands, brothers and growing sons. Women took part in violent, Sena-organised *morchas* (protest marches) in large numbers, some of them demanding the re-opening of the mills. As they claimed: 'Mumbai has always been *shramnagar* (the city of employment), not *aramnagar* (the city of laziness). We wanted the mill jobs back for our husbands....' Pathetically they narrated tales of obstructing and stoning trucks that carried machinery away from the factories, killing years of hope that 'one day, some day the factories would reopen', their men would be re-employed and they would be freed from 'their burden of poverty'.

This economic crisis generated anger in women who reiterated their 'need for aggression'. They wanted a support structure, to be able to 're-taliate'. But retaliate against whom? In reality the primary enemy for the Sena women was the urban chapter of a patriarchal social structure, which thwarted their sexuality and mobility in the public and domestic sphere. The male-dominated public framework did not allow women to be comfortable with the identity of being an economically productive member of the family.

However, 'women remain too closely enmeshed with this enemy' (Roy, 1996: 12). For the Sena women, to pass the blame onto 'an enemy at a distance', the 'evil' non-Maharashtrian migrant or the mill management, taking away the opportunities of men, seemed to be far more comforting. Yet when the Sena turned towards Hindutva, women readily went to collect funds from non-Maharashtrian Hindu corporate heads in Mumbai. This 'distance' with the enemy never remained static. Indeed, it sharpened in times of crisis and waned when proximity with the 'other' was of benefit.

Myths and mobility: spatial and social displacement

The older Sena women seemed trapped in 'a cycle of myths' around migration. The first myth was that rural-urban migration could lead to a more affluent life. All the older women moved to the city in the hope of more food and better wages. But after the textile strike some families even lost the 'luxury' of living in the labourers' *chawls* and had to move into the slums. Evidently a major source of discontent for women was the fact that their spatial mobility did not lead ultimately to social mobility.

The second myth was that 'outsiders' were blocking the social mobility of migrants within the same cultural region. Weiner, discussing the relation between migration and ethnicity, commented that 'nativism is projected as a political response to conflicting forms of mobility: the spatial mobility of culturally alien migrants and the aspiring mobility of a social class within the native population' (1978: 294). The nativist Sena movement managed to project itself to all sections of society as representative of unemployed Marathis and, according to Sugribai, 'cried for a protected labour market'. The Sena women, desperate to secure alternative forms of livelihood, readily showed militancy against migrant 'outsiders'. Indeed, they went on to play a prominent role in the controversial yet continuing eviction of Bangladeshi Muslim immigrants from Mumbai under the Sena regime. Competition was thus not viewed as a stimulus and opportunity for change, but as a force which intensified inequalities among Maharashtrians and non-Maharashtrians.

Most women claimed that they favoured domicile restrictions, and even though they felt women were far more adapted to migration, they vehemently opposed the exodus of their own people into other cultural regions. 'Restrict migrants through assaults, why go away myself?' That was the policy. Sumitrabai narrated a story about how her husband wanted to look for a manual job in Uttar Pradesh, but she struck down the idea, 'because as a native he had the first right to job opportunities in his own state.' Significantly, when asked whether she feared her husband would face the wrath of people within Uttar Pradesh seeking employment in their state, she said that other communities did not have 'the Marathi sense of justice'. She was unaware of parallel cultural movements in other states. It was neither her fear of a place 'far away' nor her loyalty to cultural nationalism that made her discourage migration to another state. She did not want to lose the alternative security, 'the sisterhood' she had achieved within the Sena. 'No more losses', she concluded firmly. She was not willing to give up the immediate, consoling self-perception of a collectivity, the real or imaginary communality of interests that had developed amongst women in the movement. Thus the demonstrations, the agitation, the circulation of myths about employment exchanges, the prevention of out-migration—these were all part of the struggle to find comfort in a distinct identity, to feel simply 'settled' and 'included' within peripheral, poverty-stricken urban slums.

Later in the movement the Sena went on to establish the *Sthaniya Lokadhikar Samiti* (Association for the Rights of Local People), which terrorised company heads to reserve jobs exclusively for Maharashtrians. It also played a role in protecting women against sexual harassment in the workplace. Even though the strong-arm tactics of the Sena were severely criticised by media persons and sections of the intelligentsia, women remained satisfied with the achievement of speedy results.

'ERASING' THE RURAL PAST, SEEKING AN URBAN FUTURE

Asked if at the end of their journey with the Sena movement the women felt their association with the party had taken away their insecurities, their answer was a clear 'no'. With age there was nostalgia, ranging from their rural youth to their militant days with the Sena, but once again feelings of isolation and anxiety about the future had resurfaced in their lives. This was primarily because the Sena's continued emphasis on violent, youth-oriented programmes could no longer accommodate older (men and) women. As Heuze (1995) points out, the party's agenda to inspire violent action prompts the ageing Thackeray to wear make-up and dye his hair to preserve his 'angry young man' image. This focus on a curriculum only for the youth made the older Sena women feel increasingly marginalised within the party.

Furthermore, unlike the younger Mahila Aghadi members, the senior Sena women had spent a part of their youth in rural Maharashtra. However, in most contexts the Sena women attempted to suppress if not erase a rural past, solely in the hope of urban integration. Yet while talking about village festivals, Sugribai burst into a song:

'My land and I, we may be apart,
But my soul drifts over your fields ...'

She stopped and tentatively said: 'Forget about village life, we belong here now.' Most older women could not forget; they continued to resurrect and 'use' the past. This was revealed most perceptibly when women energetically raked up experiences of migration from their social memory and tried to convince 'an outsider' that their movement towards militancy was meaningful and hence acceptable.

According to West, many Mozambican women who served as guerrilla combatants had a troubled engagement with their martial history. With the post-war transformation of FRELIMO (Frente de Libertação de Moçambique) politics, the discursive space within which women could participate in the exercise of power became dispersed. 'Now, as the women cope with unforeseen consequences of choices made as children and youth, as they seek to continue the stories that are their lives, DF's (female detachment) narratives lead them further from the world of shared purpose that once animated them in dangerous times' (2004: 110). Despite their energetic reflections on their urban past, the older Sena women had moved away from empowering experiences towards a constant fear of the changing identity politics within the movement. For example, the women's desperation to erase memories of their village lives stemmed from the uncertainty in seeing and representing oneself as a migrant, an outsider in Mumbai. This was partly because of the Sena's long-term mission to drive out unwelcome 'migrants', but also because the classification of 'migrants' grew more confusing over time. This is a significant contradiction. The older women wanted to display their exemplary support to the party's policies, which the women had endorsed vehemently over a long period of time, yet they now lived in the shadow of the very same policies since the latter had the potential to brand old, marginalised, rural women migrants as 'outsiders'. The urban militant movement which the women had championed in their youth now threatened to upset their fragile existence in the slums. 'The party is with you as long as you are young and active', lamented Sugribai.

Yet it was the formative years of the Sena when the blatant aggression of the men and women cadres attracted thousands of supporters into the movement, a profile evoked in a speech delivered by Thackeray at a Sena convention on 7 May 2000, after the party's debacle in corporation elections in Aurangabad: 'Shiv Sena is known for its aggressive approach on issues. Unfortunately that has diluted over time. I want the Shiv Sena to return to the early [19]70s and all steps will be taken to revive the original spirit.'[4] As creators of the 'original spirit', these women felt they deserved greater recognition.

---

[4] Translated from Marathi by writer and journalist Vaibhav Purandare. The launch of his book *The Sena Story* (1999) was organised by Thackeray.

BRIDGING DIVIDES: SENA TURNS SAFFRON, WOMEN
SUPPORT THE MOVE

The saffronisation of the Sena began in the 1970s, when the party felt a need to expand its base from Mumbai and Poona into the rest of Maharashtra, but the decisive turn towards Hindutva came in 1984 when it established its political alliance with the Bharatiya Janata Party (BJP) (a pro-Hindu political party at the national level). The literature written on this subject throws up several reasons for this definite alliance, which Katzenstein *et al.* (1998) classify under four main categories: one, the declining hegemony of the Marathas led to looking at militant Hinduism as a possible alternative ideology to help re-entrench their dominance in the state; two, a strong sense of disenchantment with conventional, unexciting forms of politics amongst the youth; three, within Mumbai, the dramatic weakening of the appeal of the anti-South Indian Maharashtrianism; and four, disillusionment of the Muslims, who formed a considerable vote bank in the state, with the 'secular' Congress government's performance and its secret support to the Sena.[5]

Sena women also yearned to expand their base of membership and 'wholeheartedly' supported this process of saffronisation. The party projected women's involvement in the process as 'their undying loyalty to the Shiv Sena' and 'because dedicated Hindu women feared their religion had come under siege'. Women, however, had different reasons for extending their support to the broader Hindutva agenda. The battle to uphold their Marathi, urban, migrant identity in Mumbai had separated women from their rural counterparts. Most cadres realised this difference when they exchanged views with their friends, cousins and relatives in the village. 'We'd sit in the kitchen during our work-chat sessions and we felt the rest of the women wouldn't realise what we Sena women were so angry and excited about! "What are you shouting for?" they'd ask us.' Rural women did not experience the same sense of personal hurt and deprivation as Sena cadres from Mumbai. For the Sena women, their proximate friends and relatives had become a 'village-they' who did not understand the 'city-us'. Radhabai lamented: 'Already our urban migration had alienated us. We didn't want any more of it.' The universe of a rural woman was radically different and a new course of action had to be developed that would bridge the rural-urban gap. So the Sena women felt it would be beneficial to stretch their identities further, into Hindu womanhood. Another reason for supporting the Sena–BJP alliance was that the prominence of a more universal and menacing enemy would

5   Newspaper reports and edits also speculated about the alliance at that time.

allow the women to add vitality to their militancy. There were thus definite reasons why women actively swung from the parochial, local-level politics to national-level 'concerns', which remained distinct from the reasoning of the Sena men.

By the time of the alliance with the BJP in 1984 the party had developed an effective network of cadres and sympathisers across Mumbai's legal and illegal slums. It also continued to garner support from a core constituency in offices, factories and middle-class Marathi neighbourhoods (Gupta, 1982; Katzenstein, 1979; Lele, 1995; Padgaonkar, 1993). With its history of anti-'outsider' and anti-communist rhetoric, the Sena saw itself well poised to capitalise on the growing popularity of Hindutva. In April 1984 Thackeray tried to give his party national stature by approaching the confederation of Hindu organisations (the Hindu Mahasangha), but because of the Sena's pedestrian image most major Hindu organisations refused to combine forces with the Sena at this stage. To prove his loyalty to the Hindutva cause, Thackeray's speeches became increasingly venomous in their attack on Muslims as traitors, fuelling anger and tension, especially in towns with a substantial concentration of Muslims.[6]

A passing report that some Muslims in Parbhani, several miles from Mumbai, had reacted to Thackeray's hostility by garlanding his photograph with a string of shoes led to the Sena demonstrating its strength by masterminding riots in Bhiwandi, Kalyan and Thane, small towns on the outskirts of Mumbai (Engineer, 1984a). Thereafter the Sena's initiation of and participation in anti-Muslim riots followed a common pattern. In each, the Sena tried to persuade its voters and sympathisers that the Hindu tradition of tolerance had made them vulnerable to the conspiratorial actions of Muslims; that Muslims were dominating the world of crime, and that they had progressively become a threat to national security because of their primary loyalty to Islam and Islamic nations. Thus it managed to portray itself as a righteous, vigilante organisation, always on the alert to protect Hindu communities from this so-called menace (S.R. Sharma, 1995). The task of women in these riots remained inconspicuous. According to the women, however, they had 'always' played a supportive role. 'Was it our war-dance during the Mumbai riots that made the press-*wallahs* sit up and take notice that even we women were fighters?' The gradual translation of communal action into war categories became a common phenomenon, allowing the more aggressive Sena women to project their new militant identity in a glorious light. Growing confidence in their combative image brought forth desires to organise militaristically into a

6 Media reports and *Saamna* edits (1984) reproduced Thackeray's speeches.

separate women's wing, to pursue their own agenda strategically and to grow independent of men.

FORMATION OF THE SENA WOMEN'S WING: SHAHAR MEIN NAYI AZADI

The Mahila Aghadi, or the women's front, was formally inaugurated in 1985, a year after the Sena formed its alliance with the BJP. By now most Sena women in the slums had developed an aggressive public image as picketers, as running abuse brigades (groups of women who embarrassed 'offenders' by shouting abuses before the latter's homes/offices for hours) and as violent demonstrators. However, by the time the Aghadi was formed, the composition of women members of the Shiv Sena had changed. The new wing did not constitute first-generation migrant women but women born or raised in the slums of Mumbai. So while the rural past informed the lives of the older Sena women, the slums had 'made' the new generation of Aghadi women. Some of these women were working widows who found security and sisterhood within the Sena camp. A large section were 'over-age' and unmarried, since the break-up of the caste and kin enclaves had prevented them from finding 'suitable' partners. But most of the lower-class women in the Sena were married, with or without domestic personal uncertainties.

There were some 'common reasons' offered by Sena men and women for the formation of the Aghadi. Some male leaders felt the Sena needed a progressive image.[7] Since all the other Hindu organisations had separate women's wings, the party 'should' emulate these models. Also the Sena felt an independent wing would help in the mobilisation of women voters, primarily in the city. The party saw how secular organisations trying to secure justice for women petitioners often became trapped in legal tangles. Hence, most women who came to these organisations with their problems, usually of wife-beating or rape, returned dissatisfied. Consequently, the party realised they would gain immense popularity if the Sena women had their own system offering swift justice. To achieve that end, the Sena needed an independent wing accessible to slum women, who would be inhibited to approach male members of the party. When asked whether the women themselves had raised a demand for a sub-group within the Sena, Sanjay Nirupam, a Sena member of parliament, said even in 'such a case' the ultimate decision to 'cut them

---

[7] I spoke with some male leaders—Sanjay Nirupam, a party secretary, Manohar Joshi, the former Sena chief minister, Ramakant More and Baba Kadam, Sena trade union leaders—at the all-party meetings, about the formation of the Aghadi.

loose' was taken by the Sena supremo Bal Thackeray. Neither the men nor the women questioned in this study deviated from this line.

However, although the women supported the 'common causes' for the formation of the Aghadi, they insisted a note be made of 'their own arguments'. First, several Sena women claimed they enjoyed taking part in public events, which had made them heady with 'new-found independence in the city' (*shahar mein nayi azadi*). They had experienced the power that lay in collective action, and yearned for more. Yet all the women seemed to be aware that their demand for more power had to remain understated within the party. They were not 'complete' rebels against their men and the paternalistic policies of the party. The women's continuing interest was to grasp as much of that *nayi azadi* (new-found independence) as possible, without upsetting the patriarchal balances within their society. One way of achieving this was to form a separate women's wing within the party and to 'respectfully' take charge of their own activities.

Some women voiced their opinions on sexual vulnerability. They felt the wing would not only address issues of defencelessness in slum women, but would also make women cadres feel secure *within* the male-dominated party hierarchy. 'Earlier the women would often have to visit their male counterparts in their homes at night to report a day's work or discuss some event. Now that's out of the question', said one of their senior leaders, Neelam. The women long felt disgruntled because these visits did not take away their feelings of helplessness, which was what they had joined the Sena for in the first place. They no longer wanted to remain accountable to senior Sena men for 'women's actions'.

Mumbai, being the financial capital of India, is also the city for the rich and powerful. Through the eyes of Aghadi women it was easy to observe how the glamorous lifestyles of people in the upper echelons of society made women more acutely aware of their poverty. They were part of the city only as subaltern elements, and even education did not lead to a change in their status. Aspirations for *gari* and *bangla* (cars and bungalows) had ensuing frustrations. Following the formation of the Aghadi women could be more conspicuously involved in a range of activities, from doing 'social service' to offering militant political leadership. These activities, according to sections of Sena women, helped develop a feeling of social worth, which partially countered feelings of economic marginalisation.

In addition the Sena women's association with the Hindutva movement had put them in control of some 'feminine' strategies (like myth-making, rumour-mongering, image-building), which the women were keen to develop further. To elaborate briefly: one of the reasons for forming the Aghadi was to permanently mark Hindu women as distinct from Muslim women. Sena women were keen not just to unite women against Muslim men, but also to use their militancy, their mobility and their organisation to magnify their differences with Muslim women. This was a conscious ploy to institutionalise their *nayi azadi* as a cultural prerogative of Hindu women, especially empowered by their experiences in the city. Hence it remained in keeping with the cause of Hindutva. This mirrors the Sena women's insecurity about returning to their own system of segregation and seclusion, and they wanted to preempt any possibility of that happening over time. So while the senior Sena women had stepped into the public arena because of several external circumstances, the next generation in the Aghadi did not want to retire from it.

The Sena women thus wanted to develop an autonomous identity as a women's organisation. They felt their social service network and ventures for women had to be granted independent recognition, and should not become fused with the activity of the party in general. They wanted visibility as women *per se*.

A QUESTION OF CHOICES: 'WHERE ELSE COULD WE GO?'

Most scholars analysing the resurgence of the Shiv Sena acknowledge that the party had organisational skills and retained the capacity for rapidly mobilising large sections of people. It also reflected the power of the ascendant Hindutva ideology (Gupta, 1982; Hansen, 1995; Heuze, 1995; Katzenstein, 1979; Katzenstein *et al.*, 1998; Lele, 1995; Padgaonkar, 1993). As shown, poor women in the slums of Mumbai who supported the political right were not Hindu fundamentalist women passively mobilised by a party into the ascendant nationalist wave; they made an informed choice based on their immediate circumstances. Furthermore, the Sena women's reasons for joining the party and displaying loyalty to Hindutva radically differed from those of the men. Women were even subverting the static, monolithic and pacifist identity imposed on them by the Hindutva discourse, and were continuously modifying their identities to retain a visible position within the party and the slums. Why then did they remain within the Sena at all? Were there other feminist options that women could explore?

According to the older women, they were aware of the presence of feminist organisations in the form of various women's NGOs in the slums. They spoke about social-service workers who 'did their rounds' and even felt that women from the NGOs had a rounded, participatory approach. Slum women had exposure to 'big big words of women's causes', but were discouraged to step out of their homes to attend these group discussions organised by social workers. There were 'too many insecurities' in the lives of women to rebel openly against their families and 'think only about themselves'. Instead they wanted to have a better life for themselves *along with* their families. And a vision of this promise lay only within the Sena movement.

According to Olson and Shopes, feminist practices, intellectual or otherwise, have repeatedly been driven by the concept of female bonding, the idea that women as a group share certain similar life experiences and social roles. 'What is often missing, however, is an explicit analysis of "different" as also unequal. Mere awareness of the diversity of women's experiences does not adequately address the fact that social differences are most often grounded in social relations marked by the asymmetries of power' (1991: 189). Most of the Sena women preferred to remain loyal to a grass-roots party than join an urban feminist group, because 'feminists' were élitist, questioned their status within the family and religion, and the practice of 'women's liberation' pushed women to take on inconvenient challenges. The ideology of a particularistic movement was far more attractive in the short term because it puffed up the dignity of married women (the largest portion of the Sena following), and ensured a 'respectable' space in the 'urban public'. Shopes' (1994) work among women factory-workers in Baltimore finally steered her away from a preconceived notion of a separate female world into their own conceptualisation of their reality as inescapably intertwined with that of their husbands.

Yet amongst all these justifications, there was one *fundamental* reason for women to join the Sena. No other organisation openly endorsed the blatant use of collective violence. Most women felt that violence in the name of social and historical justice was the most 'comfortable' route to power, autonomy and public visibility.

CONCLUSION

During the rise of the Shiv Sena, women were not given a visible role to play, and even during the party's move towards violence we see the Sena women going unnoticed as participants in the movement and its activities. Even if the women did take part in the spurts of violence, the party and the intelligentsia chose to ignore women's contributions to the communalisation of their social surroundings. Only during the Mumbai riots did an awareness of them as a militant collectivity and as a formidable women's wing within the party come to the fore. The Sena-dominated slums, controlled locally by Aghadi women, became 'a gated community' (Low, 2003) to be feared and avoided. That remained the view from above.

However, from below, we see migrant women negotiating shifting gender identities and using various forms of militancy to claim 'survival spaces'.

Women's behaviour remained partially patterned by rural life-cycles and their migratory practices were guided by their capacity to recreate temporarily those patterns in alternative settings. However, with the textile strike, large groups of women adopted identities as slum residents and urban workers. On the one hand they were faced with emotional and geographical displacement, and on the other they were haunted by a sense of loss after being uprooted from familial enclaves within the city. Women felt exploited, were forced to abandon traditional moralities and were exposed to alternative, often perverse, male sexualities in their daily lives. This 'peril in their lives' was precipitated by long phases of male unemployment compelling women to enter the cheap labour market. The Sena movement attracted the allegiance of women because the latter found crippling the new, multiple identities that developed with exposure to an urban, public realm. The Sena seemed to offer a compensatory space for women to reclaim the securities and bonding they had 'lost'. The greater ethnic identities of women were merely sharpened and a range of enemies were brought into perspective—a cause was discovered for rural women to be part of a new urban collective. Thus the fragility of slum life and affiliation with a violent movement had created these insular localities where gender equations had been partially inverted by migrant women to prolong their existence on the periphery of a global city.

The string of narratives provided by these women shows how they themselves perceive their own interests in the context of an urban struggle. The Sena is not reducible to the simplistic schema of a charismatic leader, Bal Thackeray, fascinating the masses that the party itself promotes through its propaganda. The invisibility of women within the movement and the intangibility of their political powers actually gave them the freedom to pursue their own practical ends. Since 'no one seriously watched over them', women could use the Sena as a 'tool' for relative stabilisation: securing permanent homes, steady jobs, comfort in numbers. So women did not see themselves as 'misguided' or 'victims' of a dominant ideology—only as 'victims' of urban poverty, sexual atrocities and unemployment. Sena women were already drawn out of their domestic sphere by the circumstances described above. The 'original' women members (as they chose to call themselves) joined the Sena because they were insecure in public and felt that the party would over time systematically resolve their predicament.

In this process of coping with multiple identities in their personal and professional lives and also within the Sena, the women were realising the significance and power of violence to wrest physical and symbolic assets essential for sustaining their marginalised local worlds. Once again the intelligentsia rejected these outbursts of ferocity by Sena women as hooliganism, but the seeds of women's militancy within the Sena had been sown. The saffroni-sation of the Sena women cadres for an independent agenda also remained subdued within the party. The Aghadi was finally formed which allowed the women to pursue their own plans and schemes autonomously—all of which culminated in the women's agency in orchestrating the Mumbai riots. The Sena did not control the evolution of women's militancy in the slums, it only accompanied it.

Were the experiences of men in this whole context different from that of the women? The line of distinction is difficult to perceive, but it exists. While the Sena men were agitating for their own interests and their contribution to the movement was given greater recognition, the women were perennially projected as a mere support group to the cause of the men.[8] The Sena women had played an aggressive role in taking the movement forward, but their voices remained subdued. Patai's (1991) critical engagement with the con-struction of women's oral history reveals that personal narratives systematise and order reality, thereby maintaining the dynamism of knowledge creation 'since there is never one story to tell about any situation'. The Sena wom-en's personal experiences of alienation, displacement, employment-oriented stress, their independent causes for joining or sympathising with the Sena and their move towards aggression—these transformations in their lives may have been understated. However, the accounts of women's narratives given here enable us to glance *beyond* a superficial representation of these events, to comprehend how the experiences of these various events gave purpose and meaning to women's actions.

In the process of analysing how migrant women perceived their emerging urban identities, this chapter finds itself addressing some chronic problems faced by women researchers grappling with the range of women's experi-ences. Stivers (1993), while studying the complicity between self-definition and power dynamics, comments that people conceive of themselves in terms of stories about their actions in the world, using them to make sense of the temporal flow of their lives. The Sena women are marginalised at present, they were marginalised in the past. Yet by telling stories and justifying them to an outsider, the older Sena women tried to validate their actions, and gave themselves the importance of having contested structures of domination as the latter reveal themselves in the quotidian. At the same time, in invoking

---

8 Weitz (1995), who interviewed women in the French Resistance, found that women's responsibilities in men-dependent struggles were invariably looked on (by men at least) as an extension of traditional female roles, and this led to under-rating women's contribution.

and expressing a shared spirited consciousness, the older women experienced more starkly their current disempowered status within an urban movement. But, as the following chapter shows, the Mumbai riots represented a turning point in the lives of Sena women.

3
THE MUMBAI RIOTS AND WOMEN'S AGENCY
IN VIOLENCE

Growing up in a middle-class Muslim family in Bombay, I realised that for me a 'crowd' in the city was a highly heterogeneous entity … it was the cosmopolitanism of Bombay which remained engrained in my mind while I wrote…. (Rushdie, 1991: 24)

Hindu fundamentalists razed the controversial Babri Masjid to the ground today leading to the outbreak of communal violence in the country. Massive riots broke out in Bombay following the news of the destruction, bringing an end to the city's cosmopolitan reputation. (*Times of India*, Bombay, 6 December 1992)

On the day of the destruction of the Babri Masjid the media reported that 20,000 *kar sevikas* (women fundamentalists) 'chanted in frenzy' when the mosque was being brought down by their brethren with the help of sticks, swords and spades.[1] Riots broke out in different parts of the country. Violence raged across Mumbai and the large-scale participation of women sent shock waves through the city.

    Violence covers a broad semantic field, and in the course of my research various understandings of what constituted violence emerged and then (often) became submerged within other descriptive categories. This chapter opens with an understanding of what the Sena women described explicitly as their violent role in the riots while remaining 'behind-the-curtains' (*parde ke piche*). Their actions, however, can be loosely defined as a form of female incitement that only creates the appropriate conditions for a more public parade of violent actions. It was a strategic tool that women used to ensure men's participation in the Mumbai riots, and thereby kept communal tension alive in the slums. Their most common tactics included circulating rumours about Muslim assaults and questioning the masculinity of men reluctant to take part in physical violence. There were groups of more aggressive women who contributed to direct forms of conflict (*auroton ka seedha maar-peet*),

---

[1] Newspaper reports from December 1992.

which involved face-to-face confrontation and the destruction of property. This can be more easily defined as a variety of well-organised, collective violence whereby women could create and sustain a climate of fear and use the threat of violence to sharpen their militant image in public. Whatever be the nature of women's involvement with violence, the Mumbai riots allowed the women to develop a range of action-oriented and rhetorical devices that minimised slum women's vulnerability and seclusion in the long run.

A substantial part of my later analyses of women and the Mumbai riots remains closely knit with what Schmidt describes as 'the experiential approach to violence', which looks at violence as not necessarily confined to situations of conflict, but 'as something related to individual subjectivity, something that structures people's everyday lives, even in the absence of an actual state of war' (2001: 1). In a search for various meanings and mechanisms of collective violence I have introduced understandings of domestic violence, gang violence, 'repressive' violence and 'invisible' violence, all of which constitute the uncertain worlds of the slum women. The Aghadi often used aggression to oppose wife-beating in poor Hindu households. At the same time, they openly practised 'invisible' (*andekhi*) violence, which involved subtle humiliation of their Muslim neighbours. While knowledge about the acts degrading the enemy could be shared between the community of aggressors and their victims, the world outside these communities would not see it as violence at all. The expanding list of meanings further accommodates repetitive, ritualised violence, self-harm and the ecstasy in violent action. Some of these categories are imposed externally by theorists: for example, by following the path of Tambiah (1996) while discussing crowd behaviour, and exploring the idea of 'violence as a mere sport'. However, most other forms of violence that I have reflected upon were developed as alternatives to direct violence by the Sena women themselves. Whatever the nature of violence that women suffered or took part in, they were convinced that their participation in the Mumbai riots had finally dispelled their subdued image within a violent, ethno-nationalist movement. Women were still secondary, but surely not subdued.

This chapter is largely based on women's reminiscences about a more recent past, though it carries some 'saw-it-happen' ethnography, as the effects of women's engagement with violence had spilled over and penetrated the post-riot slum life. Further, it analyses the range of practical and ideological justifications the Sena women used to advocate the need for collective violence, during and after the riots. Bajpai (2002), while locating the political roots of terrorism in India, developed at least five images of violence placed within the moral economy of secessionists: violence as an historical inevitability; violence as self-defence; violence as intrinsic to politics; violence as emancipation; and violence as bargaining. The Sena women hauled up each of these images in various forms to validate their actions. To most of them violence itself was a seemingly accepted adjunct of political expression and did not need to be questioned extensively. Bajpai goes on to argue that violence can also be an object of desire, setting up a gap between the stages of 'imagining violence' and 'acting violently'. 'Only in the terrorist, the desire for violence is translated into real acts of violence, because the terrorist, unlike the rest of us, has a rather rigorous theory about how violence can be used for particular ends' (2002: 111). Like most terrorist organisations, the Sena women did not exist outside the periphery of society. Yet the women were well aware of the instrumental uses of violence; it was seen as the most effective method of achieving gender goals while they remained within their families and the legal system. For large sections of slum women, between the stages of imagining violence and acting violently was a stage of 'experiencing violence' in their life. Several were beaten at home, while others involved in criminal activities would use arms to stave off attacks by rival gangs. Hence the Aghadi's 'desire' for aggressive or retaliatory collective violence stemmed from the normalisation of various forms of violent behaviour in the daily lives of poor women.

The riots gave the Aghadi a new lease of life, since its members felt their insular and alienating slum life had been transformed by it. Prior to the riots women had shared asymmetrical power relationships with other groups of people involved in the Sena movement. However, the Mumbai riots brought various Sena recruits, active loyalists and sympathisers (such as Hindu slum women, middle-class women and the saffronised section of the police) on to the same platform as they worked in connivance with each other. In other cases, Aghadi members felt 'empowered' to use force freely and to emphasise their asymmetry with victimised Muslim women. Several of these factors 'improved and widened' Sena women's identities and they were keen to work towards sustaining their militancy even after the riots were long over. Hence, through its active and permissive role in orchestrating the 1992–3 Mumbai riots the Mahila Aghadi eventually gained a 'controversial' but long-desired visibility.

SENA WOMEN BEHIND THE SCENES

Instigators

According to many Sena women (both direct recruits and sympathisers who came from the slums in Mumbai), they 'encouraged' their men to riot as a way of 'protecting the honour of the community'. How was the community integrity of clusters of Hindus residing in Mumbai's slums threatened, when Muslims turned violent after the destruction of their mosque? Women offered various answers to this question, which remained embedded in layers of cultural memory. Some delved into narratives of historical justice based on an imagined hostility between Hindus and Muslims during the Mughal rule. Others spoke about Partition atrocities that tied religion to a nationalist discourse. Even though Partition did not affect Maharashtra directly, women developed an artificial sense of loss and 'felt' for raped Hindu women fleeing Pakistan. Some women criticised the minority appeasement policies developed after Independence and also expressed fear of the supposed pan-Islamic loyalties of Muslims. But most important, communalism and antipathy for Muslims was a lived experience in the slums of Mumbai. Almost all the Sena women, coming from different backgrounds and experiences, wanted their men 'to fight' against their Muslim neighbours. A Sena leader, Pramod Navalkar, who went around the slums during the riots with his armed 'Hindu warriors', commented:

'At Radhabai Chawl they [the Muslims] bolted the door from outside and set it on fire. And all our [the Hindu] children, families, they were roasted.... When this hit the headlines the next day my wife told me "I should offer you bangles now."' (Quoted in Banerjee, 1996)

Many of the Sena women cadres interviewed used multiple tactics in coaxing, cajoling and chiding their men during communal flare-ups. When riots broke out in the slum areas several men who had vigorously displayed their loyalty to the Shiv Sena retreated from scenes of real violence. In Nirmal Nagar women married to 'cowards' conspired and hid their husbands' clothes. Some of the women even slipped petticoats on the men while they slept. The women 'brought out the *dhotis*/pants' only after the petticoat-clad men agreed to take part in the ongoing violence. Castigating their masculinity through language and symbols such as offering bangles and petticoats, asking n   to wear *bindis* (vermilion dots on the forehead, usually worn by married women), describing them as eunuchs or as impotent, while at the same time beating their foreheads and lamenting women's inability to 'take action', was a threat to expose the fragility of masculine identities in the slums. Pradhan, married to a Sena woman, said: 'When I came home and told my wife about the riots she said: "You didn't do anything? Are you the father of my children?" After that if I came home without a fight, my wife would probably have rubbed black ink on my face.' This questioning of the virility of men with 'frail' sensibilities, and the fear of ensuing familial and peer group ostracisation, persuaded many men to embrace violence.

Behind-the-scenes female incitement seemed to place most Sena women in a temporarily empowering position. In a reversal of roles women were vested with the authority to determine the appropriate conduct of men in public. By loudly airing their grievances the Sena women were prompting the various patriarchal discourses that they had upheld for several years to compensate for women's assumed powerlessness during conflict situations, primarily through men's violent action. This form of incitement may exist at a crossroads between ascribed agency and agency as it is presented to women. That is, women could take credit for initiating a confrontation between rival groups of men, or they may be *allowed* by men to give orders. In both contexts men are absolved of guilt if their own indulgence in violence appears too brutal. Laclau (1990), discussing the unfixed character of identities, argues that the radical relativism of social identities increases their vulnerability to social relations and introduces within these relations the effect of ambiguity. He sets theoretical limits on society, claiming there are always 'gaps' between structures which people can exploit and thus transform social relations (1990: 335). The Sena-orchestrated Mumbai riots became such a site of violence and allowed female incitement to exist in the 'gaps' between the political/public and the domestic/private. For example, an outbreak of communal riots on the streets made Pradhan accountable to his wife at home. Within these terms women were likely to find themselves with a degree of authority and autonomy. The Sena women cleverly exploited this moment of partial supremacy over men to reproduce or transform their lives (a point which is discussed later).

Sangari's study of the rhetorics of female incitement reveals that the inciting woman exercises a control over male sexuality, putting male honour, categorically linked to male sexual potency and the protection of women, at stake (1996: 479). If a Sena man did not want to fight, he was branded a coward and reprimanded by his peers for revealing his vulnerabilities. To further provoke men into action Sena women even identified their dead as either victims (cowards who did not fight) or martyrs (heroes who went down fighting). Here women were monitoring the status of men by exposing them to several forms of social chastisement for being 'unmanly' ('Are you the father of my children?'). The Sena women thus set up what Sangari describes as 'a structure of incitement', which, by polarising success and failure, can affect a man's social standing and challenge the non-negotiability of patriarchy. Several male Sena rioters felt their 'eyes were opened' by the women. Most of these men were initially hesitant to riot. Their masculinity had been challenged openly by the women and their violent actions could be seen as an expression of their subservience to women's demands. Such is the game of conflict. The fact that the men finally took part in violence and publicly caused damage to the integrity of the enemy community could be seen as a display of heroism that salvaged their reputation as aggressive Shiv Sainiks and allowed them to overcome their initial experiences of humiliation within the domestic sphere. Sena men's 'honour' was temporarily restored. But that was not the end of the game.

In their post-riot, quotidian life the Sena female cadres continued to assert power by searching for occasions to remind their men of women's 'eye-opening' roles. If men showed shame or gratitude, it was a moment of masculine weakness which put women in a stronger bargaining position within the home. If men felt women were dispensable ('Get out of my house, I don't need you'), the women's contribution to restoring male dignity during the riots was reiterated ('If it wasn't for me at that time, you would have had "weakling" stamped on your forehead'). In some shanties reminders took the form of threats of exposure ('I'll tell the world you hid under the bed when you heard the bombs'). Since the Mumbai riots had given the women an occasion to exercise their jurisdiction over male sexuality, the Sena women used the opportunity determinedly to bring about a more long-term collapse in the rigidity of a masculinist hierarchy, which over time allowed some women to gain a more dominant place within familial structures of command and authority.

Developing support structures

The second phase of 'backstage' incitement took the form of sanctioning violence by offering physical support. Many women in the Nirmal Nagar *basti* (slums) spent sleepless nights preparing tea and snacks for men who were part of the local vigilance committee formed against 'Muslim invasion' of the area. Women in small clusters also kept 'terrace vigil', looking out for suspicious groups of Muslim men. Several women would sing throughout the night to let their Muslim neighbours know they were keeping watch. In addition women domestic workers acted as agents for the Sena. During the riots, when cooperative housing societies had blackened their boards to hide the identity of neighbours, these women claimed that they aided Sena rioters in identifying Muslim homes. They even marked crosses on those doors from which traditional signs of Islam had been removed, just hours before Sena men narrowed down a colony as their next target.

A large section of women also contributed to the expansion of arms-making during the outbreak of riots. Kamla, a Sena leader in Nirmal Nagar, collected her female following in the area and went from door to door gathering glass bottles, an essential component of petrol bombs. Uma, a young Sena cadre who was in her teens during the Mumbai riots, cheerily claimed she was often more efficient at making bombs and slings than the men in her locality. There were even competitions to see who could make arms most quickly; women wanted to be equal to men and 'violence was reduced to a mere sport' (Tambiah, 1996: 278–9). Uma went on to say that the women also generously donated cloth, thread and petrol for arms-making and some of them offered to make 'country bombs' in their own homes. These were later gathered on the terraces as 'defence' artillery. So on the one hand the Sena women incited their men into offensive violence to defend the honour of the community and, on the other, they performed support functions to safeguard its physical integrity. Some Sena women, however, stayed away from the fighting on the streets during which 'the artillery' was put into direct use. Uma, though, knew all about it.

'These bottle bombs have to be thrown at a particular height. These are not regular bombs whose impact is equally great when they land. These petrol bombs have to burst while travelling through the air, because then the glass fragments go longer distances and can pierce the enemy's skin. If it hits their eye, you're lucky. That totally immobilises people, otherwise they cause injuries.'

Uma's octogenarian mother, who everyone calls 'Ai', chipped in:

'I used to tie the thread about the necks of the bottles after they'd been filled with petrol and the wick. Everyone did what little they could.'

I fell silent for a while. She suddenly became sullen and quipped:

'Didn't you say your mother used to collect donations during floods in Bengal and everyone did what they could? It's something like that.'

Maybe she felt I did not approve of her making bombs and hence expressed a need to support her argument; my silence could have evoked a sense of guilt since the job of making bombs was 'inappropriate' for women, especially of her age. Scheper-Hughes, in her various analyses of violence, underlines the fact that in most forms it is not viewed as unexpected behaviour, not condemned in any way, but 'to the contrary is defined as virtuous action in the service of generally applauded conventional social, economic and political norms' (Scheper-Hughes and Bourgois, 2004: 5). For Ai, floods in Bengal and riots in Nirmal Nagar slums were both situations of acute crisis and needed people's sympathetic contribution. If there was an enemy, be it a flood or a Muslim rioter, homes and the habitat had to be protected. Hence, she projected her peripheral engagement with violence as a quest for community solidarity and did not try to conceal her status in that role.

Almost all the slum women were involved in creating a large myth-making apparatus, which was put to use at the time of the riots. While organising under the banner of the Mahila Aghadi, the Sena women developed an incredible nexus of 'sharing information', and 'news' would travel like wildfire within a Sena-dominated community, primarily through the women's words. During relatively peaceful breaks women would circulate incredible statistics about the number of Hindus killed by the Muslims and vivid tales of other atrocities, maintaining tension within the community. A Sena woman cadre in Nirmal Nagar said: 'There were guns worth *crores* of rupees buried in the Muslim homes and mosques.' A very senior leader of the Sena told me: 'Muslims were serving *biryani* in the mosques because Hindus were dying.' These are just excerpts from a bank of 'information' that the Sena women disseminated, especially during the riots.

The fact that rumours started during riots took dramatic turns from reality was not surprising. The more threatening the experience the more likely it was to be a fountainhead of rumour. According to Kakar (1996), at the high point of a riot the content of rumours was at its most threatening and the speed at which they circulated at its highest; for it was at this moment that three of the four conditions for the generation and transmission of rumours—personal anxiety, general uncertainty and topical importance—were at their most intense level. At this juncture the fourth condition, incredulity, no longer operates since at high levels of anxiety disbelief in rumour is suspended. Kakar goes on to describe rumours during Hindu–Muslim clashes as 'the conversational food, which helps in the growth of a collective Hindu body' (1996: 20). Uncontrolled circulation of rumours helped both the Sena men and women sharpen awareness of their own kind. However, it was the Sena women who played a far more energetic role in feeding their own community with a range of 'mytho-histories' (Tambiah, 1996: 223), which were merely imaginative constructions of the already demonised 'other'.

These 'mytho-histories' were sustained even after the riots through a complicated nexus of lies; descriptions of events which were, by the women's own admissions, false. During the riots slum women would gather and heap edged pebbles and accuse their Muslim neighbours of stoning Hindu homes. These allegations made the Hindu male rioters more aggressive in their rampage against the Muslims. A Sena woman showed me where some stones had 'landed' and pointed to a house in Hoshiarpur, the Muslim enclave bordering Nirmal Nagar, from where they were hurled. When I surreptitiously walked around to the Muslim house, the owner pointed out the absurd distance and direction the stones would have had to travel from his house to land at the marked spot. When I returned later and questioned the Sena cadre about it she grumpily admitted it was 'a lie'. This illustrates how 'reality' is created out of a conspiracy between the women to control levels of intensity in a conflict. It is, as it were, a reality caught midstream—no longer a lie, but not yet a truth. In his writings on torture and the Putumayo, Taussig (2002) makes it clear that cultures of terror are largely dependent on the circulation of myth in which 'the fanatical stress on the mysterious side of the mysterious flourishes by means of rumour and fantasy woven in a dense web of magical realism. It is also clear that the victimiser needs the victim for the purpose of making truth, objectifying the victimiser's fantasies in the discourse of the other' (2002: 166). In the case of the riot-affected Mumbai slums, over a period of time there will be no evidence to disprove the lies created by the Sena women. No one will question the mysterious flight of the stones. I will be gone, the neighbours will move away, and all that will remain is the verisimilitude of these events. A tangled mesh of lies about Muslim atrocities will float around until it finally becomes 'the truth'. Hence through this myth-making apparatus the Sena women were also actively creating a memory through which future generations could justify and legitimate their actions, and in which an otherwise insignificant event would gain status by being part of a wider discursive rhetoric of conflict. Once again unquestioning acceptance of the authenticity of the women's narratives was 'necessary' for protection of the community. 'Yeh zaroori hai', 'woh zaroori tha' (this is necessary, that was necessary)—the women continued to rationalise their actions in terms of 'necessity' and 'urgency'.

The act of 'incitement' during situations of conflict gives women an opportunity to exercise power while remaining within a disadvantaged position; the wartime authority to give orders and determine 'what makes a man, a man' can adequately intimidate the men who are being subjected to it. When Sena women used several tactics to prod their men into violence, it also meant the women were articulating their personal concerns. Swaroop said: 'My husband became scared. He thought I was ordering him around during the riots, but it might become a habit since the riots went on for many months. I told him to fight for the community, not just for me.' Most women I interviewed used similar strategies to dispel alarm over the assertive position of 'instigators' within the home and the party. Even though sites of violence may end in giving voice to certain groups of women, 'incitement' seemed to become acceptable *only* if women encouraged men into action in the name of impersonal concerns, instead of verbalising any real gender interests.

It is also on this issue that the line between supportive female agency and agency that shades into maliciousness is drawn. Sangari (1996), discussing Queen Kaikeyi in the *Ramayana*, reveals how the queen is considered to be the epitome of female malevolency in mythology. Kaikeyi persuaded her husband to disown her step-son Rama in order to make way for the crowning of her own son. Since she articulated her self-interest she became the evil queen. The epic remains sympathetic to the 'powerlessness' of Rama's father Dasaratha, who conceded to his wife's demand and exiled his eldest son. Thus the onus remains on women to display whether they are custodians of good values or whether they are replete with selfishness like Kaikeyi. The selfless woman inspires and the selfish one merely incites. This polarity occupied a shifting boundary between the rationale of women's compliance and the rationale of their defiance, and helped in rearticulating women's power relationships with men in different ways. If women were giving their consent to male violence, that act itself was a resistance to their more inert roles within the family and the community. In the case of the Sena women it was imperative that they conceal their resistance to passive identities imposed by a fundamentalist movement. So they couched their actions in compassionately 'inspirational' terms.

Finally, female incitement from the background revealed some complex, related features. At one level women were motivating men into warriorhood to *preserve* a certain set of values, primarily around questions of superiority of the Hindu community. At another level the same acts of provocation were directed towards *transforming* a range of social relations which denied women social and political mobility. The Sena women wanted to gain a voice and visibility at home and within the movement without compromising the masculine images of their husbands, which in turn remained linked to women's pride and honour within the community. Since the Sena women could never clearly identify the social relations they sought to modify to their advantage, only their engagement with partial abstractions like concerns for the family, honour, religion or nation could be easily articulated.

THE SENA WOMEN AT THE FORE

Protective women

Most women within the Sena movement chose not to remain in the wings, especially during the outbreak of the riots. Indeed, a large section used the riots as a platform for direct action. As part of the Aghadi's activities a number of women had developed strategies for offering physical protection to their men. This could be considered their first step into the realm of 'direct violence'. Rioting men would find sanctuary in their homes, in cartons, cupboards, basements or water tanks. During an interview S. Bapat, police commissioner of Mumbai at the time of the riots, who was summarily dismissed following his failure to control the riots and his lack of knowledge about the saffronisation of the police force in Maharashtra, pointed out, with the help of diagrams of the main streets and its gullies, how Sena men would riot on the main road, looting, destroying property and stabbing people from the other community. Then, just when a police battalion moved into the region, they would escape into the alleys. Since the police were unable to drive jeeps into the alleyways, they would rush after the rioters on foot. They would then be confronted by women in semi-circles shielding rioters who cowered behind them. These women, who offered shelter to rioting men, were briefly mentioned in several police records.[2] According to Bapat, the shortage of women in the force was felt acutely at that time, since it prevented the police from breaking through these human barricades. As he summed up: 'If we touched the women, there would be bigger riots in the city.'

Bapat spoke about the soft line toed by the legal system towards women's criminality, which was a subtle form of lamenting the protectionist attitude of patriarchy towards women. A policeman 'touching' a woman was interpreted as violation of women's physical and sexual honour in public. Ridd, discussing the symbolic and covert powers gained by women caught in conflict, said: 'Women seen as political innocents can on occasion use their immunity to take initiatives and responsibilities of a covert political nature' (1986: 12). She points out how conditions of guerrilla war provide a number of examples of women employed as couriers because they are less likely to be handled bodily and searched by men. Interactions with Aghadi members and policemen made it fairly obvious that women's manipulation of this feminine 'immunity' to safeguard male rioters was a disturbing yet palpable public 'menace'.

Women took another step into the public realm to 'protect men' when they held demonstrations protesting the arrest of their leaders and of the men in their families. A classic case was over the arrest of Sena leader Madhukar Sarpotdar. He was a corporator from Nirmal Nagar who had been arrested for possession of arms during the riots. The women from the locality gathered in front of the police station and shouted slogans till the police were 'forced' to release him. There were also cases of women lying on the ground to prevent police vans from entering an area to arrest local boys for hooliganism. The women felt that men could not have achieved this because they could have been dispersed by a *lathi* (stick)-charge. Women on the other

---

[2] I looked at police files on the riots with former police commissioners Bapat and Sahni, former deputy police commissioner Deshmukh, riot enquiry panel lawyer Mihir Mehta and journalists who covered the riots.

hand were imagined to be 'frailer' and traditionally protected from bodily harm in public.

In this context of women in struggle, Ridd further argues that women's powers can take on various symbolic forms. A society directing all its resources towards sustaining a violent movement may exploit the power of women to represent to the outside world its determination in its struggle, in which *even* women and children play their part. This principle has been used effectively in a few Muslim, Shiite communities, such as when the media filmed veiled women who with raised, clenched fists shouted support for Ayatollah Khomeini in the streets of Tehran (Mernissi, 1987). Some of these arguments have been developed by Giles and Hyndman, who highlight the prevalent representations of women in conflict situations. Through the writings of a network of feminist scholars, the authors assembled various images of 'a woman with a rifle over her shoulder and a baby on her back, or in similar fashion, images of nationalist Croatian or Serbian mothers and daughters protesting on the street to prevent relief trucks from reaching zones belonging to the enemy' (2004: 4). They expressly blame the state institutions, media and military organisations for manipulating these images as iconic representations or symbols of women at/in war. The activities of the Sena women also appear comfortably to juxtapose the seemingly conflicting notions of the protected female and the militant woman. Instead of being manipulated by the party or the media, the women claimed they had knowingly demonstrated in public, often going against the party dictates. The primary aim was to establish women's indispensability in prolonging an ethno-nationalist movement, where the presence of women in locations of violence could both draw attention to the movement and save Hindu rioters from 'returning home in gunny-bags'. Once women's functionality was determined, the Shiv Sena's leaders did little to intervene, as an aggressive women's wing effectively increased awareness about the party's all-out commitment to resolve the vulnerabilities of the 'endangered' Hindu community.

Sections of women also stepped in to protect their children when they were arrested for rioting. The following excerpts are from an interview with a Sena cadre, Laxmi, who led a protest march to the police station when her son was arrested:

AS: 'Why was your son arrested?'
    L: [sharply] 'He didn't do anything wrong!'
AS: 'Then why was he arrested?'
    L: 'At that time all young boys who stayed out were being arrested.'
    AS: 'But the police say he was burning tyres in a Muslim tailoring shop....'
    L: 'Boys will be boys.'

AS: 'How did you manage to organise so many women so quickly?'

L: 'We had an understanding. All the Sena women would get together if any one woman's family was affected.'

AS: 'You don't think your son should have been punished for destroying property?'

L: 'He's a child. He was just having fun with friends. Why ruin his career for that?'

AS: 'Would you scold your son if he did it again?'

L: [Silence] 'I'd obstruct his arrest, otherwise he'd be branded in college.'

Laxmi's tone was in constant defence of her rioting son, whom she perceived as marginally deviant, enjoying an experimental sport under the pretext of 'teaching Muslims a lesson'. She implied that she would allow her son to riot in future, several reasons for which included: she could benefit materially from the looting; she wanted her son to be accepted in his peer group; she owed allegiance to the Sena; and if the party called for action, her loyal son should obey orders. This complex link between motivation and violence is what Schmidt and Schroeder understand as a path, 'a cultural grammar' that determines the value of material and social benefits. This grammar, the authors contend, 'gives a more permanent meaning to violent confrontation and thereby offers an additional motivational framework that holds out incentives beyond the individual actors' immediate interests' (2001: 5). Some of the motives offered by Laxmi can be understood in terms of amassing wealth. Others, which remained embedded in abstract cultural benefits like acceptance, loyalty and call of duty, created a more permanent reservoir of values for rationalising violence. Laxmi thus wove a net of motivations to support tactically her son's engagement with various forms of violence. She knew she could fall back on this net and rebound with ideas to justify her son's involvement in future communal clashes. The same net of motivations could be thrown over other women to haul them into direct or supportive action.

In times of conflict motherhood itself provides a space for collective protest. According to Jayawardena and de Alwis (1996), mothers whose children were arrested by the Sri Lankan government for anti-state activities formed the Mother's Front and held state-wide demonstrations to secure their release. In the case of the Sena women, motherhood was also a space for encouraging their children into 'just' violence. At the same time this identity could be manoeuvred to create solidarity among women, a position from which women could protest against the punitive state measures taken against rebellious sons. Since the Sena women had no codes of conduct for 'ideal' Hindu wifehood or motherhood, they freely used the broader concepts of

'Hindutva' and 'Hindu Rashtra', often to achieve cruder benefits closer to home. But in a riot situation Laxmi, like many others under her wing, realised that women's collective protest can shock traditional patriarchal structures into a response, something they had not experienced before. Also, using their own protected identity to offer protection seemed to put women in a position of power over men, who were compelled to display a level of overt dependency on mothers and sisters to safeguard their own physical integrity in public. Aptly summed up by Tara, a cadre: 'For a change, the men were hiding and women could come out of the shadows.'

The Aghadi's actions disclosed the solidarity of the Sena women in coming to each other's aid. Their accomplishments also showed the extent to which the Aghadi had pre-planned various forms of women's action during outbreaks of communal violence.

Battle for space

Sena women of all formal and informal ranks often gathered in their localities to cause obstruction to relief efforts. Areas with a small concentration of Muslim homes were called 'easy localities' because there were fewer relief workers hovering around. In the 'tough areas' women would not allow relief workers from the municipality or local NGOs to come into the slums and rebuild Muslim homes either destroyed by fire or razed by rioting men. Prachi, a cadre, said she wanted 'them' out of her locality once and for all, so she organised women to steal or remove material for reconstruction work. Interviews with firemen revealed some extreme cases in which groups of Sena women held hands and built rings around burning huts, preventing the police or the firemen from rescuing Muslim families trapped inside. However, interviews with the women also revealed that their primary reason for scaring away the Muslims was the practical concern of land reclamation. The demand for a geographical relocation of settlements was articulated largely because the women saw their families increasing and the pressure on physical space was high. As Prachi confessed: 'Since we stayed at home more than the men did, we knew the need for more space...,' adding hurriedly, 'These Muslims were taking up our space. They should go to Pakistan.' Basu, discussing the reaction of women to the Mumbai riots, gave examples of women employed in state-run agencies who boycotted their jobs until the government was 'forced' to clear Muslim slums in neighbouring areas (1998: 168). The Sena women had claimed they no longer felt safe living with Muslims.

Local NGOs who 'specialised' in dispute management were also harried out by the Sena women. When the Hindu and Muslim families were brought onto a common platform to resolve their differences, the Sena women produced humiliating clauses for the return of the Muslim families. Extracts from a *mohalla* committee (neighbourhood committees set up around Mumbai for re-establishing faith in Hindu–Muslim relations after the riots) report reveal examples of the stipulations put forward by the women who wanted:

- Muslim families to refrain from using cooking ingredients that were offensive to Hindus;
- all Muslim boys and girls to return home before dark and remain indoors;
- the right to search Muslim homes whenever they suspected any nefarious activity;
- separate playing grounds for their children and no Muslim children in the nurseries.

According to Hansen, the introduction of *mohalla* committees is an example of the way in which the Indian state has reproduced the positions of the colonial state by creating 'neutral arbiters' to resolve the conflict among 'lower classes', positioning itself as having a rationality higher than that of the 'masses' (1999: 206–7). Without an in-depth understanding of the communal situation in the slums, the *mohalla* committees in Mumbai seemed to have further aggravated the tension in the ghettoes by accusing Hindu women of being 'unfair' and 'absurd'. At a time when the Sena women were looking for excuses to frustrate rehabilitation efforts, these 'insults' gave them fresh motivation to reject all conflict resolution initiatives.

The Sena women's intolerance towards their one-time neighbours and their attempts to restrict the mobility of Muslim families had its own rationality. In his work on conflict and community in Sri Lanka, Scott asks some fundamental questions regarding practising 'toleration'. Is toleration a form of restraint in the face of hostility? Can it be understood in terms of the constitutional protection of cultural rights of minorities? Does toleration include a broader, more philosophical ethos which swings into action whenever differences turn into damaging forms of exclusion? Scott asks: 'How are the demands for a common life, for a life of shared interdependence and mutual recognition to be balanced against the demand of historical communities to live according to their own ways and their own languages?' (2000: 289). 'Enough land for all' was an answer in the Sena-dominated slums. Some Sena women had had Muslim neighbours in their villages, where physical distances between the various communities generated a culture of amicability and tolerance. Indeed, in a rural setting, where 'a Muslim neighbour lived across the field', the sights, smells and sounds of 'their religion' did not affect the daily living of inmates in a Hindu household. There were no contests over space. But in a cramped urban slum the loud noises of Hindu prayers and chanting disturbed the Muslims, and the smell of beef being cooked nauseated the Hindus. This seemed to heighten further the awareness of cultural differences between the communities, which Sena women manipulated to project as a long-term communal clash. This would then put them in a position from which they could demand land and a homogenous community life for the Hindus. This was indeed manipulation over and above interpretation, because the women were also *aware* that they were refusing to display any form of toleration, exploiting their strength in numbers merely to grab land. '*Basti ki zameen kum hai. Joh hai woh Hinduon ka hona chahiye*' (Slum land is limited. Whatever there is should be for the Hindus). This was a common phrase used by women when asked about their role in chasing out Muslims. By setting out various clauses and by insisting that repressive cultural measures were indispensable for the self-protection of the Hindu community, the Sena women were actually trying to deter Muslims from returning into Hindu-dominated regions. There were no fears of victimhood. So communalism as a lived experience in the slums seemed to hinge more upon spatial rivalries and cultural disparities than upon any dramatic ideological difference.

Conniving with the police

Women claimed that their active resistance to arrests had thrust the police into a state of 'helplessness'. However, having observed the Aghadi's close relationship with the police it seems more realistic that women received police assistance in planning their demonstrations. There has been a lot of writing on the partial role of the police during the Mumbai riots. For example, Kalpana Sharma's survey of communalisation of policemen during the riots revealed that Muslims were asked to chant '*Jai Shree Ram*' (victory to Lord Ram) to be treated with any consideration (1995: 285). Policemen were taped sending wireless messages saying: 'Kill those circumcised bastards.' There were also reports of the police specifically killing and torturing Muslims.[3] Bapat's plea of police helplessness against female aggression did not seem to hold up in relation to Nirmal Nagar, because there was a definite rapport between the police and the Sena women. One was often in alliance with the other in several matters. The two parties would meet amicably, especially while buying vegetables in the morning. The policemen, then in plain clothes, would exchange pleasantries and share local gossip. If the Aghadi women were involved

---

[3] Reports on atrocities perpetrated by the police on Muslims and excerpts from their wireless messages were published in the February (1993) and March (1993) issues of *Communalism Combat*.

in a conflict, the police would always turn a blind eye and never intervened to curb any of the Aghadi's illegal activities. Women in Nirmal Nagar would always emphasise that the policemen were good Hindus first and that, being on the lowest rung of the state-machinery's hierarchical ladder, coming to the aid of community members was their duty. In reality, the policemen were friends and neighbours who acted in collusion with the Sena women. Just how the police were 'compelled' by the women to release a violent leader (Sarpotdar) at the time of the riots is difficult to fathom.

Also some of the women running illegal trades (like cannabis or hooch dealers) felt the riots had brought them closer to the policemen. Initially they had feared the police and had to fool them to further their criminal activities, but feelings of mistrust dispersed after the riots as the two parties started working together. The women felt far less sexually vulnerable when entering police *chowkis* and were grateful that the Sena had given them the opportunity to overcome their differences with a government body. According to Neeta, a senior Sena leader: 'Now the police are one of us.'

Leadership and 'direct' violence

There were times when women felt that their participation in the violence was 'direct' (*seedha maar-peet*) and hence commendable. They felt that the greater the degree of violence exercised by women, the greater their 'fame as fearless warriors'. Rekha Kambli, a Sena leader from central Mumbai, said that at one time in her area rumours were rife that the Muslims had destroyed a local Hanuman temple. After 'hearing the news' she apparently paced in her room for a while. Unable to control her emotions, she went out onto an open patch of ground and stood there alone:

'I didn't speak but stood there looking at the closed windows of the homes around me. Even the men didn't dare to open the window and take a peek at this lone woman standing in the heart of a riot-torn area. Then all the women came out one by one, they all stood around me and I said: "Come my Hindu sisters, we must take action." The women wrapped their sari ends around them and tucked them into their petticoats [a sign of aggression or preparation for heavy labour]. We went around the area threatening all the Muslims to behave themselves. We broke into shops in the area, destroyed their property ... they would never raise their heads again, those bastards. Daring to touch a Hindu temple in our area....'

Rekha's dramatisation of the story and the mythologisation and romanticisation of the figure of the lone woman setting an example for other women to follow were attempts by her and other *seedha maar-peet karnewali* women (those who practised direct violence) to defend women's 'advancement' into the sphere of collective violence. This was the need of the hour, 'when the men were hiding'. The Aghadi's agenda was to exploit a riot situation to mobilise as many women as possible for direct militancy and thereby gain visibility as a formidable women's group. Once again women did not confess their obvious enjoyment in joining 'the sport of violence'. Instead they tried to play out a 'heroic' role under the façade of avenging an attack on their religion.

There were no reported cases of women's involvement in murder and mayhem at that time. But the riots were an opportunity for Rekha (and others like her) to bring women out of their homes and exhibit a sense of power through collective attacks on Muslim property. However, this is not to suggest that the women were incapable of bloodshed. A month after the Mumbai riots, when a local Marathi newspaper wrote against Thackeray, Rekha attacked a lady reporter from the daily with a sickle, almost cutting off her left arm. The editor of the newspaper requested that I quit my research after I informed him that I was working closely with Rekha. When asked during an Aghadi meeting if the women were capable of going on a real killing spree, the answer came in a chorus: 'When the time comes, we'll do it!' Uma's prowess at hurling bombs would be put to use 'then'. This preparation for a 'coming time' is vital to the Aghadi's future agenda to militarise their social setting.

Public assertiveness

Many Sena women who did not take part in *seedha maar-peet* involved themselves in militancy by developing an aggressive public image. For example, after the riots were over Rekha went on to form what could be described as a 'shout-and-scream brigade'. She led women into newspaper offices or the homes of academics critical of the Shiv Sena and after going on a rampage she would order the women to shout colloquial Hindi abuses and beat their chests to pressure 'recalcitrant' creators of public opinion into toning down their criticism. This is a strategy borrowed from what could be called the independent women's movement, where women activists shout slogans against families who ill-treat women within the home. The abuse brigade used similar aggression to rescue women mistreated in the family.

The Aghadi also took part in the creation of religious traditions, creating or seeking out conditions in which a strategic public role for women could be promoted. To the Sena women this was another method of sanctioning violence and was achieved predominantly through their large-scale participation in the *maha-aartis*, rituals of collective worship, which were staged by the Sena during the Mumbai riots. These were devised to compete with the traditional Friday afternoon prayers (*namaaz*) at mosques. The lack of space in the mosques often made the congregation spill out onto the streets, creating panic in the Sena ranks. According to the Aghadi, the Muslims appeared to be organised, were greater in numbers, made Hindu women feel vulnerable and put the entire Hindu religion at risk. These myths contributed to stereotyped misconceptions of the other's practices as displays of their strength and malevolent intentions. The *aartis* thus were not restricted to temple complexes; they were also held at street corners, often obstructing traffic at peak hours. The Sena *maha-aartis* convened large numbers of Hindu worshippers, but Aghadi members knew the practice would not be sustained if it were not publicly supported by the presence of women.

Some of the Sena women said their 'involvement in the rituals bordered on the edge of frenzy'. From the women's descriptions, and by sieving through news tapes on the events,[4] it emerged that women played a role in giving these public rituals a performative value. Using voice modifications, aggressive gestures and other brisk jumping movements they tried to achieve an effect through which a conventional domestic ritual could be legitimated as a public act with various implications for both Hindu and Muslim communities. The staging of this performance in a sequential form benefited the male participants because they experienced the event intensively and with heightened effect. Turner (1974), discussing symbolic action in society, argued how in all ritualised movements there was at least a moment when those moving according to a cultural script were liberated from normative demands. In this space between two ordered worlds almost anything can happen.

In this interim liminality, the possibility exists of standing aside not only from one's own social position but from all social positions and of formulating a potentially unlimited series of alternative social arrangements. (Turner, 1974: 13–14)

Verkaaik (2004), even though he specifically moves away from Turner in his study of rituals and urban militancy, makes a similar argument about the participation of women in the post-election celebrations of the Muttahida Qaumi Movement in Pakistan. He points out how women pouring into the streets to sing and dance with strangers, mostly men, allowed them to transgress an 'everyday morality'; once out in public, the behaviour of these women could not be openly controlled by the party leadership. In the case of the Shiv Sena, this so-called liberating experience of public dancing also gave fluidity to women's conduct. At the same time this shared religious passion allowed both Hindu men and women to remember and experience freely the jubi-

---

[4] The rituals were taped by several news bureaux and were available for viewing at the NDTV and Doordarshan (national-level TV news channels) archives.

lance of being associated with a violent, pro-mob movement, an experience which often became submerged under the daily eroding struggles for economic survival. The performance was also a demonstration of Hindu women's commitment to their religion. The fact that they could be 'unleashed' in public to carry out aggressive activities was meant to pose a threat to the enemy community.

The Aghadi cadres acting as vanguards of Hindu fervour helped women to view themselves as legitimate participants in public demonstrations of faith. The older Sena women had complained how their experiences in the slum had erased the boundaries between the private and the public spheres, how several women were compelled to submit sexually to husbands and male employers. But as long as they avoided confrontations, women could ensure the conjugal and material survival of the family. But when they joined the Sena they could resist the advances of male employers to construct a cherished boundary between the home and the world. In the case of the new generation of Aghadi women, however, collective action, whether directly destructive or modestly supportive, was intended to erase partially the boundaries between private and public spaces, religion and politics. Their enactment of familiar household rituals in public was meant to fortify 'the Hindu cause' as a festering collective wound. Hence the women's overt and covert participation in the Mumbai riots gave them an opportunity to overcome domestic restrictions and wilfully nurse a desire for an assertive, permanent public role.

THE ROUTINISATION AND NORMALISATION OF VIOLENCE IN THE DAILY EXPERIENCES OF THE SENA WOMEN

Pandemonium prevailed in the civic general body meeting on Thursday as corporators indulged in a free-for-all after Mayor H. Patil did not allow an opposition leader to raise a point of order.... In the fisticuffs, jostling and verbal abuses that followed, two Muslim women corporators of the Samajwadi Party, Ms Ansari and Ms Inamdar, were assaulted by a group of Shiv Sena women corporators. The two injured corporators were later taken to St George's Hospital for treatment. Witnesses said the two women were attacked by Sena leaders Trushna Vishwasrao, Vishakha Raut and Anita Bagwe, with Sena corporator Neeta Naik in the forefront. (*Times of India*, Mumbai, 17 March 2000)

AS: 'Did you really attack the Muslim women?'
　　Neeta Naik: [eyes flashing] 'I only tried to strip them. I could've killed them.'
　　AS: 'Because the women were Muslim?'
　　NN: 'Because they [the women] and their party [the Samajwadi Party is the remnant of the Muslim League] always use obnoxious language about us.' (Interview with Neeta Naik, 17 March 2000)

'After a twenty-four hour battle for life, Shiv Sena corporator Neeta Naik suc-cumbed to bullet injuries at the KEM Hospital on Tuesday. Ms Naik was fired at by two unidentified assailants outside her residence on Monday afternoon. While one bullet pierced her skull, one was lodged in her waist and a third injured her neck.' (*Times of India*, Mumbai, 13 November 2000)

AS: 'Your daughter is in her teens now. How does she feel about your aggressive image and all the criticism it draws?'

NN: 'My children know I'm trying to survive alone in a man's world. My hus-band has been in jail for many years now. He's also semi-paralysed. If I'm a wimp, how will I give them a good life? ... At least I'm not a prostitute.' (Interview with Neeta Naik, 10 August 2000)

'This certainly was not Children's Day for Pinky (14) and Hardik (10), the chil-dren of Neeta Naik. "I will kill all those who killed my mother," screamed Pinky at regular intervals.' (*Times of India*, Mumbai, 14 November 2000)

Neeta Naik's death exemplified the violence in the lives of the Sena women. Neeta, whose gangster husband Ashwin was serving a life sentence, took over the reins of her husband's illegal business. Having been a housewife for many years she found it 'difficult' to accept her new activities, which involved drug-trafficking, extortion and gun-running. She had to control her husband's henchmen and sharpshooters and, according to her, she had to take on a brutally aggressive image to keep the income flowing. Where does the Sena fit into her scheme? The party offered her a platform from which she could smoothen her relationship with the police and other law-enforcing authori-ties. But primarily the Mahila Aghadi supported her choice to control gang operations as a 'survival strategy' for women. The abuse brigades threatened newspaper critics who questioned Neeta's induction into the party, thereby displaying their solidarity with 'a woman in distress'. If the Aghadi had not stood by Neeta, she would 'have had to turn to the far more humiliating pro-fession of prostitution'. This emotional comfort is offered to several women married to gangsters and criminality. Most of these women felt it was élitist to view violence as an aberration in the daily lives of ordinary people. The Sena slums exemplified a human habitation marked by poverty and questions of survival where 'routine, ordinary and normative violence of everyday life, coexists with sudden eruptions of extraordinary, pathological, excessive or gratuitous violence' (Scheper-Hughes and Bourgois, 2004: 5).

Most Sena cadres felt that the internalisation of violence was an existential reality in the lives of women. From an early age girls would see their mothers and sisters getting thrashed by their in-laws. Many of them had faced marital violence themselves, had been raped by other men in the family, had been abandoned and had also been subjected to male supervision in the workplace. This kept them constantly vulnerable to sexual and emotional violence. Besides, life in illegally constructed slums required a state of preparedness for all forms of violence. There were several agencies striking them from all quarters, trying to uproot them from their life of subsistence. For the senior Sena women migration and dislocation was also an experience of violence against women. One of the Sena cadres put it this way:

'When a home burns down during riots, everyone shouts "violence, violence". When a home so carefully held together by a woman is blown away by storms, or maybe razed to the ground by bulldozers, then it is not violence?'

In the name of 'social service' and addressing 'women's issues', sections of Sena women developed a strategy for 'counter-violence'. This proved to be far more efficient and inexpensive for women in the slums than normal systems of legal justice. The Aghadi developed a strong-arm image and adopted a philosophy of brute justice to secure redress for women. Setalvad, in her comparative study of Hindu nationalist women in northern and western India, points out that in a society where many institutions of the state are inept in providing immediate succour to women and where the police and the state bureaucracy are racked by corruption (court cases take a decade or more to settle) the attractiveness of an organisation that delivers speedy justice cannot be overlooked (1996: 238). She cites examples of the Aghadi's activities which involved '*gherao*-ing' a senior advocate in Thane, north of Mumbai, preventing him from appearing in court on behalf of a priest accused of sacrificing a child. Similar tactics were used to prevent another lawyer from defending a rapist in court (*ibid.*). While I was working in Nirmal Nagar, a Sena leader from Jogeshwari, Rita, asked whether I would go with the women to a local school, where a clerk had been consistently harassing a teacher. I arrived late and was directed to the school premises. When I walked into the office I saw this clerk kneeling on the floor, with Rita, perched on his desk, occasionally poking a measuring scale into his testicles. The man flinched in pain. He was made to apologise to the teacher several times, and then made to say 'this teacher is my sister' and 'all women are my sisters'. When the drama was over the Sena cadres left in a hurry. Before she sailed out of the room Rita yelled: 'Make sure you're not a sister-fucker!' This event greatly hurt my sensibilities and I stood there speechless. A few days later, travelling to Central Mumbai to meet another Sena woman leader, I was 'teased' by a man on the train. He made a few crude remarks and began to follow me to my destination. I stopped at a shop and asked for directions to the Aghadi leader's house, at which the 'teaser' turned pale and to my relief ran as fast as his legs could carry him. This event did not offend my sensibilities in the least and I cheerily rattled off the story to the Sena leader when I finally found her residence. There is a point in elaborating my dilemma. Sena women justified communal violence, especially their participation in the Mumbai riots, as an extension of the entire system of serving women's interests that they had developed over the years. This was just another variety of collective violence, which would protect the interests of women in the slums. Women's aggression thus remained legitimised in advance through a discourse which perceived collective violence and rough justice as a prerequisite for the survival of poor women. The 'benefits' of the Aghadi's notorious reputation were also enjoyed by the anthropologist.

Whether humiliating a Muslim woman by stripping her or a man (who was a Hindu in this case) by trying to emasculate him, violence for the Sena women had become the favourite tool for wresting practical gender advantages. The tradition is likely to carry on over generations, as seen in the case of Pinky Naik, who threatened to avenge her mother's death.

REALISATIONS ABOUT THE 'SELF' THAT EMERGED DURING THE RIOTS

The Mumbai riots were an unprecedented moment of active violence for the Sena women. In an article on the mass suicide of Sikh women during Partition, Butalia (1993) argues that inflicting hurt upon themselves gave women agency, since they were involved in the collective destruction of their bodies, which was also a form of violence. The question here is whether we can see these women as victims or as active participants in protecting their chastity. In the case of the Sikh women, it was the apprehension of victimhood that actualised a circumstance in which they could display their agentive capacities. Fear of sexual pollution spurred the women to initiate a series of injurious acts, albeit upon their own bodies. The possibility that the Sena women had also acted in fear of being 'polluted' at the hands of Muslim rioters also seemed likely. However, the notion of the sexually aggressive Muslim male and the dishonoured Hindu female was not deeply embedded in the minds of the Sena women. Most participated in mass violence mainly to exploit a situation of action and volatility; and to heighten their communicative possibilities in the public realm.

According to Tambiah, rioting is the violation of generally established and universally valid distances, the more usual kind of destruction is an attack on all boundaries. 'The destruction of windows and doors of houses is also the destruction of the individuality and separateness of houses and inmates' (1996: 321). Besides the drive to reclaim land and use methods of destruction to humiliate the enemy, another reason for the Sena women's attacks on Muslim homes appeared to be to satisfy curiosity about their contents, which were so closely guarded from non-Muslims. 'They'd be so offended if we tried to take a peek through the windows ... but I couldn't help it,' giggled Chandrika, displaying some special pots and pans from a Muslim house, which she had kept as practical memoirs of her role in the riots. The 'ban' on entry into Muslim homes was a source of all sorts of speculation including rumours that they had armaments hidden beneath the floors.

Reinterpreting Hegel in the context of violence and community, Hoffman says:

Violence educates one to the inescapable reality of others. Contrary to my initial narcissistic assumption, I do not encompass all of being within my boundary. It is the necessary condition of my emergence as a universal, communal being ... I know reality cannot be measured by my own particular beliefs and values. (Hoffman, 1989: 144)

Rather than emerging as 'universal' beings, the Sena women's knowledge about their historical enmity with the Muslims enhanced their community consciousness. Their education in the reality of others gained through conflict helped them project their own values and subjectivities as superior to those of the enemy. However, the riots provided increased opportunity of communication between several groups and classes of people *within* the Hindu community, which allowed the Sena women to forge new relationships within the narrow frame of nationalism.

During discussions on the Mumbai riots, repeated emphasis was placed on the fact that women from nearby high-rises, MIG (middle income group) colonies and those in the slums who were not direct Sena recruits had joined the Aghadi in their efforts, 'even if the men remained indoors'. This was highlighted in Rekha's description of the situation in which—on the spur of the moment—she offered leadership to women from many layers of society. In the absence of conflict the slum women had steered clear of the 'air-conditioned women' (most of whom were not active Sena members) from the high-rises, lest their grubby hands smeared their dry-cleaned saris. Some of the slum women who worked as domestic help in the high-rises often discussed the special silk clothes that their employers kept out of the reach of careless maids. Yet during the riots many of the upper-class, upper-caste women offered food, clothing and money to the Sena women. Some of the 'air-conditioned women' even left the comforts of their apartments, temporarily dissolving unequal power balances, to work closely with Aghadi members and protect their locality from Muslim attacks. An obvious relationship of co-dependency emerged at that time: Sena women needed funding and the high-rise women did not want Muslim trouble-makers near their homes. Yet, when talking about their experiences of women from different class, caste and kin groups sitting together to keep vigil, holding protest marches, making bombs or preparing food, the Sena women insisted that there was a new feeling of fun and sisterhood; women enjoyed being part of a highly interactive, decision-making process which often remained independent of male interference. According to Girard, the internal divisiveness and conflict within a group or collectivity may drive its members to seek out a scapegoat and kill it sacrificially to gain an uncertain unity within the group, making of this a cleansing and a sacred act of generative unanimity (1977: 23). For the Hindu women there was a converging and coalescing of class and caste interests for a while, giving them a monolithic experience within the folds of waging a religious war. The uncertain unity, however, spilled over into the post-riot slum life. The various groups of women carried on being 'friends', and even though class differences were not erased, the Sena women felt 're-spected enough to get invitations for high-rise weddings'.

The participation of the women in religious violence in public also contributed to a strengthening of links with several other groups of people. After sharing a relationship of distrust for years, the Sena women embarked on a common platform with the police force, which played an overt partial role during the Mumbai riots. Sita, a Sena woman who had sold marijuana on a station platform for the past fifteen years, felt that a sympathetic association with the police guards developed after she played a visible role in anti-Muslim propaganda during the riots. It staged a turnaround in her relationship with the policemen and she experienced a definite toning down in their earlier hostility towards her. According to Sita, 'They're also scared of me now because if they mess with me, the whole gang will be at their throats as well.'

The riots also provided the women with a means of reasserting and reaffirming their identities. Even though there were minimal social connections between the Hindu and Muslim women in the slums, there was also little difference between them when thrown into the same physical space. For example, in Hoshiarpur, bordering Nirmal Nagar slums, Muslim women did not wear a *burqa*, though their mobility seemed to be restricted within the home. So points of difference needed emphasising. In the absence of real economic differences with Muslim women, the Aghadi emphasised differences through Hindu religious identity and communal violence. The formation of the Aghadi was at the root of one such mission, and the participation of the women in the riots was another way to overcome the danger of confusion. After the riots the Muslim women continued to see themselves as victims, but the rioting Hindu women could now be more easily identified as aggressors. For the Sena women, taking part in conflict defined and legitimated both personal and collective identities, and also effectively marked their boundary with the enemy community.

The violence displayed by the Sena women provided an umbrella under which personal, familial, commercial and other local scores were settled. For example, land occupied by Muslim homes that women wanted taken over during the riots was seen as a collective resource, not individual entitlement. This immediately removed a sense of guilt in the women who developed outrageous clauses for the return of Muslim families to the slums. Since rescuing Rama's birthplace from treacherous Muslims was justified at the national level, Prachi's desire to 'reclaim land whose rightful owners should be Hindus' at the micro-level was projected as legitimate. So there appeared to be a careful merging of Hindutva issues with local interests. Women learned that if they stated their personal stake in this form of behaviour (usurping land and looting), then it would acquire a negative connotation. They would then be envisaged as materialists, knocking their men off a moral course. So the Sena women tried to ground their actions in the 'selflessness' and 'heroism' as demanded by a fundamentalist discourse. Human actors are not mere subjects, automatically following rules or autonomously exercising existential freedom. Their actions cannot be understood in terms of 'obedience to a directive', but have to be comprehended in terms of exploiting real possibilities and realistic strategies. With all its strengths and its limitations this is an essential theme running through Bourdieu's explanatory practices (1990, 1991, 1998). The Sena women's primary agenda was to exploit the temporary endorsement of women's public action within a struggle to confront inequalities in the social and material structures of patriarchy in their slum life. In the process they were constantly negotiating with the same discourse to which they displayed their undying loyalty.

The riots also gave several women within the Sena a chance to offer militant leadership on a larger scale. For example, after narrating her story Rekha admitted that her situation was also 'a process of learning' for her. It revealed the value of exhibitionism. She knew what effect dramatic demonisation of the enemy could have on an admiring spectatorship. Rekha also realised the significance of mass oratory skills as a potent energiser in mobilising women, and of the naked display of women's 'power', 'all of which [she used] later, as strategies for making women enrol in the Aghadi.' Thus the riots gave rise to a crop of aggressive women leaders who learnt to utilise 'rowdiness' as a method of generating fear psychosis.

What was striking about the Sena women and their role in the riots was the repeated narration of their participation in unfettered violence. They were unlikely to tell these stories to journalists because of the party's drive to present a moderate face to the world outside the Sena camp, but within the ranks these stories on the riots were widely circulated and reiterated. Writings on violence state that it is usually the victims who remember, and tell and retell the story of their experience of victimisation. Repetition allows them to mould their narratives into a ritualised form of mourning, which is then progressively shared by the afflicted community as a collective memory. The collectivity of aggressors would in time prefer their individual remembrances, especially acts of brutality against a weaker community, to be eroded by amnesia (Das, 1995; Tambiah, 1996). In the case of the Sena women, however, the telling and retelling of their role in the violence helped crystallise the event into a collective reminiscence about Hindu women's heroism and their daring step towards ending a state of victimhood. This form of retelling also helped develop mechanisms of collective hallucinations. For example, one of the Sena female cadres felt that when she joined women in the slums and ransacked a police station to demand the release of their men (husbands) the skies had turned red reflecting their *sindoor* (vermilion; sign of marriage smeared on the forehead of Hindu women), which had turned so aggressive. Other women who had staged this attack repeated the same story. One would tell the other: 'Do you remember the colour of the skies?' The other would say: 'That was the power of our *sindoor*.' Quite likely the skies were red because of the number of fires and pyres lit during the riots, but for all the women to view it passionately as a miraculous sign supporting their endeavour reflected their faith in their glory as women soldiers for justice.

Bowman's analysis of violence and identity reveals that violence cannot be understood merely as a force that manifests itself in the destruction of well-maintained margins; violence also creates certain identities and integrities which define, extend and reinforce boundaries. 'Violence—rather than being a performance in the course of which one integral entity (person, community, state) violates the integrity of another—may as well serve to generate integral identities in inscribing borders between something in the course of becoming an entity and its surroundings' (2001: 26). The Sena women demolished Muslim homes to pollute, humiliate and attack historical boundaries between the two communities. Yet their participation in the riots allowed them to look beyond their insular slum life to view formerly 'unapproachable' men and women as friends, supporters, sympathisers and co-conspirators within the boundaries of Hindu nationalism. Aghadi women's militancy marked their difference from more docile, restricted women of other communities, settled disputes within the slums and also gave the Sena women an opportunity to offer political leadership. Women discovered various strategies, some real, some hallucinatory, to recollect and celebrate their collective 'victories'. The riots thus spawned numerous dynamic identities for women, which made them realise intensively the usefulness and centrality of conflict situations in altering power equations.

CONCLUSION

This chapter has traced the progression of Sena slum women from a life of alienation to one of vitality. For the senior women the sporadic use of collective violence to gain space, assets and employment proved beneficial for wresting gendered advantages. The consistent organisation of women's collective action by the Mahila Aghadi culminated in women's active participation in the Mumbai riots. Women's 'new-found success' reiterated that collective violence could satisfy the Aghadi's quest for visibility, solidarity and partial equality in the public realm.

According to Daniel (1997), the primary question that faces the violent group is how to be assured of the continued recognition it desperately desires and needs. One option is to pursue the path of exclusionary violence and annihilate the Other (*ibid.*). A second could be to extend violence until it compels the Other into submission. The latter option is preferred by the Sena women as their form of historical justice. The Aghadi women would rather impose limitations upon the choices of Muslims, confine their movement and hold Muslims accountable for their actions towards Hindus. Complete annihilation of the Muslims would be followed by a period of certainty, which would prove detrimental to the interests of Sena women. If the target of their aggression was lost, their mobility could be curbed and they could even be compelled to return to a life of seclusion. If the enemy group were only subjugated, there would always be the insecurity created by the possibility that it may reorganise its forces and launch a fresh attack, like the Mughal invasion of Shivaji's territories. So the women would always need to be on alert and order themselves militaristically to ward off a new Muslim offensive. In addition the enemy could always be repeatedly accused of being a community with flimsy values and provoked into retaliation. For example, during the placid phases of the Mumbai riots the Sena women scoffed at Muslims for not offering a stronger resistance to the Sena rampage; for sacrificing their 'honour' in exchange for life and security.

Women suffer when poverty collaborates with patriarchal structures to claim success (in keeping women at home) and failure (in protecting women from being violated during a communal struggle). The Aghadi women were consciously trying to create a space where women could step out of their homes and also be equipped to protect themselves in public. Through its active and permissive involvement, the Aghadi sought to validate the donning of macho identities by women. Their ultimate goal was to achieve the militarisation of society (a combatant, Maratha, Hindu nation), through which women would acquire mobility, power and self-worth. Despite rational deliberations involved in the resolve to use violence, once given a free rein, violence creates its own dynamic. The following chapter discusses life after the riots and focuses on the Aghadi's strategies for mobilising women, most of which revolved around freeing women's aggression from male supervision.

4

MOBILISATION AND ORGANISATION

After the 1992 riots the Mahila Aghadi's reputation as an independent, militant women's group increased, but this did not dissolve the insecurities of the Sena women about the future of the wing. There grew a need to expand, to gain stability and to retain a visible position within the party. Hence the Aghadi gave emphasis to developing organisational strategies.

The Sena supremo Bal Thackeray lauded the Aghadi's militant history, but he also glorified the more restricted roles of 'everyday Sena women' as carriers of domestic and religious culture. The first section of this chapter analyses the apparent contradictions in Thackeray's speeches, in which he both puts women squarely within the four walls of the home and urges them towards public martiality. However, instead of highlighting the inconsistencies in Thackeray's approach to the position of women's warriorhood, the Aghadi tried to develop a powerful image of themselves as women who could swiftly and successfully shuttle between domestic duties and public aggression.

This chapter also analyses the fluidity of ideologies and organisational activities within the Sena women's wing. An organisation seldom consists of unchanging groups of peoples and beliefs. It is constantly in the making and thus remains fluid and fluctuating. Wright (1994), discussing the anthropology of organisations, suggests that instead of presuming a static thing called an organisation with a boundary against the environment, the *continuing* process of organising should be underlined. Although she is trying to address principles of corporate cultures, she opens up an analytical space within which 'organisation' is seen as a process of adaptation, generating symbols through which various kinds of activities are mobilised, including the construction of boundaries. Since most women in the slums had peculiar histories of segregation, migration, urban displacement and dispossession, adherence to a narrow fundamentalist ideology with strictly defined codes of conduct for women would have limited appeal to the wide range of *nouveau*-politicised Aghadi members. The Sena women thus created a flexible, assertive, 'woman-friendly' Hindu nationalism even while protecting their boundaries from 'invisible' veiled Muslim women. The Aghadi cadres further used their martial image and their notorious reputation to create and sustain a system of local brute justice, especially in favour of slum women. The Sena women also used their greater nationalistic credentials to wrest, violently, temporary social and economic benefits for poor women (ranging from material benefits like illegal taps and electricity to more intangible advantages like women's safety and mobility in the face of male predatory behaviour).

In addition the Aghadi maintained its unique militant image, but did not consist solely of violent women or women emulating their aggressive leaders. The Aghadi's strategies to mobilise homebound and mobile, young and old, active and subordinate women from the expansive slums of Mumbai into a violent hyper-masculine movement were so successful that they challenged the feminist movement in Mumbai, the latter becoming demoralised by its failure to collectivise slum women on a secular platform.

Although the Aghadi brought various women and their various worlds under one umbrella, unequal alliances inevitably materialised. But while emerging hierarchies broke the surface of unity, they were also submerged beneath new forms of compromise, cooperation and internal negotiation. The Aghadi's primary agenda was to maintain an organisation based on sympathy, loyalty and shared (not homogenous) identities; but although the Aghadi's existence was dependent on a parasitic relationship with the larger nationalist agenda, its success and continuity was not. The wing thus used a number of economic and institutional resources to develop a mobilisational base, which in turn legitimised daily, diverse battles for poor women. Right-wing women's struggles therefore reveal multiple dimensions of domination and resistance, and the many thresholds of women's endeavour and organisation to have the potential to transform local level gender dynamics.

This chapter outlines the various efforts made by the Aghadi to subtly re-adjust the mechanisms of power that frame the everyday lives of poor women. It also illustrates the self-proclaimed need of the Sena women for organisation, aggression and a large cadre-base to achieve that end. Without threatening the integrity of the party, women wanted to obtain power which was not derived from men, as well as to appropriate an independent arena of operation which was partially free of male management. The need for subtlety, which resulted in the shrouding of women's personal interests in a wider, cultural/Hindu nationalist cause, became essential for the Aghadi to refine 'that human machinery that assumes responsibility for and places under surveillance women's everyday behaviour, their identity, their activity, their apparently unimportant gestures; another policy that guides the multiplicity of bodies and forces that constitute a population' (Foucault, 1977: 77).

WOMEN AT HOME, WOMEN AT WAR

Thackeray's speeches on women, published in various sections of *Saamna* (a newspaper which acts as the Sena mouthpiece), had within them apparent contradictions. The Aghadi manipulated this ambiguity in the role ascribed to women within the Sena movement in order to develop 'an identity of convenience' for its supporters. Although Thackeray remained elusive and paradoxical, the local level female leadership (in collaboration with the women cadres) tried to develop a benefits-package for women retaining the essence of Thackeray's varied dictates, while fusing it with their own interests. Hence their loyalty to the party's supreme philosopher was enthusiastically displayed, which in turn legitimised women chalking out their own agenda and acting upon it.

In a speech to a women's convention on 6 June 1994 Thackeray said:

'I don't understand why the traditional ideas and perspectives on women's freedom once established *have* to change.... Now all of you are educated and go to work. But your children are left with *ayahs* [maids]. The child doesn't receive the mother's love, which is the mother's duty to give. Do all your social work, but at the same time stay at home, taking care of your children and your family. In America people get married in the morning and divorced in the evening. So precarious is the situation.... Girls these days don't wear *kumkum* [vermilion], which is a sign of good fortune. It does not represent backwardness or illiteracy!'

And later in the same speech:

'We need to form a squad to fight the atrocities against women ... for every problem there must be a specialised squad.... Get out of your homes.... Give guns to the women.... Take guns and see what happens! [Applause]. It is not enough to clap your hands. You must become the reincarnations of *ranraginis* (women soldiers).... Applying lipstick is not enough ... like the red in your lipstick, you must be a blazing fire. Women in Mumbai are robbed, stabbed and killed. I have something to tell them. Instead of your lipstick and comb, carry some chilli powder and a knife. The lipstick will not be able to save your life. If you are confronted with a miscreant, throw the powder in his eyes ... drive the knife into his chest. You may also use a gun to save yourself ... no matter what happens. After this it is my responsibility to see that you are saved from the police.'

The Aghadi members were aware that Thackeray's pronouncements related to women in the roles of mothers and simultaneously as soldiers ('stay at home' and 'get out of your homes') would not prove beneficial for the women's wing if interpreted as inconsistent. The primary support to the Aghadi came from lower-class, slum women who were compelled to enter public spaces in which their traditional notions of fidelity, morality and ideal motherhood were usually compromised. The slum women, whether educated or illiterate, had entered the labour market which often required granting sexual favours to employers, dealing in illegal trade and also leaving their children at home for entire working days. Hence the Aghadi did not interpret Thackeray's views on working women as restrictive, moralistic or judgmental and instead consciously used his prescriptions to develop an image of the Sena woman as one who performs her domestic duties well and is granted her public militancy as a reward.

In the all-party Sena meetings[1] married women wore their *kumkum* (vermilion) and their *mangalsutras* (black-beaded necklace worn by married women) and deliberately spent time discussing their domestic duties. But in their daily lives the women were keen to gather into 'squads' and enlist themselves as equal participants in the 'struggle'. This gave them the 'right' to carry weapons and acquire the freedom that was previously enjoyed by men. The Aghadi thus manipulated Thackeray's speeches to co-gender what Jeganathan (2000) describes as a 'space for violence', where the performance and practices of masculinity create conditions for the possibility of violence, which is easily recognisable within a community as terrorising. Thackeray's encouragement to form 'specialised' squads was also appreciated, since not all the women could play similar roles in public. According to Tulsi, a cadre:

'Like me, the ones who can't be part of a team going into an offensive, can do their bit ... and make their contribution in some other way. So everyone is important and has a part to play in the camp.'

Despite the exhibition of obedience to Thackeray's dictates, the women specifically used the Aghadi to develop their individual strategies of rebellion against male dominance in the slums. Some of their actions even contested the values upheld by their supremo. Although Thackeray openly chided women who wore lipstick, the regular application of make-up was used by a few Sena women as a form of dissent against their families. Sena cadre Neena, for example, wore a very dark lipstick even though her husband's family disapproved of women using cosmetics. Feeling that she could not apply it 'perfectly' and that it invariably smeared on the sides, whenever she spotted me her eyes lit up and she would drag me into a corner, hold out a lipstick, and stretch her lips for that smooth look. No words were ever spoken during these conspiratorial exchanges. Later though she said, 'I want to let them [her in-laws] know that I don't care about their impositions anymore.' Neena claims she learnt to resist her husband's tantrums and restrictions only after gaining the Aghadi's support.

[1] The Shiv Sena invited members from all its wings to attend specific meetings.

'My husband and my in-laws know that the Aghadi would be at their door if they clamped down on me. I wear the lipstick to remind them conspicuously that they mustn't mess with me ... the day I stop they'll think I've become submissive again.'

However, Neena was sure that despite all she preferred to be married than single, because 'people think that a single woman and a single cot have only one purpose, they have to be laid.' 'First it was the Aghadi business, and now it's this madam from England', complained Neena's husband after he caught us engrossed in a lipstick-application session. He obviously wanted to believe that 'foreign' elements were putting unholy ideas into Neena's head, she having been brought into his shanty as a 'regular and good wife'. In fact, women are known to resist their subordination in various low-profile ways.[2] However, the Aghadi operated in a clandestine way to assure more freedom for Hindu slum women and open up their chances for small rebellions. Hence they rarely encouraged women who wanted to take part in Sena activities to stage open revolts against the family.

Militant goddesses, avenging women

'Be true subjects of Durga and Kali, mothers. Those perpetrating injustice should feel your terror.... Why did Phoolan Devi stand up in protest? She was raped by ten men. She did not sit shedding tears. She rose up in anger. Took the gun in her hands. Caught those ten demons, tied them to a tree in the village and pumped bullets into them. She avenged the wrong done to her.' (Thackeray's speech at the women's convention on 6 June 1994)

By invoking the militant goddesses Kali and Durga, and the notorious female dacoit Phoolan Devi, as the ideals for his female wing Thackeray tried to justify women's militancy in public. However, most Aghadi women remained unmoved by the invocation of heroic goddesses from Hindu mythology as modern-day female icons. 'That's very common. We're always asked to be powerful like Kali or Sherawali [an incarnation of Durga]', said Tulsi, half yawning. Instead of laying emphasis on their status as human goddesses and expecting devotion for being painted in that light, the Aghadi women were more keen to draw on the violent revenge factor in the heroic tales of these women, real-life or mythological. On the one hand, as avengers the Sena women could project themselves as selfless devotees of justice, which would help shift the focus from their own interests. On the other hand, their

[2] According to Jeffery and Jeffery (1998), for example, the husband treated like a lord or a deity to his face may be derided behind his back and given excessively salty meals.

depiction as a women's retribution team allowed them to perpetuate their combatant image in public and legitimised the display of organised violence. According to Sarkar's later studies on the RSS women's wing (the Samiti), the absence of communal clashes in parts of northern India have forced the Samiti women, who had enjoyed an energetic public role during the Ayodhya movement, to return to their homes (1999: 134). The Sena women were often haunted by the fear that militant goddesses in the Hindu mythology returned to domesticity when a crisis situation was diffused. Perhaps the fate of women in their sister organisations had created a need to manipulate representation in order to highlight the more long-term, violent, public position for women suggested in Thackeray's speeches. They felt the possibility of sustainability, if 'the communal crisis was never resolved', explained Chanda-tai, an Aghadi member. The feeling of anger could not subside. According to Tulsi,

'Phoolan avenged the assault on her, Durga wanted to kill the demons who had taken over the skies ... the men proved weak and the women played a big role in defeating the enemy. People know that no one is more fearsome than a woman in wrath.'

Sena protects women, women protect themselves

'The police mercilessly beat up the women who were protesting against the renaming of the Marathwada University. They just ran amok ... tell me what bravery there is in beating up women ... if the women squads were ready then, would this have happened?' (Thackeray's speech at the women's convention on 6 June 1994)

The Congress has a corporator called Haji [a Muslim]. His men doused a woman named Gitakumari with petrol and set her on fire. The Shiv Sena will give women protection. (Thackeray in *Saamna*, 30 November 1994)[3]

Through his speeches Thackeray helped the Aghadi to identify enemies who had the potential of being a permanent threat to women's physical integrity in public. In the extract above, the name of the woman in question, Gitakumari, was also significant since the act implied the burning of a sacred Hindu text, the *Gita* (a virgin girl is usually called *kumari*, but the term is also used to represent 'purity'). While describing the burning of Hindu women by Muslims during the 1992–3 Mumbai riots, some Sena women would equate it with the enemy reducing the whole Hindu religion to ashes: 'It's the same because Hindu women are the biggest reservoirs of religious symbols'; 'burning a Hindu woman is like blackening the face of the religion.' However, they re-

[3] Apart from *Saamna*, the event was not reported elsewhere in the press.

fused to view Muslim women as 'culture-bearers' in a similar way. By breeding resentment in women through these narrations Thackeray also strengthened the bonds within the Aghadi. He created a parallel reality at the behest of the Sena women (a hostile world out to get Hindu women), which enabled the Aghadi to focus on its homogeneity, instead of dwelling on internal differences. Once the riots were over the Aghadi cautiously had to keep their mission of counter-retaliation alive, since it was through their role as religious warriors that women could advance into the public realm. So Thackeray had to play upon the idea that atrocities against Hindu women would never cease, and that women had to protect themselves. By capturing a vision of remaining sexually vulnerable to the secular police (the lowest government mechanism) and as being a material enemy to the aggressive Muslim male (who in the speech above also happens to be a man of the government), the Aghadi could establish prolonged hostile relationships with these enemies, which, since those enemies could not in reality be 'defeated', also gave the Aghadi the opportunity to develop long-term strategies to organise militaristically.

Women as 'culture carriers', women as 'commodities'

Q: 'Why does the Shiv Sena not protest against the Miss World pageant in Bangalore?'

BT: 'But I like to see the beautiful women in the pageants! What is the problem with these women activists? And what hypocrisy is this? You look at pretty women next door through the keyhole, but when beautiful girls walk the ramp, you sanctimoniously look elsewhere—even though you are eager to have a good look—and condemn the fashion shows! What humbug! Why can't they just let the shows be?' (Interview with Thackeray, *Saamna*, 8 December 1996)

Q: 'Why are the Sena women protesting the release of the film *Fire*?'

BT: 'Because I have told them to fight and protect their own culture! How can we allow some people to get away with distorting relationships between women on screen? All this they are showing [a lesbian relationship between two sisters-in-law] are Western imports and not part of our tradition!' (Interview with Thackeray, *Asian Age*, March 1999)

According to Bacchetta (2002), to configure a female-friendly Hindu nationalism the RSS women's wing often reproduces RSS representations but interprets them differently. Sometimes the Samiti ideologues draw from sources the RSS ignores to construct feminine identities beyond the RSS imagination. 'As a result, different aspects of the Samiti discourse are coherent with, or asymmetrically "complementary" to, or even antagonistic to, the RSS discourse' (2002: 47). Within the Sena, Thackeray's shifting 'beliefs' about the representation of Hindu women helped the Aghadi to develop a flexible brand of Hinduism such that the Aghadi could often gain an amount of public visibility and mobility by acting as the culture police, even though the boundaries of what was defined as 'culture' remained blurred. Most of these speeches of Thackeray were delivered well after the Mumbai riots and after the women had gained prominence as active participants in situations of violence.[4] By that time Thackeray is likely to have realised the potential of the Aghadi as a vote bank and as an influential organ of the party, and consequently delivered his speeches to appease the female wing. On the release of *Fire*, Aghadi picketers ransacked all the cinema halls where the film was showing and forced the distributors to withdraw it, albeit for a brief period of time. So Thackeray likely got wind of the women's discontent over the making of *Fire* and their nonchalance towards the cultural acceptability of professional modelling, and delivered his dictates accordingly. During my time in the field most Sena women leaders kept Thackeray and other senior male leaders aware of their major grievances, though usually not through 'official' channels (letters or memoranda). Rather, they utilised other means such as discussing their inconveniences, as if casually, in the presence of senior leaders, most of whom held proximate relationships with Thackeray. Consequently, the Sena supremo not only gave birth to a set of constructions (like the imagining of a common enemy), he also echoed aspects of a growing vision within the Aghadi (like the necessity of women's militancy) which the women wanted publicly reiterated before their male counterparts.

In her analysis of female garment workers in Dhaka, Feldman (1993) reveals that *burqas* were not affordable to poorer women, who justified their apparently deviant position by describing *purdah* as 'an internal state of being'. Thus Feldman posited that contradictions in ideology and material needs could give rise to new forms of appropriate female behaviour. Thackeray tried to resolve the contradiction of women's seclusion and mobility within the movement by allowing the men to believe that it was *they* who were setting their women free. In this way Thackeray could avoid giving controversial recognition to women's agency in securing their own autonomy. Since Thackeray had thrown a blanket of security around the women, promising to acquit them if they were accused of indulging in violence, men felt 'reassured' about their women's role in public. Tulsi's husband hesitantly said, 'If Bala*ji* (Thackeray) says it's OK, I guess it's alright. Otherwise I would've felt guilty about putting my wife in danger.'

[4] Prior to the Mumbai riots there were no recorded speeches of Thackeray exclusively for women. He gave general speeches at the all-party meets.

According to Nettl, 'some forms of legitimacy are characterised in terms of an analogy with the theatre; the relationship between the ruler and the ruled being presented as an actor–audience relationship' (1967: 219). Thackeray's acerbic speeches, his aggressive body language and his saffron robes certainly had a strong dramaturgical effect on women and played a big role in whipping up passions in the crowd. His speeches during the destruction of the Babri Masjid, for example, were instrumental in sparking the riots in Mumbai. Besides cheering loudly and clapping during the Sena women's meetings presided by Thackeray, the Aghadi members often rounded off these gatherings by parading around the meeting grounds and then around the city shouting slogans, thus displaying their undying loyalty to Thackeray—who they declared was a man of God.

According to Weber:

The term 'charisma' will be applied to a certain quality of an individual personality by virtue of which he is set apart from ordinary men and treated as endowed with supernatural, superhuman or at least specifically exceptional powers.... The group which is subject to charismatic authority is based on an emotional form of communal relationship. (Weber, 1968: 49–50)

By this definition, Thackeray was indeed a man with charismatic authority over the Sena. Rhidhi, an Aghadi leader, believed, 'Whatever Thackeray says is always right. It's almost as if he's been granted special powers by God.' In her bedroom Rhidhi kept a large photograph of her being blessed by Thackeray. All the Sena women kept photographs and posters of Thackeray in a strident posture in their prayer rooms, on their walls, on their tables, even in their wall clocks. For a long time they tried to convince me that Thackeray had 'divine sanction' for being at the helm of affairs in the Sena camp. This was the official face of the Aghadi.

Overt resistances

However, Thackeray was not above criticism from within the Aghadi ranks. On a day he inaugurated a factory run by a Marwari (a man from Marwar, a region in Rajasthan) in the Bhayander area, there was general discontent in the Aghadi meet. The Marwaris (occasionally slandered as 'Marus', a distortion of their regional identity) are perceived to be a prosperous and 'open-to-migration' community, which unscrupulously gained wealth and power in many parts of India. Thackeray's act violated the Sena's commitment to cleanse Maharashtra of its alien population. According to Yogita, the Bhayander Aghadi chief, 'Now he'll get only Marwaris in his factory and offices. Bala*ji*'s making a very big mistake.' Most of the women complained about their men and children not having enough jobs and 'Bala*ji*' compromising his position for 'this ugly Maru'. So when the interests of the Aghadi clashed with that of the supremo, the women became restless and critical. The gossip was that this 'Maru' had made a tidy contribution to the Sena to get its high commander to snip the ribbon on the factory door. Apparently the businessman had 'pulled this stunt' to secure immunity from Sainik attacks, since he was setting up his factory in a notorious Sena-dominated locality. 'I'll pay him a visit later and do my own round of his factory. He'll know who he has to deal with on a regular basis', said a scowling Yogita. However, the women were not keen to air their grievances to male members of the party.

De Certeau (1984), discussing diversionary practices within operational models of popular culture, argues that the finality of any order of things is an illusion. He points out how people (or human artists) 'develop count-less ways of refusing to accord the established order the status of law, an ultimate meaning or a fatality', and describes these popular tactics as 'an ethics of tenacity'. Since Thackeray was the supreme leader and philosopher of the Shiv Sena, the Mahila Aghadi as a crucial wing of the party had to display adherence to Thackeray's dictates. But the daily functioning of the women's wing incorporated ideas and actions which considerably digressed from Thackeray's opinions on the ideal behaviour for Sena women. Yogita's personal programme to visit the factory and let the owner know 'who is boss' showed how the local female leadership pursued their independent agenda. They were not hesitant to terrorise candidates befriended by Thackeray and establish the Aghadi's hegemony at local levels. Thackeray's caustic speeches for women thus represented a certain style of politics, but whether it really had an all-powerful impact on women remains doubtful. His instrumentalist use of symbols—like the stigmatisation of the threatening 'other' and the invocation of militant goddesses who had been reinterpreted and given sig-nificance—aided in constructing a shared, ethnic and/or religious identity for women. But the real task of mobilising women was not achieved through the formal and expressive symbolism that characterises party politics (de-scribed by the Sena women as 'microphone and podium politics'). Rather, mobilisation and organisation was carried out through a continuing process of confidential negotiation amongst Aghadi women in the slums.

Women and political participation

Most analyses of power admit that a subordinate is never in a state of pow-erlessness. According to Giddens and Held (1982), those in dominated po-sitions within social systems are frequently adept at converting whatever resources they have at hand into some degree of control over the conditions of reproduction in those social systems. That was one of the main organising principles of the Mahila Aghadi, who wanted to exploit the limited economic and ideological resources available to women within the Sena to wrest a more powerful and permanent social position for women. Since women thinking independently would become an obvious diversionary practice, Thackeray tried to curb this trend by passing several demands aired by the Aghadi as his own concerns for women. For example, he contradicted himself several times over the issue of reservation for women in the political arena. In a speech given on 30 November 1994 Thackeray said:

'The government has promised to provide reservation for women. What *aarak-shan* [reservation], women want *samrakshan* [protection]! Go and ask them. The Shiv Sena did not just raise slogans. We provided jobs for so many women. Go to Air India [the government-owned international airline] and see, all the women there say "Jai Maharashtra". Because of whom?'

Several Sena women leaders were not happy with Thackeray's remark. Indeed, many women reported that their greater political ambitions would be thwarted if Balaji kept 'blabbering nonsense' about women's issues. Later, when asked in a *Saamna* (8 December 1996) interview, 'What stance will you adopt when the Women's Reservation Bill is tabled in Parliament?', Thackeray replied:

'Why 33 per cent, I favour setting aside 50 per cent reservation for women. And reservation alone cannot guarantee justice. Even the fate of the reservation rests in the hands of men. Also, instead of just harping on the rights they have been denied, women must carefully consider the rights they have right now and enjoy them fully.'

In the first extract Thackeray refused to acknowledge the value of women's reservation in Parliament. By the time of the second he had clearly changed his stand and advocated a greater percentage of reservation for women. While he cautiously reminded women that they should not overlook the rights they have at hand, in the first extract he urged them to be content with the, albeit limited, mobility and employment opportunities they had procured under the protection of the Sena male bastion. Thus the dominant power (Thackeray) tried to retain its dominance by shifting stands and accommodating the concerns of the dominated (the Sena women).

Thackeray squarely put women within the sphere of domesticity and also urged them to become a militant battalion in the same public speech. The Aghadi overlooked the contradiction to converge both strands of thought and develop an attractive, rounded image of the Sena woman as one capable of passively carrying out domestic chores, even while fulfilling public duties which required the display of violence. They expressed full support of women's role in counter-aggression against the enemy, but did not disclose this support as an independent thought. The Aghadi needed to convince their male counter-parts that their militancy in public was justified, since they remained under Thackeray's protective wings. At the end of his writing on charisma and insti-tution-building Weber (1968) concluded that charismatic authority is specifi-cally outside the realm of the everyday routine and the profane sphere. In this respect it was sharply opposed both to rational and particularly bureaucratic authority, and to traditional authority, whether patriarchal, patrimonial, or any other form. However, Thackeray's sway over the women was primarily legitimised because it contained substantial elements of patriarchy. Thus the promise of protection largely allowed Aghadi women to organise themselves and draw other women into the fold.

MOBILISING WOMEN, SHARING LOYALTIES: A DAY IN THE LIFE OF AGHADI LEADER YOGITA PATIL

This section explores how the independent and assertive activities of a wom-en's cadre enabled it to operate as a new-age local vigilante group, adapting to and evolving within a situation of poverty and conflict. According to Ismail (2000), studying the politics of nation-making in Sri Lanka, not every group can occupy the same position in the vertical structure of the nation. In his study he views nationalist movements as a set of constitutive ideas that creates overlapping spaces of identity and difference, consensus and dissent. Here we see how the Sena Mahila Aghadi used diverse mobilisational strategies (persuasion, raw justice, threats, ostracism etc.) to gain the sympathy of poor women and partially modify their life-cycles in urban slums.

From my diary:

Yogita gave me a call in the morning and asked me to visit her. I must have been irritatingly persistent, begging for a meeting ... because she had that tone ... 'OK come and see me pest'... I am getting used to it now. I put on a saffron *salwar kameez*. I hate doing this when I go to visit a new *shakha* [local party office], but it was a waste. She was not a member of the hardcore saffron brigade I had thought her to be. I walked straight into her tiny LIG [Low Income Group] flat. The door was wide open and there were five women sitting on the floor. There were Walt Disney cartoon characters painted on the walls; a children's slide and water tub was pushed against a corner. The women smiled at me, they must have known I was planning to visit and one of them popped their head into the adjoining room and announced: 'Yogita-tai, that girl from England (*woh Englandwali ladki*) has come.' Yogita walked into the room in a pale blue *salwar kameez*. She sat in one of the two chairs while I occupied the other. 'What is there to tell about me', she began when I brought out my infamous notepad. 'I'm *shakha pramukh* (chief) in Bhayander area for fifteen years now. I'm bored.' Yogita looked at the women around her and said: 'I'm training these women to be my successors. Initially I used to take them along wherever I went for work. Now they go on their own.'

Radha: 'I'm her neighbour. When I came into this neighbourhood, I was such a docile housewife. My husband didn't let me go anywhere. Yogita-tai convinced my family to let me join the Sena ... (hesitant pause)... for a better cause of course. Now she says "Be my successor"! I get a lot of freedom now, but even today my husband says if you go anywhere for work, make sure you take Yogita-tai's name. Everyone here fears her.'

AS: 'What was the better cause?'

Radha [looking at Yogita]: 'Uh ... social work, Hindutva....'

Under the aegis of 'Uh ... social work, Hindutva', Sena women from various social and economic backgrounds tried to develop a shared identity as a women's collective. The Aghadi members initially approached women who were partially free from male guardianship. This target group consisted of women who were heads of their households, widows, women abandoned by brothers/husbands and often unwed mothers. In the case of single mothers the Sena leaders approached 'uncontroversial' women on whom traditional sanctions had eroded over time. The leaders also pressured unmarried women and older women living among kinsmen, usually with no hope of marriage, to join the women's wing. Some women felt isolated in a life of poverty and vulnerable because of the absence of protectors in their household. Others were house-bound women with sick husbands or workers who had acquired a degree of freedom after establishing their economic independence. These women felt protected and 'empowered' as part of a martial women's organisation. Having established a strong group of women in the *shakha* the Aghadi pursued slum women restrained at home and persuaded them to take part in the front's activities without offending their immediate families. By their own admission, this was not a unilinear process. The strategies to recruit restricted and independent women intermingled when implemented at the everyday level. 'We'd tell all the women, "Why sit at home in your spare time? Work with us." Women from all walks of life would come one by one ... not that some women came before others did', said Rama-tai, Aghadi leader.

Women from restricted backgrounds: negotiating their mobility

According to several feminist scholars, women's seclusion and segregation are forms of punishment and instruments to manage female sexuality (Dube, 1997; Karve, 1990; Leslie and McGee, 2000; Uberoi, 1996). Most Sena women were sensitive to this interpretation and experience of female confinement. They were aware that if slum women were encouraged to leave their homes to protest a life of captivity, it would only lead to increased detention. Instead the Aghadi members tried to reassure men that they viewed restriction as an extension of the concern and caring properties of their male kin, which was geared primarily towards protecting women from exposure to a harsh public life. Aghadi chief Meena said:

'Some of our men initially escorted us to the Sena meets. But after a while, when they realised we wouldn't be harmed, we started to attend the meetings by ourselves.'

The Aghadi did not brashly do away with the tradition of male supervision as symbolic shelters for women. Instead they preached a balanced vision of women's mobility in which women entering the public realm remained under the protection of the grand male—Thackeray—at the macro level. Meanwhile at the local level the women tried to overcome their defenceless status by carrying the violent, hyper-masculine Sena tag. 'We were marked as the notorious Sena women. No one would dare to touch us ...' became the common belief. Over time most men were reassured that the fear psychosis generated by the Aghadi was enough to ward off attacks on mobile Sena women. Since the Aghadi largely promoted youth leadership and membership, the considerable collective physical strength of a large band of aggressive women 'warriors' was found to be comforting for men. Yogita's husband Ashok said:

'They [the Aghadi women] had each other and since they kept growing in numbers, their force increased daily. I became complacent about Yogita's capacity to take care of herself and her flock.'

Even though some of the Sena men lifted the restrictions and conventions of women's complete confinement, it was difficult to draw out women used to years of familial control. Some housewives in the slums worked out of home and contributed richly to the family income; yet they were denied autonomy. Some slum women faced corporate control on their mobility and/or denial of sexual gratification for 'offences' like stepping out of the house (often to fetch water) without permission. These women were so steeped in their condition that the Aghadi improvised constantly on its strategies of persuasion, cautiously and persistently urging housewives to review the benefits of joining the women's front.

Scholars dealing with notions of segregation in South Asia have commented that villages in India have certain areas outside the home earmarked as exclusive domains for women. Dube (1997), for example, identifies the area around the well and the days scheduled for women's devotional music as spaces considered to be an extension of the women's quarters; women use these places briefly to shed their patriarchal fetters through gossip and banter (1997: 60–70). Sena leaders began to project the Aghadi as such a 'feminine place' outside the home: a physical and emotional space which did not overtly threaten male structures of domination yet remained free of male surveillance at all times. It was almost the re-creation of a village space in an urban context, where the freedom of association between women gave them a chance to share their daily grievances.

Several slum women looked upon the Aghadi as an active social network outside their homes. Most of the younger Sena women, recently married into slum life in Mumbai, had realised that the household was not just a domain of responsibilities, but was also a domain of power. Sena women expressed that they felt their power was curbed within the home for several reasons, a chief one being the presence of senior men and women in charge of the negligible space and resources available in a slum home. 'The new bride had no say, and no space to hide', complained Rama, a cadre. However, the Aghadi offered alternative social and political engagements which allowed women to gain a sense of social worth through involvement in 'social work, Hindutva', as declared by Radha above.

To allow restricted women opportunity for interaction the Aghadi leaders worked certain schedules and celebrations around the structure of women's daily lives in the slums. Some Aghadi meetings were strategically located near markets and tube wells. Policy-maker for Sena women, Poonam, said: 'When women were spared that hour for doing groceries, they could also attend a meeting.' The Aghadi further organised collective celebrations for women, such as *haldi-kumkum* (turmeric and vermilion) and *karwa chauth* (prayers to prolong a husband's lifespan) festivals for married women. These public re-inventions of traditionally domestic rituals attracted the attention of some scholars, including Banerjee (1996) who suggests the celebrations for married women can be interpreted in three different ways. First, they can be seen as the Sena's way of fastening women to the status of wives to counter their liberating experiences as workers. Second, the Sena could be giving out a message of female autonomy, fusing it with familial iconography to make it more appealing. Third, the Sena could be subverting attention from a display of feminine energy by espousing 'Hindu power' through these rituals (1996: 223). According to the Aghadi cadres themselves, promoting these rituals exerted a Hindu solidarity in the slums. But to most women it was also a ploy 'to convince the Hindu slum men that women could contribute to Hindutva if allowed to act collectively', said Jaba, a cadre.

Rewards for 'bad conduct'?: male leaders endorsing Aghadi solidarity

The Shiv Sena's upper male leadership had noticed the functionality and powerful impact of women operating in solidarity, so some of them conspired with the Aghadi to create an everyday space where women could interact openly without coming under suspicion. During the Mumbai riots the Aghadi had played a visibly aggressive role, which had benefited the Sena men. Consequently Madhukar Sarpotdar, a notorious Sena corporator who was arrested for supplying arms to Hindu rioters (discussed in Chapter 2), decided to develop physical support structures to ensure that the Sena women's strength and solidarity did not suffer erosion within a quotidian slum life. When Sarpotdar became an MLA (Member of the Legislative Assembly) he was allotted an amount of money to extend civic facilities to the people in his assembly. He invested part of that money in building three decorative Ganapati temples with expensive bathroom tiles. This appeased the Sena women because it gave them a fancy place to meet and sing *kirtans* (devotional songs) in the evening. Women were not condemned for gathering in these temple areas and hence they could freely exchange their ideas for recruitment and social work. These *kirtan* sessions were infused with an atmosphere of enjoyment created by the energy of the place when all the women sang, laughed, cried and conspired together. Most women, who mourned the lost vitality of community life in villages, seemed to have regained their traditional group solidarities. Thus the Aghadi gave slum women a chance to assimilate into a new social and political network, within which they could resolve their urban insecurities and experiences of alienation. Furthermore, some of the male leaders in their limited capacity helped the Aghadi increase their scope of mobilising these women.

Targeting 'independent' women, transferring male dependency

Yogita: 'Women in the slums have to work ... otherwise they won't be able to survive. But someone has to be there to tell them that if anyone hurts a hair on your head, we'll thrash the life out of them! We had to make the women realise they were not totally dependent on men for their survival.'

In the slums of Mumbai several conditions led to a breakdown in systems of permanent dependency on men, and women developed fresh insecurities when faced with new challenges for survival. The socio-economic conditions surrounding poverty had created a group of 'independent' women employed in the organised and unorganised sectors. The effects of migration, industrial strikes and the breakdown of kin enclaves on women, and how migrant women were compelled to take up income-generating activities in the city, were all discussed earlier. A number of women experienced a trend, somewhat liberating, where they became economically independent of men. However, the social conditioning in the slums was such that the position of women was still rooted in their marital status. Several Aghadi slum-dwellers were the sole breadwinners in their family, yet they remained in abusive conjugal relationships. Some of them joined the Aghadi to divert their domestic frustrations into active militancy and productive 'social work'. 'That's how far these women can go right now', Aghadi leader Kamla would comfort me whenever I became distressed over bickering slum couples.

This section of women (irrespective of their marital status) seeking urban employment for the first time faced various forms of sexual and economic exploitation. Some of them, widowed after coming to the slums, had little scope for returning to their native villages since the city, at least, provided them with a livelihood. Several, despite being economically independent, felt helpless and humiliated when husbands abandoned them to set up new families elsewhere. The women not only faced an uncertain future, they often became the targets of lecherous co-workers, supervisors and neighbours. Neha, a woman whose husband ran off with his mistress, surprised me with her insight:

'You urban people would think that migration either leads to greater sharing of responsibilities between spouses or the strengthening of the family bond. I'm not saying that doesn't happen at times. In your case, that's what happens when you become a *chhota* [nuclear, small] family, isn't it? In our case, it often leads to a loss of affection between spouses, children, infidelity and other marital problems. We're separated from our larger family, there's a breakdown of family norms, the men are independent of senior patriarchs and suddenly realise there are no sanctions for running after more *chikna* [beautiful] women.'

Neha's husband did not return to her, but after she joined the Aghadi a band of women went and beat their chests in front of his new home. One of the senior Sena women also 'punched his face' and broke his nose. Neha had her revenge. The Aghadi delivered similar forms of 'justice' when vulnerable women were harassed in the slums.

Women were greatly affected by the changing experiences of 'family joint-ness' in their urban milieu. Most slum families went through periods of togetherness and isolation since urban employment made the male members professionally mobile. At times the families became so depleted that the women tried to develop alternative structures of male dependency. For example, Juthika, when widowed, tried to run a boarding house for men in the hope that they would act as the protectors of her family.

'But there were no permanent residents and not all the men were good. You don't know what is good? Good means good. Bad means *bad*. When I began to work with the Sena, everyone knew me as a Sena woman. I was also *bad*. My vulnerability went away. I didn't care what people thought.'

Over time Juthika realised that most men were untrustworthy and willing to take advantage of a 'defenceless' widow. She took the initiative to develop a notorious reputation as an Aghadi cadre, primarily to protect herself and save her family from financial distress. 'If I'm a bad poor woman, so be it. I've seen how good men have treated me', she concluded. The Aghadi created a common ground for women to share their employment problems and its repercussions in their personal lives. Through their militant image and methods of extending violent justice the Sena women grew in popularity for offering protection to working women and/or women 'alone'.

However, the Aghadi ensured that the two categories of women, the mobile and the less mobile, did not develop a relationship of envy. The wing constantly emphasised the common sentiment that all women must coalesce their interests. 'The Muslims are attacking us', 'the Christians are attacking us', 'the police are attacking us', 'our employers are attacking us', 'men on the streets are attacking us' and hence 'we must stick together and fight back' (were the opinions shared). It is significant that the militant, mobile Aghadi women did not want to mass produce other women in their image. The fluidity in the organisation and flexibility in its approaches to incorporate women from varied backgrounds reflected the Aghadi's desire for sympathy, support and an extensive base of cadres. This phenomenon possesses parallels with the operations of other 'fascist' organisations, such as the Ku Klux Klan in America, where the swearing-in oath for both men and women stated: 'Female friends, widows and their households shall ever be the special objects of our regard and protection' (quoted in Annan, 1967: 266). In this context, Blee (2002) argues that there was a marked difference between the propagandist messages of the Klan and the real motivations for women to join its women's wing, Kamelia. While the official line was to attack the racial others (African-Americans, Jews etc.), women were drawn into the movement for 'much more mundane concerns like education, physical safety and family life' (2002: 113). This is also true of the Sena, because the women definitely benefited physically and financially from their association with the Aghadi. Though there is little scholarship on Kamelia, a substantial difference with the Aghadi was probably that the women of the latter were consciously and conspiratorially protecting their own gender interests even while projecting a selfless, self-effacing image as nationalist women.

CHALLENGING THE FEMINIST MOVEMENT AND
SECULAR PARTIES

Some of the feminist writing critiquing the Hindu right (Agnes *et al.*, 1996; Banerjee, 2000; Butalia, 1993; Sarkar *et al.*, 1993; Setalvad, 1996) condemns the Aghadi for blatantly hijacking the symbols and actions of the feminist movement and using them for their own purposes. The Sena women's front were candid about their enterprise to outwit the autonomous women's movement and the associated 'bourgeois' welfare organisations to secure the loyalties of slum women. Several feminists were outraged when their slogans like '*hum Bharat ki nari hain, phool nahi angarey hain*' (We are the women of India, not flowers but burning embers)—used to protest violation of equal rights for women—were used by rioting Sena women during the post-Ayodhya outbreak of violence in Mumbai. Even the transformation of their logo *Stree Mukti* (women's freedom) into *Stree Shakti* (women's power), the latter being more representative of Hindu female militancy, angered some academics. Rekha's initiative to form the 'shout-and-scream brigade', often to deliver justice to slum women neglected by their families, was a strategy borrowed from the independent women's movement (where women activists would shout slogans against families ill-treating women within the home).

Despite their blatant emulation of feminist practices, the Aghadi was careful not to develop the image of an élitist 'NGO-type' organisation where 'the women sitting on soft sofas in air-conditioned offices thought troubled women from slums would come to them for help.' Instead, the Aghadi went in search of 'their women'. Visiting local NGOs and speaking with the women leaders from other political parties it became clear that no one knew the interiors of the dark and damp gullies, every turn, every open gutter, the way the Aghadi leaders did. Women leaders and their associates regularly visited each household in their constituencies to keep them informed about the party and its activities. Over lunch and tea, or through gossip and rumour-mongering, the Aghadi cadres made themselves familiar with all the women in the locality, their families and the problems locked up in each shanty. This kind of active social networking built a *bonhomie* and camaraderie among the women in the slums. It also allowed the Aghadi members to devise, surreptitiously, strategies for alleviating the misery of individual slum women. These plans had to be implemented without annoying the family members and creating tension in their immediate surroundings.

'Who are the ones who truly represent the masses? Us or them [welfare organisations]?' asked cadre Rama when questioned about the Aghadi's sway over the slums. Feminist Mumbai filmmaker Madhusree Datta once commented on the Sena women:

'Our [feminists'] weakness is we didn't realise this desire to belong. We thought of need, of rights, but not the desire to belong. Rebellion does not make a movement, does not make a craze. Rebellion remains an alienating, isolating factor.' (Quoted in Banerjee, 1996: 228)

The Aghadi put no pressure on women to deviate and gave them time and advice to think and work their way around their familial problems. Over the years the wing developed a strong base in the slums of Mumbai. Since the local leadership was chosen from among the masses, it was the personal relationships between leaders and cadres that went a long way in harnessing the loyalty of slum women. But the women who joined the Aghadi were not passive recipients of dictates from an influential organisation. Most women carefully weighed each option offered and calculated the extent to which they would profit from joining the Sena. Others made a commitment to the Aghadi and took part in its activities only after testing the waters over long periods of time.

The Shiv Sena aimed to impress secular parties (who took mass support as a sign of legitimacy) further with the strength of the party's claim to be a political successor/competitor. Hence at the local level there was an attempt to cover up divisive issues. In Thackeray's words:

'We do not need to pass any resolutions at this convention. The people do not want formal expressions like resolutions, they want justice. And justice will be obtained at all costs. But do not run to newspapers in case there is a clash within the Mahila Aghadi or within the party. Quarrels in the family can be settled at home. Stay away from the lure of newspaper publicity. Mediapersons are always waiting to write about dissension within the Sena. Do not play into their hands just because you get your name printed in the papers. There should be no "my group" and "your group" in our party. All groups are Shiv Sena groups. You must have Shiv Sena stamped on your entire being.' (Women's convention, 6 June 1994)

Thackeray feared that evidence of intra-party discord would ruin the reputation of the Sena, especially since dissension within organisational wings had provided cause for concern in the past. Indeed there was considerable disagreement within the Aghadi, but despite occasional clashes, there was a search for consensus and not just the containment of conflict. Women developed inward-looking policies for creating *bonhomie*, rather than providing a cover up in order to avert criticism from the press or other parties. While the Sena's primary concern was to mobilise the masses to assert its own legitimacy, the Aghadi wanted to create a real base for expressing the interests of women.

SATISFYING PRACTICAL GENDER NEEDS

The Aghadi used several tangible schemes to mobilise women and to divert attention from their underlying programme in order to forge an identity among them. An important part of this strategy was holding health camps, which gave advice to women on how to gain control over reproduction and health. Elaborating on this, former Aghadi chief Sudha Churi said,

'We often held camps to make women aware of breast cancer. The men were comfortable with allowing women to attend such gatherings. While the women became aware of their health, they also interacted heavily, shared their problems, reiterated that the Aghadi was helping them and this helped us to bring about a desired unity among women.'

Some of these camps were held at regular intervals in the local *shakhas* so that women did not have to travel distances to gain health benefits. Some camps were held for free immunisation of children and others during an outbreak of Hepatitis B, to counter the spread of the disease. They also dealt with current women and childcare issues and did seem to benefit poor women in the slums. There were also formal inaugurations of public toilets for women, dustbins in the slums with the Sena symbol on them, crèches for working mothers and evening literacy classes for women. Also, the women harassed local suppliers to set up illegal taps and fuses in homes with water and electricity shortages. Clearly the health camps and the like did not always serve an ulterior motive, but constant and demonstrative extension of these practical gender benefits made the Aghadi visible and kept the slum women indebted to the organisation.

A part of the Aghadi's operation was also to *create* necessities. For example, the Sena announced its own ambulance service, especially for the poor. This propaganda led to cadre Ruchika lamenting: 'No one but the Shiv Sena does anything for us these days', which summed up the general feeling in the slum regions. However, imagining urban slum dwellers needing an ambulance service to government hospitals was difficult. The ambulance could not enter the gullies and once a patient was brought out to the main street, most government hospitals were nearby. Yet the Aghadi leaders went around their localities praising the service and declaring that people in the slums would finally be saved.

Thus the Aghadi manipulated the economic and ideological resources available within the Sena movement to fulfil ceremoniously the real and imagined needs of poor women and children. In the process the wing created long-term dependencies between the Aghadi and women in the slums.

ADVOCATING A BRAND OF FLEXIBLE HINDUTVA

Yogita: 'Come and see my shop ... I started a butcher's shop here. When I came to Bhayander I realised that it was a Christian-dominated area and there were no meat shops. It was lucrative for me to start a business here. I began by building a shack around a severed tree trunk. See my hands ... [she shows some gashes] ... they're all from cutting frozen meat ... and I used to be a model, imagine! During Christmas I decided to bake cakes ... people could smell my cakes from a mile ... I sold them to the local churches ... no one dares to buy meat and cakes from anywhere but my shop. I also employ a few women now. See ... I don't believe in preaching ... I want to set an example for my women and I do it in reality. Start your own business and get your contracts by hook or by crook ... you have to survive! I also run a crèche in my house where some women work with me.'

The Aghadi played a prominent role in publicly assaulting and privately torturing building contractors, small entrepreneurs and businessmen to procure local jobs for slum women. During an interview Sena writer Vaibhav Purandare related that the Aghadi women once cornered 'a government welfare official to give out sewing machines to the Sena women. When the man protested he would get in trouble with his seniors, the Aghadi leaders allowed him to hand over token machines to a few Muslim women.' During my fieldwork I saw the Aghadi chief Meena bully an official for a contract to make mid-day meals for government schools in her constituency; later she handed over the project to Hindu women in the slums. The Sena women became gainfully employed, receiving remuneration for doing what they did easily, i.e. preparing food, and the feeling of collectivity that the Aghadi wanted to endorse was achieved through mass participation in community cooking. Meena gave the workers daily wages, and those who worked during slack periods within their regular jobs also received wages according to their contribution. The chief refused to admit that she kept a large share of the profits for herself, saying,

'We do a lot of research, madam, before we implement such schemes as the *khanawali* [food-makers] project that I run. We made sure that when the women were out cooking, the full responsibility of running the home didn't fall on the daughters, which is usually the case. So we ran shifts for all the mothers, so that their girls could go to school during the day or in the evening.'

The Aghadi leaders did not openly advocate freedom from domestic responsibilities for girl children. Instead the women were trying to develop a convenient schedule so that the girl children could at least attend school and not lose out on an education. Some of the women in Meena's constituency came and secretly joined in the scheme when their men were at work, so they could earn extra money for themselves. The conspiracy of silence to protect these women was an indicator of the extent to which the Aghadi had created a feeling of comradeship and intimacy among the slum women.

Discourses on power and opposition open up spaces where women can develop counter-resistances within regimes trying to create a uniform, masculinist and totalitarian culture. According to Foucault, for example, resistances are all the more substantial because they are formed right at that point where relations of power are exercised; resistance to power does not have to take the form of an external force to be real, nor is it predictably frustrated by being the partner to power. 'It exists all the more by being in the same place as power; hence, like power, resistance is multiple' (1980: 142). The Aghadi's veiled attempts to provide financial, emotional and educational benefits for slum women and girl children digressed considerably from the Sena's decrees on women. The wing would have been accused of defying the dictates of Hindu nationalism if their covert resistance to women's domestic and economic burdens became apparent. But the system of offering employment with some amount of flexibility appeared attractive to the slum women, and they flocked around the Aghadi for more of these 'down-to-earth, not manifestly deviant propositions' that reduced hardship in their daily lives. Hence all the women negotiated; yet no one moved away from this zone of power and resistance. The women, the men, the movement and the discourse of violence remained and struggled ahead in the slums.

Within the ambit of profitable economic transactions, the Aghadi maintained a façade of undiluted commitment to Hindutva by sponsoring small enterprises for Hindu women. The Sena women often used strong-arm tactics on people with secular credentials to sell finished products. Yet when it came to promoting businesses for poor women 'Hindu fundamentalism' became a malleable concept. It allowed Yogita and her cadres to chop beef (even though nationalists seek a ban on slaughtering the cow, a holy animal to Hindus). Yogita then used her reputation as a dangerous Aghadi leader to force-sell her goods to local Christians (even though nationalists demand a boycott of social and economic interaction with proselytising non-Hindu minorities). While wildly shaking her fist against cultural imperialism in public, Yogita painted Walt Disney cartoons on her walls because 'it draws more kids into the crèche, we make more money.' Thus the Sena women were willing to acquiesce to various demands on their conduct only in a public space. In their homes and workplaces women used the Sena as a tool for gaining greater control over their bodies, their mobility and also their earnings.

The Aghadi also drew supporters, if not recruits, from sections of women who found social service 'very glamorous'. These women were keen to skirt the tedious process of acquiring a degree or other qualifications in social work. Since the Sena women were informal 'social workers', their time was flexible and the nature of their work was also haphazard. Hence it was easier to approach the Aghadi as volunteers than turn to other professional welfare organisations. However, for these cadres, garlanding a bust of martial Hindu king Shivaji, especially in front of a cheering crowd, was also social service in the form of 'cultural activity'. While attending one of my first Aghadi meets, a young girl walked into the session and offered her services. I was quite taken aback by this sudden intrusion, but over time I became used to it. One of the leaders explained: 'The trend has increased dramatically because of the popularity of a TV serial called *Damini*.' (The protagonist, a woman from an 'ordinary' family background, won accolades for trouble-shooting in the homes of oppressed women.) So the Aghadi was willing to take recruits who had no pretence of being associated with the cause of Hindu nationalism. This reflected the leaders' enthusiasm to incorporate all sections of women to increase their base.

This aspect of flexibility visibly separated the Aghadi from the women's wings of other fundamentalist groups in India. Many critics of right-wing Hindu fundamentalist parties felt the similarities between the RSS and the Shiv Sena were striking. In debating the influence of leadership in shaping a nationalist identity, Brass suggests: 'They shape group consciousness by manipulating symbols of group identity to achieve power for the group' (1974: 45). This is true for the women's wing of both parties since they innovatively use religious and cultural functions first to bring women together and then to promote their ideology. However, the Sena women preached a far more adaptable Hinduism and unlike the RSS had few codified systems of punishment for religious deviants. The RSS women's wing also made its members undergo formal processes of ideological indoctrination such as sessions for reading and analysing religious texts, exercise classes for carrying able-bodied Hindu sons etc.(Bacchetta, 2002; Sarkar, 1996). The Aghadi, on the other hand, allowed its women to use and abandon religious symbols according to their own convenience. The Sena women thus had a far more instrumentalist approach to Hindutva. Being 'a Hindu' and being 'a fundamentalist' was a flexible concept within the women's wing and this lack of rigidity attracted many women into its fold.

Yogita: 'Our girls are not always radical. Once we had news that a cadre, a young bride, was being beaten up by her husband. We went and rescued her at once and sent her back to her family. After a few days we discovered she was back with her husband. All our effort went to waste and we were a laughing stock for a few days. But we can't blame the girl really. She must've been ill-treated in her family home as well. It's natural that she wasn't used to the idea of being a married woman staying with her parents. Since we don't run destitute homes or anything like that, we can't be judgmental about her behaviour. Over time she'll know that her situation is unbearable and then if she comes to us, we'll help her again.'

The Aghadi leaders seemed aware of their limitations as temporary relief teams offering no real alternative support structures to women. Yogita was affected by her loss of face, but she realised the cadre involved was not yet prepared for any extreme action. She would wait for the moment when the young bride felt pushed to the brink. Nonetheless, the comfort of belonging to a collectivity was offered unconditionally to the girl. People seemed to be drawn to Yogita because she sympathised with the aspirations of poor people, she claimed to 'understand' their circumstances. 'Oh, that must be taken into account. Only then can my work be legitimate, and the strategies effective', she said. The women leaders were aware that programmes imported from alien cultural settings—such as the West, élite institutions or male-centred Hindu nationalism—would fail when applied to the gendered, patriarchal, patrimonial systems operating in marginalised urban slums. Hence the Aghadi tried to develop indigenous channels of social work, which took into consideration cultural factors like the role of the family, attachment to one's roots, kinship groups, emotional dimensions of poverty and community involvement, and reinforced rather than distorted them.

CONSOLIDATING SYSTEMS OF BRUTE JUSTICE

Yogita: 'During the rail riots I took my women and burned a whole train. The corporation didn't give us any water on Holi day [festival of colours] ... we couldn't bathe ... everyone was so angry![5] I knew the local police wouldn't dare to touch me. But unfortunately the matter came up with the Railway Police in Delhi and they arrested me. On the day of my trial some of the Aghadi women from my area jumped into a jeep and whisked me away while I was entering the courthouse. I lay down on the floor of the jeep and the women sat on me. Later people told me that they thought a group of women were just picnicking around the area! The women took me to Thackeray's house where I stayed in a cellar for two months. After two months I left the city and went to live with my uncle in the districts. The police frantically hunted for me ... and finally the search orders were lifted. See these newspaper cuttings ... [the headlines read: "Yogita Patil abducted from

5 During the festival of Holi men and women are smeared in murky colours. On this occasion the municipal corporation could not provide water to houses in Bhayander, which angered the residents, who, lead by Yogita Patil, protested by burning trains stationed in the area.

courtroom", "Massive manhunt launched for Yogita Patil" and finally "Yogita's case dismissed by judge".] I didn't see my family for months.'

The Aghadi tried to project itself as a general law-enforcing body which did not operate exclusively for women. Yogita led all sections of affected people into taking violent action during the infamous Bhayander water riots (March 1998). *Shakha* leader Kamla once received a complaint that a local shopkeeper had dumped plastic bags in the drain, which clogged the sewage system. She and her companions marched to the man's shop, assaulted him, dragged him out, and made him climb down into an open sewer and clear the bags. On another occasion Aghadi leader Laxmi smashed a cigarette and betel nut shop because the shopkeeper, a *chakka* (a eunuch/gay), would tease small boys by lecherously calling '*aaja raja*' (come, my king). At a sit-in demonstration against the municipal authorities trying to evict illegal tenants from government owned land, the Aghadi women had me join them in shouting the group slogan:

'If Pakistanis and Bangladeshis can come and stay on our land, why can't we who serve the country stay on this land? [Twice] Down with the government, up with the Shiv Sena [handclaps].'

The women then went on to break the iron railing set up by the local corporation to mark their territory. As I watched, one of the cadres said: 'Stay with us, you'll learn so much.'

However, the Aghadi gave special attention to women's grievances and the demands kept pouring in for gender justice, which the women were far more effective in delivering than the men. While women were constantly busying themselves assisting people in 'distress', men rarely addressed 'insignificant' local problems and generally only became active during larger political turmoil. Yet even during Thackeray's arrest over his role in the Mumbai riots the women were more active in resisting officials sent to bring him to court. Although the Aghadi cooperated with both men and women in the slums, the women were far more passionate about their association with the front. Yogita, in her fifteen years of social service in Bhayander, had won over the women cadres to such an extent that they were willing to risk their lives to stage their local leader's dramatic getaway. According to Rani, 'She rescued us from so many situations, how could we let her languish in jail?'

Yogita: 'We do the most for women because it's always a woman who has to deal with mundane affairs. This woman here [pointing to a woman on the floor who was busy putting *vadas* (salty doughnuts) on a plate] ... her husband left her with a child. She was helpless and came to me for help. I kept her as a maid in my house.'

Rani: 'After sometime Yogita-tai told me that I was a good cook and should start my own business to support my child. She threatened some bank official and got a loan sanctioned even though I didn't have any assets. I started a *vada pao* [salty doughnuts and bread] stall and now I've bought a small flat. I have to pay just 20,000 rupees to clear my loan. I'm sold to her for life.'

For clearing sewer systems, controlling misdemeanour, protesting evictions and procuring loans from banks the Aghadi women used and promoted physical and destructive violence. However, they would not blatantly contest the practice of 'customs' even though they were willing to use aggression to set limits. For example, in cases of torture over inadequate dowry, Sena women would ferociously protect young brides, which would often lead to incidents of violent confrontations with the groom's kin. Aghadi leader Seema said:

'It's hard to fight age-old customs face on. What I did was simple. My team almost broke the backs of a few men who treated their wives badly for getting insufficient or no dowry. Now we just visit all the weddings in my locality, take a survey of the dowry and declare that it's enough. After that no men would dare to demand more or beat their wives.'

The Aghadi women were not battling for an abolition of the system of dowry. Indeed, the leaders claimed the exchange of gifts was auspicious during a wedding, though their inhibitions could be determined by their own desire to demand a dowry when marrying off their male children. The Aghadi also remained concerned about its popularity as a social service group with limited resources, and probably tried to strike a balance between tradition and radicalism. Thus the wing tried only to relieve the bride's kin from the pressure of gift-giving. Chandrika, a cadre, said: 'We didn't want the men to use the idea of inadequate dowry as an excuse to beat up their wives.' The system of raw justice aimed to redefine the concept of dowry to free it from commercialism and thereby curb cruelty on women.

Yogita: 'Why did I start a crèche in my own house? I used to teach in a Christian school in the area. They threw me out because I worked with the Shiv Sena. They can exert their Christian identity and I can't exert mine? I promised myself I'd start a children's school in seven days time. And I did. I painted the walls and invested the money for other playthings.'

The rivalry between the Aghadi women and members of other religious communities existed at the grassroots level. The women wanted to oust Muslims from the slums for more land, to eradicate competition in businesses etc. Thus the larger issues of 'serving historical justice' were clearly manipulated to resolve local level rivalries. Sometimes enmities arose over minor frictions. After one Sena meet I went with some Aghadi cadres to a crowded beach to have *golas* (crushed ice dipped in syrup). Looking around for a spot to rest, their eyes fell on a group of Muslim women. Having first loudly accused the *burqa*-clad group of women of reproducing rapidly and probably being married to the same man, the Aghadi cadres took off their slippers and started throwing them at the women, who, in a state of shock, gathered their belongings and ran as fast as their legs could carry them. The people on the beach looked on nonchalantly; either they were used to the Aghadi's antics, or they endorsed anti-Muslim behaviour. Although this attack on minority women was a case of pure harassment to acquire some space to sit, the women projected it as a spontaneous display of religious nationalism. The Hindu women threw slippers, the Muslim women fled, the spectators, probably Hindu, did not intervene: this whole public performance of honour and humiliation reflects how nationalism becomes refreshed and rearticulated as localised forms of anti-minority vigilantism. At the end of the day the battle seemed to be for space, be it through the mosque/temple argument at the national level, for housing space at the slum level, or just a place to sit at the insignificant level of an outing by the sea. The Sena women, though, had a simple justification: the majority wins.

These actions, which appeared to be outbursts of irrational social behaviour, were forms of ritualised violence—brief demonstrations of the Aghadi's obedience to the Sena and to the religion. Displaying hostility towards Muslims gave the Aghadi a forceful visibility in their surroundings. The Sena women were aware that their impoverished Muslim neighbours did not pose a real threat; yet they needed to gain a more central role within a violent, anti-Muslim nationalist movement. So they exploited the more general insecurities created by an understanding of the 'Islamic world' as promoters of world terrorism. Since 'ideological fantasies were often forms of knowledge about the other, that appeared as a construction beyond argument or falsification' (Zizek, 1989: 24), the women could circulate myths about their neighbours (the Muslims had guns hidden in their tin shacks; they were eating *biryani* to celebrate the death of local Hindus), keeping wider hostilities towards the Muslim community in perspective. The Aghadi *needed* to sustain communal conflict and to keep the threat of the Muslim Other alive to maintain a longer-lasting status as women warriors. This strategy, when implemented successfully, allowed the women to offer better practical solutions to gender concerns within slum areas. The Aghadi's participation in a fundamentalist movement became more about claiming civil and political space for women, while couching it in chants of 'Jai Shri Ram' (Victory to Lord Ram) and 'Jai Maharashtra' (Victory to Maharashtra).

Yogita: 'Who are you?' [A man with fresh bruises on his face has just entered.]

Man: 'Yogita-tai, I accidentally hit a man with my autorickshaw this morning. He and his friends turned out to be some rich man's sons and they beat me up so badly. I kept apologising, with folded hands, but they went and complained to the police about me! Please help me out.'

Yogita: 'Leave the FIR number with the *shakha*. First get yourself to a hospital. Nothing'll happen to you.'

AS: 'How do you know this man's telling the truth ... he could be ...'

Yogita: 'Poor people don't need to lie about such things.... I've worked with these people for ages ... they're all criminals in your eyes ... but they're all fighting to survive.'

The Aghadi's popularity grew primarily because they quickly redressed grievances, especially for the poor, in a society marked by 'untrustworthy' institutions of justice. Once, news spread that local women employed as domestic servants in Middle-Eastern countries were victimised by their employers. Some of these maids, who had been bundled back to Mumbai, went to women's NGOs for help. But with no aid coming from either the government or the embassies, the NGOs finally gave up. A few weeks later the women informed the NGOs that their problems had been settled. The maids had decided to approach the Aghadi. The Sena women located the employers' relatives in Mumbai, marched to their homes, threatened and/or thrashed them and recovered the dues for the maids. Over time the Aghadi task squads became enormously glorified as covert and swift revenge groups.

The popularity of some films was also an indicator of women's apathy for turning to state institutions for help. For example, the film *Zakhmee Aurat* (Wounded Woman) was extremely popular in the slums. It focused on a raped police officer, who organised a team of victims to castrate rapists let off by the law (Setalvad, 1996: 239). I took some of the Aghadi women to see *Pukar* (The Call), a film about an unjustly court-marshalled hero and his lover who foiled a terrorist operation by Pakistani militants. The hero delivered nationalistic dialogues such as, 'Pakistan is a small country, I'll squash it under my shoe.... I don't need to be part of the army to do that.' The Sena women cheered and applauded. Since many state institutions were perceived to be redundant and the police, the army and the bureaucracy were racked by corruption or incapable of providing prompt succour for common grievance cases, an organisation that offered ready justice, even (or especially) if it involved the use of brutality, enjoyed a special appeal.

Rani [in Yogita's absence]: 'D'you know what she did once? She'd gone to her village and was sleeping with her aunts and uncles when some *dacoits* attacked the house and injured everyone. They hit her in the stomach with a rifle butt. In that state she drove her uncle's motorcycle to the next village and came back driving a jeep. She piled all the bodies of her kin into the jeep and drove it straight to the hospital. Since it was night the doctors refused to come, but she dragged the doctor out of his house at knife-point. The doctor saved the whole family and after he came out of the operating theatre and announced the good news, she collapsed from the pain in her stomach.'

Yogita walks in and scolds Rani: 'How dare you talk about this event to anyone? [Rani looks at the floor.] I was supposed to be awarded for national bravery, but they didn't give me the award because I was an Aghadi woman and had threatened the doctor into saving the lives of the people I love.'

From Rani's narration it was apparent that she immensely admired Yogita's heroism. Clearly the Aghadi's system of delivering justice through organised violence allowed women to be equal participants in a masculinist discourse and not just as valued accomplices in public; the use of guns and knives or the freedom to drive vehicles also gave the women a chance to overcome pervasive feelings of envy against men. During my stay in Mumbai there was a spate of killings targeting Sena men (after I left Aghadi women also started to be murdered by contract killers.) Most of the male leaders at the time had security guards carrying sophisticated arms. At one Sena meeting I asked a guard if I could shoot his gun at a tree. Seeing people swarm around the tree he promptly turned down my request, but permitted me to hold his gun. Having put the strap across my chest I found myself surrounded by Aghadi women who had been observing the exchange from a distance. They applauded loudly but quickly dispersed when I accidentally pulled the trigger. Luckily the safety lock was on. On the one hand I could identify with the Sena women in the childlike glee at having handled a toy that usually only boys played with, which was equivalent to crossing a frontier. On the other I shied away from a collective glorification of the image of an armed woman in public. Here the juxtaposition of one's 'status' as a woman against one's 'identity' as a woman creates a contrast poignantly described by Mies when discussing the methodological problems faced by female researchers studying provincial women's struggles (Mies, 1979: 13–17). According to cadre Aruna, 'We are heroines. We prove our might in the face of adversity. We deserve an ovation.'

The Aghadi's system of raw justice also became an effective means of countering the efforts of men to recreate particularistic, non-competitive and unadaptive social structures in the slums of Mumbai.

Yogita: 'Priya here is an interesting girl. At home she keeps quiet all the time like a good housewife. Her folks thought she was the docile, obedient sort. After joining the Sena she became very active in all our violent operations. She would shout and scream during the Sena protests. Her family was quite shocked. But they couldn't complain because she was socially active for a good cause and she doesn't open her mouth in the house.'

Priya: 'At least they shouldn't take me for granted, no? They know I have many sides to my character now. I may be docile at home, but I'm capable of more.'

Several families in the slums saw women's raw aggression as a form of deviancy. Some women joined the Aghadi to show their families that even though they were silenced at home they were *capable* of deviant behaviour. Priya, for example, used the politics of the Aghadi as a platform to raise consciousness in her own home about her subjugation, and to show that she had the capability to fight back. Hence complete domesticity did not come 'automatically' to most slum women, even though they had been practising it for years. And although this kind of endeavour without a support group appeared frightening, they were willing to be part of a collective strategy to wrest more public space. The women were also content to achieve their end in phases, without toppling their immediate family structures.

Jenkins (1997), studying ethnic problems in Northern Ireland, commented that the vision of a researcher studying ethnic communities could be structured to *see* an intense solidarity among the group, especially if the group is forcefully displaying it all the time. I often sat among the Aghadi members and wondered whether I was missing sharp differences of opinion among them. Although there were arguments and clashes of ideas, there was also a sincere effort to organise all kinds of slum women. There were no fixed policies. Initiation of new members seemed to add vitality to the wing. There was all-round excitement and sweets were given out to reinforce the group solidarity. There were no formal incorporation rituals. The inflow of women was not always contingent on clear demarcations between being an insider or an outsider. Some women would join the Aghadi cadre base and take part in its activities right from the start. Others would sit at the door of the party office, or simply follow Aghadi members around, either to show their quiet support or to make themselves silently visible; all these women were also considered part of the Aghadi. More active members expressed how the process of expansion would reawaken a cadre's sense of responsibility to the group and would also reassure her that she operated within a structure on which she could depend. The intensity of the reciprocal relationship apparently made the women feel 'invulnerable' to the world outside. According to senior cadre Sandhya:

'Each new face reminds me that this girl's come because she believes in what I believe in ... and makes me think afresh about what I want ... and since I'm already an old member of the group, I feel more responsible because there are new faces that'll depend on me … and it'll be my job to keep them with the wing, protect them from the world outside and also help them face it….'

Furthermore, the estrangement that came with relocation into a peripheral urban setting slowly faded with support from a clearly defined group. New member Neha said: 'I want to stay in a small, stable and less mobile community. I want to stay in the Aghadi.' The women in the Aghadi sought unity, but did not want to be depersonalised to the extent to which they believed Muslim women in *burqas* experience uniformity. Jaba said, 'In our culture we don't make our sexuality apparent. But they [Muslim women] look like a flock of black crows! You can't tell one from the other.' The Aghadi women obviously enjoyed their visibility and the fact that in each area they were marked out as women to be seen and feared.

CHOICES AND SANCTIONS

An example of the way in which the Aghadi concentrated on earning merit within their surrounding network of Sena members was by considering women's choices. The cadres first took advantage of the built-in choices available to women (such as trips to the market) and then exploited the choices developed for them (such as attending Aghadi meetings while at the market). 'Choices usually curtail or reinforce one another' (Dube, 1997: 9). In the case of Yogita's 'loss of face', she did have the choice of ending an abusive marriage, but since she could not support herself or return to her natal home her choice became devoid of meaning. The Aghadi, aware that 'disadvantaged' women could not relate to feminist stands, instead turned itself into an alternative organisation, informing women about the 'unconventional' choices available to them. For example, collectivisation of women's labour through the catering systems fused emotional bonds with sources of income. It partially reinforced the choices available to women because they realised the value of financial and emotional fallbacks when faced with personal crises. Furthermore, the Sena women's front continued to be concerned about the future of the Aghadi, and hence women's strategies were oriented to gain long-term sustainability for the organisation.

Yet the Aghadi did not always maintain the image of a patient and benevolent giver of social and economic goods. The refusal of cadres to contribute to collective action in situations of crisis, whether actively or through support functions, was penalised by the Aghadi through systems of formal or informal sanctions (such as ostracism from the collective). In such situations there were few choices available to women. During the Mumbai riots, for example, a Sena mob attacked a bus and dragged out six passengers identified as Muslims. While five of them tried to escape, one man having received a head injury fell down and fainted. As he lay unconscious, the mob poured kerosene on him and torched him. While the man lay burning, Sena women threw stones at Muslim passengers fleeing the scene. One of the women later approached Mashwara, a legal aid centre in Mumbai, to avoid a police crackdown on her pro-Sena family. She admitted she had taken part in the violence, but only to avoid being branded a deserter, which was common if cadres did not respond to the call of the Aghadi. She was hesitant to display such extreme violence and had made an ethically difficult decision to assault a group of terrified men; ultimately, she had been afraid of incurring the wrath of the more militant leaders and of losing the support of the Aghadi altogether. So while trying to instil discipline in its operations to deliverer immediate, social, or historical justice the Aghadi functioned through a system of positive *and* negative incentives. This was in keeping with the ideals of the Aghadi to develop a reputation as a martial women's organisation. The stress on intolerance of any breach during a display of group action upheld the Aghadi's faith in structured violence.

The Aghadi's ultimate goal was to create a militaristic Hindu society in which women had the freedom of mobility, assertiveness and association, although this 'freedom' would remain couched in women's nationalistic credentials. When Abu Azmi, a member of the Samta Party made a comment against Hindus in India, all the Aghadi leaders marched to the town centre and burned effigies of him. After a few days, when the agitation did not subside, Azmi apologised in public and withdrew his comment, after which there was revelry and the success of the Aghadi movement was extolled. The women's wing had displayed its anger against an imaginary alien so that their battle against the enemy within, their patriarchal fetters, remained submerged in the din of protests and celebrations of success.

CONCLUSION

The link between understanding (one's reality) and agency is formed by identity ... it provides us not only with a conception of how we should act under certain circumstances but also with the motivation to do so. (Poole, 1999: 61)

Both in the field and outside it the mobilisational strategies of Aghadi women seem perplexing. One school of thought finds women's mobilisation by fundamentalist movements in South Asia reactionary (Das, 1995; Madan, 1997; Menon *et al.*, 1995; Moghadam, 1994; Pandey, 1993; Sarkar and Butalia, 1996; Vanaik, 1997a). Das (1995), discussing the rhetoric of suffering, argues that fundamentalist discourses idolise the 'regressive' role of women in a past society and project it as integral to the ideal society of the future. In the case of the mobilisation of the Aghadi women, the covert scheme was to partially set aside the oppressive roles for women in the past and integrate the contemporary militant role of women with the society envisaged for the future. So the Aghadi's 'political action' seemed to be more expressive than political in nature. For example, Sena women were not totally disinterested in making a serious bid for state power because it would mean greater resource mobilisation in favour of women; to that extent it was political. But what women wanted was to *express* their collective strength and their marked presence in a public role, which meant a bid for cultural hegemony rather than real political sovereignty.

One way of viewing mobilisation is as a process that not only draws apolitical people into public action, but also monitors their levels of involvement with a movement. In the case of the Sena women and the implementation of their strategies, the women certainly could not be described as the sluggish and submissive section of the slum population. And they did not take part in the Sena's political acts purposelessly. Having joined the Aghadi only after considering the material and symbolic resources on offer, their agency in all kinds of political action was premeditated. Their expressive participation depended on whether women felt they had benefited enough from the Aghadi and whether women's political actions would ultimately benefit the Aghadi. Political participation merely allowed the women to pass the 'passion' test in public. So while the Aghadi members tried to show that their purpose for action was in keeping with the political ends envisioned by the wider party, women's stake in taking part in violent mass politics was actually different from that of the men and was in fact born of conscious choices designed to achieve certain ends exclusively for women.

Scholars from both feminist and non-feminist points of view observe that political mobilisation is related to, but not identical with, spreading political awareness and increasing participation (Butalia, 1996; Feldman, 1993, Hasan, 1994). According to Bayly (1998), for example, growing popular awareness is an aspect of political mobilisation, but the process also involves ideological dedication and the fulfilment of this commitment in perceptible political action. However, whereas political participation tends to focus on the rate of individual performances, particularly the easily charted act of voting, political mobilisation involves a converging of ideas, issues and circumstances that engender or alter political activity within an organisation. The Aghadi women were a politically mobilised society and an organised group. Since they were aware of national-political issues and avenues of participation, they sought at least some of the all-party collective objectives through political channels and repeatedly engaged in some form of political action. What lay at the basis of this participation, however, was not a political crisis but fundamental social changes. Customary ways of conducting relationships, conventional patterns of social and economic activity and traditional values typical of rural community life were gradually transformed in the urban slums and replaced by an alternative moral economy. Economic changes produced different occupations and production relations (especially after the textile strike), and the women felt they had borne the brunt of these 'changes'. So the degree of mobilisation achieved by the Aghadi in the slums of Mumbai depended on the changing internal relations of the collectivity brought about by changing external circumstances.

According to Mernissi, the public visibility of women terrifies and angers most men (1987: xi). Although she was referring to the male-female dynamics in a Muslim fundamentalist society, this terror at seeing women in public roles seems partly to be at the base of the ideological revitalisation of suppressive religious movements in urban settings where socio-economic shifts compel women to enter the labour force in great numbers. Although the thrust of a fundamentalist movement is to recreate a moral order in which the simplification of reality would dilute any role conflict between the sexes, the Sena movement operated differently. Since a large part of the Sena women comprised workers, it was difficult for the Sena to develop a gender discourse which put women uncompromisingly within the home. Hence Thackeray's speeches were not inconsistent but situational. Even though he emphasised the role of women in upholding tradition, he expressed his support for the large numbers of Sena women who were obliged to enter the public realm to provide for their families as well. He was making particular arguments in favour of specific sets of women. Thus Thackeray's charisma was not just related to his standing and achievement, but to the different social conditions which validated his emergence and legitimised his influence over slum women.

Women were mobilised into the Aghadi, and they desired the stability that came with sharing an identity and common interests within an organisation. At the same time they did not desire the stability which remained embedded in clearly defined sex roles, a family life and passive religious orientation. Thus women created and organised the Aghadi according to 'female desires'. While recreating the moral universe as committed members of the Hindutva brigade, women were trying to conceive of a more flexible construction of womanhood. The Sena men only saw the 'culture masks of women' (Moghadam, 1994: 16) because they uncritically assumed their claims *on* women; unlike the RSS, the Sena had not clearly defined its position on women over time. The Aghadi, however, saw the real faces of women marked by multiple insecurities and made covert claims *for* them, which formed the basis of its organisation strategies.

On the one hand the Sena women had a pragmatic and utilitarian approach towards political participation, but on the other negotiated through the Aghadi to create a transit space—where women's honour would be tied to women's autonomy—between the reality of the current community and the imagined Hindu nation. The eternal ambivalence of 'nation' as narrative strategy as well as the conceptual ambiguity of 'culture' (flexible Hinduism) allowed the women to persistently manipulate these two ideas and keep up the pretence of a struggle for a Utopian Hindu community. If, however, this community were achieved then all Hindu women would have to return to their homes. In other words, the autonomous space for women lay in perpetuating the struggle and not in reaching its goal. Thus, for the Aghadi women, organisation and mobilisation entailed the creation of an 'artificial reality', i.e. women needed to struggle for the greater Hindu community to come into being. This parallel universe was created in response to what the women felt was an 'actual reality', i.e. women enjoyed their visibility in a struggle. This theme will be discussed further in later chapters.

The informal channels of 'social work' developed by the Aghadi, marked by everyday and extraordinary forms of violence and conflict, provided temporary relief to women through social intervention. What the Sena women yearned for was long-term sustainability and hence most of its mobilisation policies, based on organisation and terror tactics, were developed because the women's front believed that these strategies could attract more women into the camp. In turn it would extend the organisation's influence in the slums of Mumbai. The Aghadi wanted to be indispensable in the lives of female members, to create prolonged dependencies among them and to rely on mass-based actions to gain permanence.

To differentiate between leaders and cadres in the Aghadi was always difficult and hence who formed the policies and who implemented them has not been specifically articulated in this chapter. In many areas women who had been cadres and did not acquire/want official positions wielded tremendous clout over the slum women; on the other hand, several others like Meena Kulkarni, the Aghadi chief, were noted for their humility and refusal to flaunt their senior status. Converging with the socialist model of party politics, Meena once said in a speech given at an Aghadi meet:

'I was a cadre before I became a leader. What difference does it make? We all do the same work. The idea within the Aghadi is to absolve this leader-cadre difference through social work.'

As the next chapter shows, this constant façade of women's unity, the display of female militancy and the changing gender dynamics within the family had a substantial impact on children raised in the Sena-dominated slums.

5
SENA BOYS AND 'SURVIVAL'

This is a paper I did not want to write because I would be happier if the data did not exist. (Graburn, 1987: 211)

My most troubling experiences in the Sena-dominated slums were with militant children. This chapter discusses how groups of boys from Sena families were trying to develop a knowable world, a framework for understanding and negotiating disruption in their daily experiences, and their attempts to withstand that disruption. There is a growing corpus of research which tries to uncover the problems of aggressive children, primarily through the concept of child agency. Korbin, for example, points out that 'children's own voices and perspectives have been largely absent from the anthropological literature on childhood and violence' (2003: 2). This chapter tries to remedy that by drawing on the stories and voices *of* children *on* children. Initially the focus is on boys rather than girls, primarily because at the time the fieldwork was conducted the gendering of aggression among the Sena children was at its nascent stage, and the need for securing family and community survival was articulated more frequently by boys. Mostly, different groups of Sena boys seemed to be making attempts, however contrasting, to counter the unpredictability in their lives. Becker (1997), examining processes by which people create continuities, points out how—after a disruption to life—the ongoing interpretation of events and experiences enables people to make sense of their personal worlds. A sense of continuity is captured in the ordinary routines of daily life, the comforting sameness of repetitive activities. Although Becker's ethnography is drawn from North American societies, she asserts that certain activities that give structure and logic to people's lives are universal.

In all societies the course of life is structured by expectations about each phase of life, and meaning is assigned to specific life events and the roles that accompany them. When expectations about the course of life are not met people experience inner chaos and disruption. Such disruptions represent loss of the future. Restoring order to life necessitates reworking understandings of the self and the world, redefining the disruption and life itself. (Becker, 1997: 31)

She goes on to argue that the ideology of continuity is based on an array of disparate cultural components, which includes values of personal responsibility, perseverance, control over the environment and an orientation towards the future. The main agenda of the Sena children, who encountered layers of sudden and sustained aggression, was to construct a 'safer' future. It was an anxious aspiration for surviving the present and reaching the future which informed children's initiatives to regulate their unstable existence in the slums. Before conducting my fieldwork I did not have, to use the words of Siegfreid Sassoon, 'the sufficient imagination to realise that children could suffer from such continued agonies' (Sassoon, 1945).

For the children 'order' (*reet, padhyati*), 'normalcy' (*samanya paristhiti*), 'stability' (*stheeryata*) and 'survival' (*jeevit rehna, astitva rehna*) became the primary constructs which could offer an antidote to different scales of disruption. In the case of a child, the 'long-term' planning of actions and ideas covering a time span of twenty to thirty years may seem improbable. Nevertheless, this chapter provides an insight into children's perceptions of their own capacity for endurance and their attempts to encompass their experiences and develop certain prolonged permanencies in their lives. The boys admitted that order and stability meant achieving calm; but that that stage could be reached most often through the path of violence and at other times through restraint.

Sena boys identified five main spaces in which they had to overcome disorder. First, they wanted to redefine intra-household conditions. They wanted militant women (the mothers) and aggressive boys (the children) to play a reciprocal role in ensuring the survival of the family. They also wanted to construct a 'rosy' future in which romance and steady marriages survived to face personal and external instabilities. Second, the boys identified the local *shakha* (the Shiv Sena branch office) as the only permanent structure in the slums, as a reservoir of symbols and representation of stability in their lives. Third, the boys felt they had to operate as children's 'gangs' on the streets and believed that staving off enemies through collective action would ensure the survival of children. Fourth, they sought out forms of 'knowledge', especially in the classroom, through which their endeavour to develop a militant, Hindu identity would be sanctioned. Finally, the children felt alienated from the NGO movement, which remained sympathetic to the minorities, and hence felt a need to counter the NGOs' efforts because those efforts destabilised children's ideas of what constitutes 'right'.

The boys concerned were all aged between nine and sixteen and most were 'school'-going. However, 'school' was an ambivalent category in the slums. Anyone asked whether their children went to school would nod. Children who went to schools where they wore a uniform and paid a fee had a higher status than those who went to schools (usually evening schools) run by governmental or non-governmental organisations. A third category of boys went to 'schools' that were just informal classes in reading and writing run by some educated people in the slums, who accepted a fee (but required no uniform be worn). The concept of a school drop-out was ambiguous because a few of these schools held classes up to only the eighth standard. If boys had completed the eighth grade but did not sit any school-leaving public examination, they would still claim they had completed school. Boys usually helped their parents in their work, putting in a few hours in their shops or hawking some of their goods; but almost all of them pick-pocketed, shoplifted or ran off with belongings accidentally left by people on public transport or on park benches. Later they sold their acquisitions on the street, or to established dealers of stolen goods. But they would not steal from people they knew (they claimed they did not steal from familiar faces or from people who could not absorb a loss). Despite the fact that they carefully examined my micro-tape recorder several times, it never went missing, even though I often left it lying around.

My ethnography uncovers some aspects of the lives of slum children in their intra-household relations, and how their worlds were informed and modified by external engagements with a fundamentalist discourse. Even though I lived and worked with violent women, I remained acutely aware of my status as an anthropologist, different from that of a social worker. Having come to the Sena-controlled slums after spending many years as a 'child liberationist', I retained a hope in the capacity of children to know what is best for them and maybe redeem adult behaviour. Fleeting disillusionment may thus have crept into this chapter, reflecting my helplessness while observing the regeneration of militancy among the Sena children. Even though my research findings seem to reiterate what Mead (1929) and Benedict (1934) claimed a long time ago, that children brought up in cultures of conflict are bound to become violent, I suggest a more nuanced view which also recognises children's resilience and enterprise in the face of great disadvantages. Furthermore, I must still insist that the excerpts from the lives of the Sena children that are detailed below were not my happiest memories of them. I also danced with them in the Mumbai rains.

THE HOME: SENA BOYS AND CHANGING INTRA-HOUSEHOLD RELATIONS

It is easily forgotten that children 'create parents' as well as parents creating children. (Giddens, 1977: 130)

Because of the external social and political engagements of women and children internal relations in Sena families underwent many changes. The boys tried to ensure the survival of their families by accepting and openly supporting the immediate, limited breakdown of gender hierarchies brought about by the Mahila Aghadi. Some riot-affected boys drew up schemes to protect their families from the 'enemy'; others decided to encourage their militant mothers to act as protectors. While some children practised group violence to compensate for passive mothers within the Aghadi, others displayed ferocity to complement the militancy displayed by their mothers. Further, a large number of the boys felt that building protective, romantic relationships with Sena girls would in the future offer the family unit stability during crises. Thus by switching roles between 'the protector' and 'the protected', the boys felt they could prolong their fragile slum lives. This was how the children wanted to be raised and this was how they imagined a stable family.

Survival at present: mothers, grandmothers

The children's primary concerns were about gaining control over and making sense of their immediate environment. Becker (1997), discussing agency and resistance in the context of disruption, argues that the effort to create a sense of continuity after disruption raises issues of power. Indeed, people's initial anxieties are about the loss of personal power over their lives and how to regain it. Some slum children had been affected by riots and their primary concern was to acquire enough power to protect uprooted families (especially the women). Other children, who had 'grown up' on grandmothers' tales of Hindu–Muslim animosity, focused on living up to a Hindu family's expectations of valour. Most of the boys, in some way or another, tried to re-classify intra-household gender hierarchies to enable Aghadi mothers to 'save' the children and rescue the community from erasure. The children started using new categories, developed new attitudes and looked for new ways to bind their families together.

Some of the boys who had been injured or uprooted during the Mumbai riots felt the only way of ensuring the family's survival was to create a permanent home, and keep it free from external threat. With the outbreak of riots in the slums it seemed that usually women and children were shunted off to safer places. There was a sudden rupture in family life, the children were isolated with the mothers in alien places and some of them felt 'scared' to see their mother's fear of widowhood. There was a tremendous indignity in fleeing, especially since they had been told Hindus were the dominant community. 'I saw, I saw how my mother cried when we had to leave the slums and

my father stayed behind. Yes, our slum had lots of Muslims,' said Guddu (13).
He wanted to grow up and 'be tough, so that my parents wouldn't have to
separate again.' When they recalled these conditions the children's language
became a fountain of abuse towards Muslims, and they repeatedly justified
the use of violence to 'save' their families in the future.

The medical files of three children (two boys and one girl) who were separated from their families during the riots and had to go to the local municipality hospital for treatment indicated the following common 'symptoms': constant fear of losing parent; massive temper tantrum when one parent leaves
the house; phobia of leaving the house themselves. These children spoke about
their longing to join the Shiv Sena party and 'learning to be warriors'. Waiting for adulthood might be too late to quell their fear of attacks. The children
argued for counter-violence and securing equal status with the other Sena
families who were proud at having stayed put in their homes during the riots.
Extra manpower, even if it came from children, would prove advantageous in
their more defenceless slum environment.

Several boys who were not displaced by the riots openly supported revenge against Muslims simply because it would enhance their family dignity.
Most of these boys felt privileged to conspire with 'more experienced' family
members, especially their grandmothers, to protect their families. In these
families child rebellion was not about the young against the old. Since a common enemy was seen to be the threat to the physical and emotional integrity
of the Hindu family in the slums, tremendous in-family bonding was the result. Although the older Sena women in the family may have felt marginalised
because of their inactivity within the youth-oriented party, when it came
to zealously protecting their property and creating a safe all-Hindu, familiar
environment in the slums, they gave vigorous support to the belligerence in
the younger generation.

Raju (16): 'I love my grandmother. She always told me stories of Shivaji [the martial Hindu king who had fought off the Mughals and from whom the Shiv Sena
took their name] and I grew up on tales of valour and heroism. I knew all along
how badly the Hindus suffered in the hands of the Muslims.... Today if she tells
me "Go Raju, go and fight against the Muslims", how can I hold back?'

During the Mumbai riots, when Raju was only eight years old, he gave his
grandmother the trophy of a chair he had dragged out of a furniture shop
owned by a Muslim. The shop had been smashed by rioters. 'I've been doing
my bit since then,' proclaimed Raju. Most boys felt they got fresh 'ideas' about
adding to the family pride from elders, and children's motivation for violent
action was often modelled on the elders' notions of historical justice.

Parallels can often be made between children in conflict zones, for example, in relation to vengeance.[1] In some of the Sena children exposure to conflict had created what seemed to be an overwhelming sense of humiliation, and even though they had moved into a Hindu-dominated environment, they reiterated their need to overcome their embarrassment as boys who came from families of Hindu victims. For other 'more lucky' boys, whose need for revenge had been created, sustained and supported by older and wiser members of the family, their duty was to pre-empt the possibility of defeat. This sense of honour, however, was prescribed.

According to Becker (1997), when the normal and the habitual are disrupted, redefining family relations gives way to new possibilities. When children affected by disruption wanted to inculcate some new qualities in the family they took the initiative to support or change certain intra-family relations. For example, while some of the Sena men were unhappy about women's participation in the martial activities of the Mahila Aghadi, many boys tried to cooperate with their Aghadi mothers, believing it would contribute to the integrity of the family. Most Sena boys repeatedly spoke about supporting their Aghadi mother's move away from full-time domesticity. These actions were bound to the children's own understanding of what constituted child honour and child dignity in the slums. For example, the husband of Mohini, a popular Sena women's leader in the Mahalaxmi washermen's slums, came home one night and in anguish pulled out all his teeth. When admitted to a mental hospital, it was discovered that his work-mates had consistently mocked him for being 'the woman of the house'. When the whole slum area was buzzing with gossip, Mohini's two sons stood by her and did not want her to retrace her steps back within the four walls of the house. As Mohini's elder son Chintu (13) said:

'My mother's a fighter. I feel proud when people say your mother has solved another case. She and some other Aghadi women thrashed the life out of a man who raped his own daughter every night. His neighbours knew all along but didn't stop him. I saw the girl when she came to my mother. Her own father! I would've killed the man and I know that my mother would've stood by me if I'd followed the path of justice. I'll stand by her when she does the same.'

What later 'absolved' Mohini of her 'sins' (in front of the slums dwellers) was her complete devotion to her husband while he convalesced.

[1] According to Smyth (1998) and Byrne (1997), who conducted studies in Northern Ireland, if they were vulnerable to an enemy (as against a natural disaster over which they had no control) even small children placed stress on 'vengeance' to cope with communal strife.

There were several boys in the slums who felt, like Mohini's children, that their mothers should play an active public role even if that involved organised violence 'unsuitable' for women. From their point of view, contesting atrocities within the family and the slum community often made the use of force imperative. Since the Aghadi women did 'social work', it was their conspicuousness in the slum life which enhanced the status of their children. 'People know you're so-and-so's child. If your mother's a leader, they give you a lot of respect,' said Hari (15). The boys thus felt assured of a 'child pride' that was integral to their search for survival.

Some boys, especially those from fragile, friction-ridden families, felt that if children became supportive instead of resentful towards Aghadi mothers then some of their domestic insecurities would be partially resolved. This was especially true in those families where the mother was the primary breadwinner. Pappu (10) and Babu (12) knew their mothers to be working women and their fathers to be alcoholics.

Pappu: 'Whenever my mother gets beaten up she can't go to work and we don't get enough to eat. After a period of respite the process starts again. The Aghadi has really helped her. When I see her shouting slogans on the streets, I feel she's getting stronger. I like that.'

The children did not seem to entertain the idea that families should split up and bring their experiences of hunger and domestic violence to an end. The boys were relieved that the Aghadi could provide their mothers with an amount of sustenance, which they deserved for bringing home *rotis* (bread) at the end of the day. 'Sometimes I think my father's good. But when my parents fight, my mother becomes like a zombie (*chalta phirta murda*). I want her to go out on Aghadi work because she becomes alive again,' pondered Babu. According to the boys, women becoming infused with life meant they would be temporarily distracted from domestic woes and this in turn could keep the precarious family unit together.

The boys were also keen to give up the hunt for inspirational male role models and quite readily justified the emulation of women leaders closer to home. Bappaji (14) saw his mother bring his father home from the Mumbai riots a defeated man. After displaying an initial show of strength Bappaji's father was caught in a police trap. His mother, along with other Aghadi women, had staved off imminent arrest and rescued their men from a tough situation. Bappaji's father was also unemployed. 'My father's a loser,' he concluded. 'I'm on my mother's side. I'll grow up and not become a weakling like my father.' Erikson (1968) wrote that boys, shattered to see fathers returning crushed from the battlefield during the First World War, felt an important need to discover an alternative 'rebellious' role model. Even though he was discussing the effect of Hitler on children in Nazi Germany (and a parallel could be drawn with Bal Thackeray as the fanatic supreme leader of the Shiv Sena), several boys in the slums of Mumbai felt no need to emulate an iconic male leader at a distance. In the daily experience of violent clashes witnessed by the children in the slums the Aghadi leaders mostly emerged winners. The sex of the winning leader had ceased to be relevant and an ungendered notion of heroism was being created. Hence, 'I want to be like my mother' was a common declaration of the Sena boys, especially those who had very militant women in the family. Thus their drive was to discover role models who embodied public militancy, since the boys felt that such icons could fortify the community.

In their desire to be accommodating children some of the boys were willing to follow the path of self-sufficiency. Notorious Aghadi leader Yogita's children, for example, often came home to find their mother out doing social work. They learnt to throw together a meal for themselves, which usually consisted of bread and omelettes. 'At home she's a good mother. Outside she's a good fighter. But when she's out we should try and run the home,' said Raj (14), Yogita's eldest son.

The Sena easily won the loyalty of those children who realised that their otherwise marginalised mothers had been integrated into the larger 'extended family' only by overtly supporting the party's cause. This was especially true in the case of children who had little or no experience of a father. In Nirmal Nagar, for example, some single mothers were assimilated into the Aghadi after they participated in its activities. They also received special attention as independent workers within the Aghadi's economic schemes. This made children like Rakesh (12) happy because they felt 'people' talked to them 'normally'. As he put it:

'I don't feel like the son of a prostitute. Most people think that single mothers are prostitutes. I'll repay this debt. I'll kill all the bad people of the world [thumping his chest].'

AS: 'What bad people?'

R: 'The people my mother says are bad.'

Chimpu (13), also the child of a single mother, had to do 'something extra' to display his support to the Sena community. 'Whenever I pass Hoshiarpur I pick up a stone and chuck it at a window', he said. He claimed this act had 'its own thrill and also a heroic appeal'; but mainly it won him trust among other Sena children, who had accepted 'an otherwise marginal child' like him because of his mother's close association with the party. These mergers formed in the face of social antagonism created conditions in which even small children could move from 'imagining violence' to 'acting violently' (Bajpai, 2002). The boys believed this was one of the ways of ensuring cohesion within the community. It also ensured 'peer-group acceptance', which was imperative while resocialising into the Sena child gang culture (discussed later).

Growing up in a Sena-dominated slum, children who had comparatively passive parents felt they had to indulge in excessive forms of violence as an apology. Tipu (12) said:

'Whenever my parents stayed out of a conflict the other children would taunt me. My mother did say a few bad things about Muslims, like she didn't want to get involved because the Muslims weren't even worth having a confrontation with. But that wasn't enough.'

Staub, describing the birth of genocidal behaviour in societies, comments: 'People who were initially bystanders become involved in the destructive system and become perpetrators' (1989: 18). Tipu's parents tried to justify their own passivity by devaluing the victim, which did not make them a visible force, but meant they played a nominal role in demonising the enemy for their son. Thus Tipu 'knew the enemy' against whom his peer group demanded more visible acts of aggression. So he had to indulge in stone-throwing and the occasional sexual harassment of Muslim women to compensate for a shortfall in the level of visible violence most children expected of Sena parents.

In summary, the boys felt that reshaping the realm of intra-household relations, especially the redefinition of the relationship between male children and women in the family, would ensure the survival of the family and the community. The boys often rattled off a Taliban joke about Muslim women being asked to lead men because in reality they were being used as 'nuke fodder'. The Sena boys felt proud and secure that their 'mothers were better off than these Muslim women' and were 'real leaders'. In collaboration with their mothers and grandmothers (maybe using different paths), the boys felt they could build group honour, solidarity and endurance. This strategy of accommodation and adaptation was not restricted to the immediate functioning of the family and spilled over into the children's imagination of their future roles as boyfriends and husbands.

Survival in the future: girlfriends, wives

This section attempts to provide a window into the real and imagined relationships shared between sections of Hindu male and female children in the

Sena-dominated slums. Some boys felt that building stable, romantic relationships with members of the opposite sex was an important 'method' of constructing a 'better' family and a sound future. This, they thought, was a clear deviation from parental dictates of male authority, arranged weddings and suppressed conjugal relationships. Since several gym facilities were attached to the *shakha*, the boys wanted to do body-building and practice martial arts which, though they appeared to be in preparation for Sena warriorhood, were primarily for seducing girls and keeping them in happy marriages. This was also a covert deviation from Hindu fundamentalist values as the ideology was laid out in the minds of children. Indeed, these boys were willing to exploit the facilities provided by the Shiv Sena to achieve their ends. However, the boys did not want their parents, the Sena or the media to know about their intentions. '*Yeh andar ki baat hai*' ('this is what lies inside'), a boy told me mimicking a television advertisement for underwear. Boys rather than girls liked to talk to me about their ambitions because they believed I could give them valuable tips for wooing girls. They also found it intriguing and perhaps novel to talk about topics reserved for boys-only discussions to an older woman who did not take an overt moral stand against them.

Most of the children harboured a desire to 'fall in love'. Several boys wanted to be sensitive to women and to take into account the changing notions of femininity in the slums, where plain machismo was becoming *passé*. The slum girls, being raised in the city, were not subject to complete confinement. Exposure through their workplace (some of the girls worked at factories and households from an early age), co-educational schooling, unbound slum life and so on allowed most of the girls to be choosy about their mates. This freedom of mobility among girls also seemed to permit a more flexible morality in the slums where boys and girls talking or going out together—though not practising sexual intercourse—was not frowned upon. While the Sena mothers often had to put up a covert fight to wrest valued securities, the new generation of girls were more blatantly aggressive and mobile and easily resorted to verbal abuse or violence to ward off unwarranted male attention. Over time their families' involvement with the party had also thrown a shield around them. If a girl had a Sainik father or an Aghadi mother, it was assumed she would face no danger in the slums.

Girls said that they felt the factors discussed above made the role of men as protectors or aggressors in public quite 'useless'. Most boys felt they could no longer play the roles of male guardians and could not 'get' girls by using force (for example, by dragging a resisting woman by her hair). Bollens (1999), discussing gender roles in deprived households in Northern Ireland, comments that communities affected by conflict are marked by male 'rolelessness'. Since feminine roles are more clearly defined, girls become involved in childcare and home-making activities to regain stability. Boys, however, are left to search out 'worthy' roles for themselves within the family. The Sena boys felt that if they could be loving husbands in blissful marriages, then they would have the vital role of giving permanency to their families. To achieve that end the boys had to seduce women into steady, working relationships in the first place.

To develop attractive bodies most of the boys took up body-building and karate. 'The girl has to come to you, she can't be teased or lifted off the streets anymore,' said Prakash (14). 'So it's important for us to look good. There's too much competition,' he rambled on. Hence the boys regularly haunted the local *shakha* gym and did various body-toning exercises. They would lift weights and bend and coil their thin frames. I was often shooed out because women were not meant to watch the means, only to admire the results (which were short, reed thin bodies with even slimmer waists and lit- tle lumps for biceps). The boys also pored over film magazines to develop the 'right' postures that would attract women. For example, when a young girl passed by the boys would slip their thumbs into the corners of their trouser pockets and throw their head back to lift the hair off their foreheads. This was a common mating call.

According to several scholars, the Shiv Sena introduced a large-scale trend towards masculinity, especially among the lower classes. Heuze (1995), for example, traces these trends to virile, *Kshatriya* (warrior-caste) models in- herited from a Maratha upsurge dating from the end of the nineteenth and beginning of the twentieth centuries. He concluded that the increase in wom- en's permanent residency in the slums of Mumbai cultivated the need for a contest in the display of male vigour, while the absence or minimal presence of women in the slums earlier (when most women remained in their villages) did not promote a need to reflect upon and acquire an attractive sexual image among the men.

However, the boys were certain their body-building attempts had nothing to do with commitment to a masculinist discourse. 'We're actually using the facilities made available to us by the Sena [where no one would monitor the activities of the boys] to seduce women. I *know* this isn't what the Sena elders would want,' said Rakesh (14). This contrasted with other more conservative Hindu nationalist organisations like the RSS, where boys in the *sangh shakhas* build their bodies to become stronger, Hindu warriors. RSS male cadres are strictly instructed not to be weakened by women and their body-building is part of a period of development called *Brahmacharya*, which is traditionally described as a stage of learning and abstinence. According to Rakesh (14),

'Nothing's certain in our lives anymore. I need a partner to love and who will love me. There's joy in permanencies. That way life becomes liveable.'

In Nirmal Nagar the pressure on boys to develop a good-looking male body increased dramatically with the rise of Hrithik Roshan, a film star whose debut film *Kaho Na Pyar Hai* (KNPH—'Tell me you are in love') was a massive box-office success. Even the popularity of this new film star in the Sena-dominated slums was partially informed by the presence of a Hindu fundamentalist discourse. Hrithik's fame was greatly lauded by both *Saamna* (the Sena mouthpiece) and *Panchjanya* (the RSS mouthpiece)[2] as being the long-awaited Hindu challenge to the seemingly interminable reign of the Khans (Shah Rukh, Aamir, Salman, Arbaaz, Saif Ali and Fardeen) in the Mumbai film industry. The newspapers alleged that the Khans were being propped up by the notorious Muslim mafia based in Dubai, which was apparently responsible for attempts on the lives of Hindu film producers who refused to pay extortion money.[3] Finally, the boys felt they had a Hindu hero to look up to and 'openly' emulate. Hrithik's bulging muscles and dancing prowess seemed to have all the girls in the slums mesmerised.

The release of *KNPH* led to a dramatic change in the body-building sessions carried out by some of the boys. Before the film's release boys went to the gym twice or thrice a week, often according to their whims and fancies. After the Hrithik Roshan phenomenon swept through the slums, however, they were seen at the fitness centre every day and would often practise their hero's dance movements to songs from the film, leaving the boys sweating and tired. This became a classic case of real life emulating reel life in Mumbai. All because wooing women became real hard work and 'lifting women off the streets' (using force) was no longer an option.

Boys believed the girls 'these days' wanted tender sexual relationships with their husbands. 'One of the most appealing aspects of Hrithik Roshan is his eyes, you see, they're soft brown and very sensitive,' explained Naren (12). 'The girls like that.' Cornwall and Lindisfarne (1994), discussing the fluidity in gendered identities, showed that weaknesses in male sport icons, like Paul Gascoigne and Andre Agassi crying in public, were hugely appreciated by sections of British women. 'The caring and sensitive heterosexual male thus has recently been celebrated as the new man' (1994: 15). Indeed, a dominance of certain idealised male icons does not preclude the possibility of men developing fresh images which emerge from women's everyday agency in resisting traditional forms of masculinity. Such a transformation of identity

2 Both issues were published in June 2000.
3 Hrithik's Roshan's father was also shot, sparking off a controversy.

seemed to be rapidly taking place in the slums of Mumbai, within the context of a supposedly conservative Hindu nationalist movement.

Why did the romanticisation of marriages become so important among the slum boys? Most of the boys felt that demonstrative, stable, romantic love was missing in arranged marriages. 'Our parents aren't lovers. That's why they have *serious* fights. One can't afford that when there are such uncertainties in our surrounding living conditions,' commented Raj (13). In addition, the chances of arranging a wedding in the slums were gradually reducing. According to the boys in Nirmal Nagar, this was primarily because they were becoming increasingly detached from their rural brethren. Also, their insecurity, lack of space and poverty in the slums made them poor candidates in the rural marriage market.

Oliver's (2003) and Zimring's (1998) studies on aggression among marginalised groups establish a causal link between violence and ambiguity among teenagers in defining their social, sexual and masculine roles. The Sena children were mostly in their pre-teens, but had already developed enormous clarity of thought on their masculine roles within and outside the family. Their supposed firm understanding of their past, present and future also justified the use of violence to sustain their social and sexual responsibilities. Thus the Sena boys put enormous emphasis on the suitability of their future mates. 'I'm in the city now; I don't want to marry some rural woman who spends her days looking after cows and buffaloes,' said Naren. Naren's contempt for rural women as partners stemmed from his semi-urban upbringing in the slums and also his belief that village girls had not gained exposure to concepts of 'love and romance'. 'I actually have nothing against arranged marriages as long as the girl's from the city,' he said.

According to Boyden (2001, 2004), who studied the impact of war on displaced children, a view of children as dependent and of limited competence encourages an understanding of those children exposed to political violence as helpless and traumatised, dependent on adults for their salvation and protection. A study of the Sena boys actively contributes to Boyden's resistance of an understanding of children as passive victims, as opposed to effective *survivors* of conflict. Certainly an understanding of what constitutes childhood 'is constituted in particular socially located forms of discourse' (Jenks, 1992: 23). In the Sena-controlled slum areas of Mumbai the Sena boys were only physically framed as 'children', and when it came to seeking out a stable future for their families and the community the boys did not come across as 'pre-logical beings' (Hockney and James, 1993), innocent and ignorant of the ways of the world. Indeed, the boys sounded perfectly cogent when they explained how they were deviating from the Hindutva discourse while building bodies for seduction and in the process deviating from parental dictates on what constituted an ideal, urban marriage. 'Domestic squabbles can be very disturbing. We have to break free of the old model,' said Raj. Because the family unit still provided anchorage in the face of instability, the boys were only trying to alter the nature of the family, of conjugal relationships while seeking happier futures.

However, it was also crucial for the boys not to be perceived as 'weak children' (*kamzor bacchey*) by the enemy community. The boys would reiterate that they would never woo Muslim women and hence there was no need to show restraint in their behaviour towards them. 'We're very clear in our minds about "our" women and "their" women. Muslim women must be treated violently. The main thing is that Muslims must *not* think Hindu men are becoming soft because they're now treating their own women with love and respect,' said Amit (12). To counter 'myths' about the correlation between 'romance' and 'weakness' some of the Sena boys told me they had to indulge in 'target practice'. A trip to Kamathipura, Mumbai's most renowned ghetto for prostitutes, revealed that Muslim and eunuch prostitutes were in great demand by Hindu boys (not just men) who were their main customers.[4] These prostitutes were beaten up by Hindu boys during intercourse. Some eunuchs (considered unfit for living in a pure, Hindu society) were tortured, abused and smeared with spit in a process that stopped only after the persecution had been brutal enough to satisfy the customers. The demand for Muslim prostitutes increased during the time of *namaaz*. According to Islam, devotees in prayer must not let anything interrupt their exchange with God. The boys would often barge in on praying women and tease and torture them to test their patience. 'Hindu boys can be kind to their wives. But they can also make brutal warriors. Right now it's war,' said Raj.

Most of the boys considered brutality towards 'other' women a necessary form of revenge and retribution, yet they remained mindful of their projected image as the strong, well-built, yet kind Hindu male. Some said that Hindu boys were usually incapable of such violent action: the children were merely emulating the combat strategies of Muslim men, since 'the Muslims had to be given a dose of their own medicine.' One must remember in this context that these children were growing up in an environment of female militancy, which was partially justified on the basis of countering vulnerabil-

---

[4] A women's cell next to the Kamathipura police station offered to help Muslim and eunuch prostitutes, but little could be done for them. They could not afford to choose clients according to their religion. Consequently, most customers were Hindu. Although some were familiar, others were not and they could not tell who might turn violent and start abusing them and/or Islam.

ity to the violent sexuality of the Muslim male: hence the children's awareness of the supposed predatory qualities of the enemy community. Since the
boundaries between usual and unusual behaviour were constantly shifting
among the boys, most of them did not want to take the risk of informing the
Hindu girls that they visited prostitutes. It was likely to tar the boys' attractive image, or if the girls decided they liked non-violent men, then it would
become one more thing the boys would have to negotiate. 'That's why these
talks about *randilok* (prostitutes) are for laughs between the boys only,' said
Naren who regularly went to red-light areas in other localities solely to locate
Muslim prostitutes.

The boys were clearly trying to conceive of two parallel roles in the future: a 'controlled and kindly' Hindu man before their own women and a
'violent' warrior before 'other' men and women. They felt a merging of these
roles would ensure the survival and honour of their family, neighbourhood
and community. A significant comparison could be drawn with Grossmann's
(1983) study of a group of radical sexologists called the 'League for the Protection of Motherhood' in 1920s Germany. The League recommended sex
and erotic pleasure classes for women since a fulfilled sexuality gave birth
to healthier children. Their diagnosis struck a responsive chord because over
150,000 Germans joined the organisation. The massive support from men,
which shocked the world, rested on the belief that women who found fulfilment with their lawful husbands would not succumb to adultery, lesbianism
and masturbation (Grossmann, 1983: 154). The same men who took the sex
education classes to appease their wives feared that 'others' may consider
their enterprise a sign of racial weakness. So they cheered the Nazis when
they sent Jewish women to the gas chambers (*ibid.*). In a similar pursuit to
secure the sexual and emotional fidelity of their girlfriends, which apparently
could not be ensured through force any more, most of the Sena boys tried to
acquire sensitive, romantic personas. However, they were willing to coerce
Muslim women sexually to show they were not enfeebled by their new endeavours. The girls in the area did not openly express that they sanctioned
violence on Muslim women or on eunuchs, or that this would be an indicator
of Hindu male virility for them. But they *did* want their men to be attractive
and loving. 'There's no fun in life otherwise,' said Chipi (16), one of the girls
in the slum.

On 22 December 2002 *The Indian Express*, an English daily, reported the
founding of Shiv Sena martial arts camps in the slums of Mumbai:

Ten saffron flags flutter neatly along the angular boundary walls of a *maidan* [large
open playing-field] on the outskirts of the city. Inside are school students lining
up for free Shiv Sena T-shirts complete with party logo—handed out on Day One

of the Sena's Commando Camp 2002. The boys will wear the uniform for training to be karate kids and sharp-shooters, *sainik* style. No entry fee.

A few years earlier there had been no such Sena commando camps. Possibly they were built after the Sena leaders observed the attraction of body-building and martial arts among the boys. Thus, the emphasis on organising these camps within the Sena movement may not have been contrived by the Sena leaders; instead the organisation may merely have followed the popular evolution of life among the lower classes. The boys' initial agenda was to create order by building stable families, which in turn would overcome personal and communal crises. A few years later these boys with stronger bodies were being officially recruited and incorporated into the party mechanism.

THE LOCALITY: SENA BOYS AND THE SHAKHA

Crowds and crowds of little children are strangely absent from the written record. (Laslett, 1972: 104–5)

Relating the complexity of children's thoughts and actions to their words and expressions is often difficult. According to the Sena boys, their conduct in public and private spaces was closely affiliated with the sense of Hindu 'dignity' and 'purpose' propagated by the Sena movement. This section discusses the boys' search for a secure place in the locality that signified order, stability and normalcy in their lives and hence explores the centrality of the *shakha*, the hub of local Sena activity, in the lives of much younger boys. According to Katzenstein, the slums did not provide adequate recreational facilities for children, and since parents were away for long hours to earn a livelihood, the Sena youth turned to the *shakha* (the local party office)[5] to kill the loneliness of freedom (1979: 116). Thus the vagaries of slum life—the temporary nature of shacks, constrained space, fear of police arrests, marginalisation as street children—enhanced the appeal of the *shakha* as an inspiring symbol of 'safety'.

Child life in the shakha: activities and identities

The *shakha* served as a gathering ground for boys during 'special sessions' involving children. These sessions fostered discussions among adult party

5 The party office usually comprised a big room with a desk, lots of chairs, some busts of Shivaji, some paintings or photos of Shivaji, a saffron Sena flag in one corner and a couple of steel cupboards bursting with files. The more prominent *shakha*s had adjoining gyms, classrooms or empty rooms for health camps or large gatherings.

members about the prospects of the movement. Long-term survival strategies were developed and circulated around the office, and the young boys
were free to 'grasp' whatever they found comprehensible. Ideas about building stronger collective identities and steady futures fascinated the children.

As part of the Sena's 'survive the slum' strategy, health and awareness
camps exclusively for Hindu women and their offspring were held in the
shakhas. These formal camps dealt with issues of female infanticide, child
education, AIDS awareness and child abuse. However, the Sena boys were
quick to point out the stark absence of child opinion in the organisation of
children's camps. Rajesh (11) said: 'I'd like to talk to someone about what
children should do when they see their parents, two people they love the
most in the world, are ready to bite each other's heads off. Where's the camp
for my problems?' Despite these shortcomings, some of the camps involving children's issues appeared to be progressive—even to the children. For
example, during one of the Sena women's events a couple from the slums
was fêted because, despite being fertile, they had adopted orphaned children.
Another couple was congratulated for fostering a baby they had picked out of
a garbage can. The *shakha* also provided a space where children could be approached directly to take up career-training courses, and the Meenatai Educational Trust,[6] run by the Shiv Sena, instituted computer classes for children
in central Mumbai. The boys interpreted this initiative as an encouragement
to be better equipped in future workplaces. A tour of the computer section
inaugurated within the *shakha* premises revealed that they appeared to be
technologically advanced.

'Bala*ji* says we should be prepared to fight the enemy in every field. We'd
have better jobs and better futures, no?' asked Jaggu (11), after reading about
the computer classes in a *Saamna* editorial pasted on the *shakha* door. The idea
was not just to reduce competition by defeating the enemy through physical
combat, but also to extend the war zone to the sphere of progressive family
values, good health and professional calibre. According to the boys, attending
these *shakha* camps increased their awareness about the movement's multifac-
eted designs to outwit the 'other' community and build 'economically sound,
healthy futures'.

The children also gathered in the *shakha* to lend a hand during political
meetings. The boys felt that taking part in nationalistic activities sharpened
their identities as Hindus, took away their sense of 'rolelessness', and allowed
children to imagine themselves as worthy contributors to the Sena movement. These party meets were always a cause for great excitement. Most boys

[6] Named after Bal Thackeray's wife.

were in charge of stools and tables and the distribution of food and beverages to attendees. During the more fierce demonstrations and protest marches originating from the *shakhas* the children were often used as shields against counter-attacks by law enforcing authorities. During a Sena *bandh*[7] to protest the arrest of Thackeray, children aged 8–12 years were gathered in the *shakhas*, dressed up in saffron, ceremoniously marched to local stations and dropped on the tracks to bring the intra-city train service to a standstill. The look in the eyes of the children huddling on the tracks was unforgettable. Several weeks later the children said they had been afraid, but that their parents had asked them to be 'brave'. Asked whether they thought giving immunity shots to the children and then exposing the same children to such enormous risks was inconsistent, the Sena cadres answered with a wall of silence.

The children were made to uphold this legacy of 'bravery' through their participation in various cultural activities. Shivaji Jayanti (a festival to mark the birthday of Shivaji) generated enormous festivities in the slums for which the *shakha* became the unit of coordination. In Nirmal Nagar, besides the food and the finery, the occasion was celebrated with parades and the performance of Shivaji plays in the local *shakhas*. The children loved to enact the story of Shivaji killing Mughal general Afzal Khan with tiger claws. However, who would play the parts of Shivaji and his victorious general on the one hand, and Afzal Khan and his defeated army on the other was—not surprisingly—cause for a big row. Most of the time children practised on the *shakha* premises. When they rehearsed without parental supervision they would interrupt their usual Marathi dialogues with Mumbaiya colloquial Hindi abuses (often accompanied by the body language of film stars), which degraded the Muslim community. This made the children roll with laughter.

Shivaji: '*Abey chutia Afzal, tu mereko marega? Mereko? Rand ki aulad, tu us din mar gaya tha jis din tu landya ban gaya.*' [You fucker Afzal, you'll kill me? Me? Son of a whore, you died the day you were circumcised.]

'That means he died as a child,' one of the children explained, rubbing the tears of laughter from his eyes. While the performance of violence sustained the larger Sena movement, the children's involvement in the pseudo-struggle was also determined by the 'violence in performance' (Jeganathan, 2000: 52). Keeping the Marathi plays on Shivaji alive was also a crusade among some of the older members of the Aghadi. Shobha, a distractingly beautiful retired stage actress, said:

7 *Bandh*, lit. 'closed', refers to a protest meet forcing a shutdown of government services.

'My drive is to keep the Shivaji performances alive through the children. It shouldn't be a dying art. But after watching too many films the children try and act out the role of Shivaji as Amitabh Bachchan [a Mumbai megastar].'

While some defended the 'authentic' folk versions, the parents often refor-mulated the plays along modern lines and these new adaptations became popular among the children. 'Since the next generation shouldn't forget the Shivaji tradition, let's repackage it.' On one occasion, when the army of Shivaji was dressed in modern paramilitary (camouflage) combat outfits with automatic toy weapons, the children were relieved to see that the army appeared more menacing and well-prepared for warfare. Nonetheless they were not totally averse to traditional performances 'as long as Shivaji beat the Mughals and proved we won.'

The *shakha* created the façade of a permanent space where the boys be-came more intensely socialised into 'a Hindu community'. The organisation of militant Hindutva rallies created a setting in which most of the children learnt that 'being a Hindu' was something that needed to be celebrated and defended. Through the routine enactment of attacks on Muslims, some-times modernised and often traditional, children learnt the mytho-history of antagonistic relationships shared between the two communities. Passions were whipped up through the repetition of the same hostile dramas and when alone the boys distorted the original dialogues, reducing them to a crude abuse of Muslim leaders in history. According to the boys, 'once in the *shakha*, we're aware all the time that Muslims are the bad guys. We're aware all the time that once together Hindus can also fight back.'

'Triumph of fear'

The *shakha* also signified a hope for overcoming various vulnerabilities. The boys felt that it was mainly within the *shakha* walls that they had learnt to use fear as their biggest weapon. For example, the concept of 'we won'—bla-tantly encouraged among the *shakha* offspring—extended to competitions with other clubs for gathering donations during cultural programmes. Most households gave money to the Sena children, either because they were loyal, or because refusal meant being marked as detractors. (The children were well aware that detractors were severely punished.) Although the cultural programmes were intended to represent the non-political image of the Sena, when the boys returned to the *shakha* with their collections they felt that 'It was the triumph of fear.' Furthermore, within the *shakha* the children felt safe from the recurrence of fear in their own peripheral urban lives.

There was a protector-protected affiliation between the Sena children and the *shakha*, which, the children felt, drew parallels with relationships with Aghadi mothers. For example, the *shakha* remained beyond the reach of the police. The children were grateful that a small yellow-bricked office with a saffron flag fluttering on the door could symbolise fear, safety, security, identity and entertainment. Hence, the local party office provided daily shelter to children who indulged in illegal activities—running illegal errands for their parents, pick-pocketing, selling marijuana for quick money, running illegal roadside stalls for stolen goods. During clean-up drives the police let the Sena children off. ' "If you know my mother, don't touch me," I'd tell the police. They all feared my mother. And if I hide in the *shakha* the police can't touch me there either. They all feared the *shakha*,' said Dinu (12). A number of girls were also being pushed into illegal rackets because they stood less chance of getting caught. 'The *shakha* would be a hiding place for both boys and girls, where we would run after shoplifting,' he said. 'But we always shared the profits.'

'Sharing' made the boys see themselves as Robin Hood-type characters, which was encouraged by the Sena elders. They would imitate 'good dacoits', indigenous versions of Robin Hood, who played central characters in many Hindi films. The boys were perceived as playing 'a positive community role' by helping out during *shakha* camps and demonstrations, taking part in cultural programmes, learning to share their loot and claiming to be child warriors. Thus the children's indulgence in petty criminal behaviour was eclipsed by greater efforts to organise themselves into nationalist task forces.

'Systems of offering justice'

Sharing their parent's disregard for formal law and order institutions, the children were relieved that the Hindu communities had their own rules which emanated from the *shakha*. For example, the *shakha* decided the minimum exchange of dowries between poor families. Thus 'justice' was always assertively upheld, maintaining order and stability within the slum areas, and the *shakha* became the equivalent of a courtroom where the use of force to counter situations of tension was calculated, debated and thus legitimised.

Although the children supported the Aghadi's aggressive policies, they believed several women had limited capacity to deliver violent justice. Thus the '*shakha* boys' often had to make up for the weaker women law enforcers. Furthermore the children began to view the *shakha* as a unique training ground to 'take up future responsibilities of maintaining order'. When the film *Godmother* was released it became very popular among the Sena women.

(Ironically it starred Shabana Azmi, a Muslim actress who also played the lead role in *Fire*, the film on lesbianism that the Aghadi berated.) *Godmother*, a story of revenge, was based on the life of an ordinary Gujarati village woman who was forced to join the world of crime, and later politics, after her criminal husband was killed by rival gang members. Soon thereafter a newspaper article reported that the real life character of the film, Santokben Jadeja, had mocked the police and had pressured them to release her son, who had been arrested for burning a bus that had honked loudly and overtaken his car. 'He did the right thing,' claimed Supu (15). 'When you get used to power it's hard to digest insults. Mothers can't *always* do violence well. This boy was lucky. *Shakha* boys who don't have such powerful mothers have to take a lot of responsibility themselves.'

To practise their skills at delivering justice the children would also play anti-Muslim 'riot games' or Indo-Pakistan 'war games'. The *shakha* not only provided an open space for these games but also created the ambience of communal hostility where violent games were easily endorsed. The children would divide themselves into hit squads and revenge teams and wear straps around their waists as ammunition belts. They explained how wide exposure to television had increased their interest in military toys. Also, instruments of violence were easily available in the slums so children had access to knives, swords and sticks for play. Most scholars discussing war games among boys in battle-ridden societies feel children improvise on earlier games like 'cops and robbers' or 'cowboys and Indians', which were based on pre-existing cultural biases (Komarovsky, 1971; Tuttle, 1993). In the case of the Sena children, 'Indo-Pak army clash' often substituted the more common 'good *vs* evil' game of '*chor* (thief)-police'.

The *shakha* thus provided a space where children could develop their own understanding of being Hindu, being male and also being a child. The children were at a stage in their (slum) lives when they felt a need to take charge of their own survival, deal with their own ideas of uncertainty and danger, and at the same time ensure the protection of their home and hearth. These experiences generated in the children a faith in gang culture. Emulating the adults, the boys wanted to create their own organisation and solidarity group where they could pursue their own agendas for survival. However, since the *shakha* could not provide adequate space for holding large group meetings, these self-styled children's gangs poured on to the streets around the slums.

THE STREET: SENA BOYS AND THE RISE OF GANG CULTURE

It is not a dead-end world,
I have discovered,
They are not dead-end people. (Kim, 1991: 73)

The Shiv Sena children and their parents both agreed the street was an important point of interaction and intersection in the lives of slum dwellers. It symbolised and regulated certain identities for them. Parents were forced to adapt to a life on the streets, as hawkers, peddlers and stall owners, because it offered a livelihood. As for the children, even though they put enormous emphasis on the importance of the family and the home, they could not remain cooped up in small shanties for most of the day. Thus, the street was an alternative space available to the children where they could 'hang out' and expend their energies.

In wanting to overcome the status of being segregated street children and develop a more glorified status as groups of Sena area soldiers (*ilake sainik*) boys formed Hindu 'kids' gangs' in their localities. They insisted that forming child armies was an important way of dissolving vulnerabilities in their slum life. According to Becker (1997), people's efforts to create linkages with the past during times of disruptive changes—whether societal, such as those caused by a revolution, or individual, such as those caused by illness—have been readily observed. People maintain continuity with the past amid the facts of change by interpreting current events so that they are understood as part of tradition. Like the adult Shiv Sena members, the Sena boys tried to justify their gang-ism by stressing Hindu majoritarianism, Marathi martiality and a long-established system in the Sena-dominated slums to control spaces, maintain order and group solidarity.

Tags as 'street children'

Several parents did not want their offspring to be labelled 'street children'. Since children with working parents did not get much familial supervision, their parents preferred that they not spend long hours in the streets and instead gain a more 'respectable' identity as '*shakha* children' or 'Sena children' in general. They would rather their sons rose above the street culture and belong to an umbrella organisation, fulfilling group expectations and turning their associations with the party into a learning experience about 'appropriately living within a community'. Some Aghadi mothers preferred their children to spend their time only within the protective boundaries of the *shakha*, especially in their absence. Lakha (12) said,

'My mother can't be around to save me every time I have the urge to make a few quick bucks. But she knows that if I hang around the party office, I'm occupied otherwise, I stay out of trouble and even if I get into trouble people from the office and the locality will come forward to help me.'

'Being on the streets is like a stigma,' complained Lakha's mother. 'What will he learn by hanging out on the streets? The *shakha*'s not the home, but at least it helps people to create bonds that'll help us later,' she said. A very small proportion of children agreed with their parents. For example, Niranjan (10) said: 'My mother hawks on the streets, she has a reputation to maintain. Even if I just loiter on the streets, I'll be branded a thief. I don't like it because some holier than thou people tell my mother your son's a crook.' Some other boys, however, could not entirely overcome the sustained exposure to the glorification of street realities. This exposure lay in watching tele-serials and in keenly observing the activities of the older Shiv Sena vigilante groups among whom a criminal lifestyle was already in vogue. The boys seemed to be fascinated by the occasional triumph of 'deviant' children raised on 'waves of humanity rather than by a sea of money' (dialogue from a popular serial *Nukkad* or 'Neighbourhood'). Most of the boys admired the strong physical presence of local vigilante groups (which consisted of men and women aged eighteen to twenty-eight) and easily grasped how working as a gang could enable its members to gain and retain control over their social environment.[8] They were also deeply influenced by the Aghadi's strategies for collective action to resolve local problems. An experience of power and self-protection was something the children aspired for; hence they rapidly spilled on to road corners as 'gangs' or 'armies'. However, the boys felt their association with the Shiv Sena had given them a prior esteemed identity as 'Sena boys', so even if they operated as child squads, they would not be seen as stereotypical 'ordinary' street gangs.

The terms 'gang' or 'army' are used here to represent the groups of Sena children solely because that is how the children identified themselves. During casual discussions they would often refer to themselves as a *dal*, which could mean gang, group, party or collective. When asked how they collectively identified themselves, they always said: '*Hum bacchon key* gang/army *hain*' ('We're a gang/army of children'). 'Gang' may not of course be a concept the children learnt in school. It was another common English word, like

---

[8] The vigilante groups were area watchmen/women and were often significantly different from the gangsters, who were hardened criminals. The gangsters were closely affiliated with the Sena, but would not be seen in public as a group, primarily for fear of police retaliation.

'problem', 'taxi' or 'culture', which was used by everyone in the slums. In the movies as well, which greatly influenced the children, groups of boys in slums heroically warding off attacks by land sharks were always referred to as 'gangs'. One Hindi film, for example, which told the story of such a group of justice-deliverers was called *Gang*. Another, about a group of young civilians armed to the teeth and seeking social revenge, was called *Army*. There were also various adult, criminal groups in the slums who referred to themselves as gangs. Thus, the children seem to have developed this collective identity as a 'gang' through daily exposure to life in the slums. But they were clear to demarcate themselves from homeless children who lived together in the temporary squatters' or rag-pickers' colonies. 'We haven't been abandoned by our families and nor have we run away. I'm talking about those children on railway platforms, you know,' explained one. 'We have access to party money to back us,' said another. So the Sena children's gangs had access to other collective identities like family and party and also to their resources, which separated them from other groups who operated collectively in the streets.

Control of space

The gangs' operations largely represented the control of street space. Gaining ownership of the street seemed a predictable yet prominent exercise in the Sena slums. In Nirmal Nagar, for example, most of the street hawkers were women, who would spread their wares at the same place everyday and would get into scuffles with other vendors who tried to usurp them. However, the control of territory became fuzzy the moment the issue of its maintenance and management was raised, the responsibility for which would promptly be transferred on to the unwanted neighbours. 'These Muslims are so dirty, they regularly mess up the place,' said Gauri, who sold her costume jewellery close to a few Muslim households. Watching these ambiguous battles for space apparently inspired the children to wrest and mark their own hang-outs as well. The boys 'snatched' and marked parks, street corners etc., taking over spaces not designed for them. Protection of those spaces from invasion, primarily by the local Muslims, also required that the children 'stick together' as a gang. 'We used to watch our mothers and knew that if one has to get one's own space in the street, one has to fight for it,' said Topu (15).

Different 'gangs' of children gave different overlapping reasons for trying to control the streets in their localities. Most boys were suspicious of local Muslims and feared being on the streets alone. To address this fear they developed certain gang codes of conduct. For example, they set times to meet together at preordained spots. One of the child gangs in Nirmal Nagar invited

Babu Rao, a known (adult) felon and a Sena gangster, to join their group for a while and pat their backs. The children treated the gangster as a distinguished guest and fortified their strength by showing others that their gang was under the protection of stronger forces. The boys also displayed menacing postures when Muslim neighbours passed by. There was a particular 'boils in your armpits' walk, when the boys would puff up their non-existent muscles and try and develop a surly, burly look. 'We're not beggars just because we stand on the street. We have to rake up ingenious strategies to prove that we're powerful,' Ishwar (15) said.

But the children had other enemies, who they feared more covertly. This need for controlling space, the collaboration for confrontation, seemed to stem partially from a long-term fear of eviction by government forces. Since social security functions were poor and the municipality provided inadequate housing facilities, the children felt they always bore the brunt of eviction. For example, following a massive eviction in Ambedkar Nagar slums on 1 May 1998 several children died of sunstroke and diarrhoea (Cehat Medical Report, 2000: 45). 'Even if the mothers hold their children to their chests, there are still forces that might separate them, take their space away,' said Sheru (9), talking about that eviction. Arbitrary evictions with no resettlement plans seemed to keep the children in a perpetual state of uncertainty about their own spaces and dwellings. Hence, the boys felt they had to develop and carry out their own role in protecting the home and the community land.

The slum children's desire to control space was intensified by the idea that 'the meeting spots' could be draped in notions of purity and pollution. For example, Gappu (10), explaining his need to belong to a gang said: 'We always guard our hangouts, even at night. No women with provocative postures are allowed to stand there,' he laughed. Although the boys went to prostitutes, they still considered them 'unclean' enough to protest such women occupying 'their corner' at night. However, even though they took part in all kinds of illegal activities, the boys carefully avoided sexual networking, i.e. involvement in the flesh trade (as pimps). Asked for their reasons, one of them said: 'We may be a gang, but we're respectable. We wouldn't compromise on women's causes within the slums. Look how our Aghadi mothers are fighting for it.'

Memories of riots

A large section of Sena boys turned to memories of various communal riots to justify their entry into gang culture. Although the children often came from families of aggressors, the boys still complained of a common fear of being attacked on the streets, and they frequently said how loud noises reminded them of the bombs and gunshots exchanged during riots. The boys believed they could overcome these 'fears' by functioning as a children's collective.

Those boys affected specifically by the 1992–3 riots claimed their idea of operating as a successful gang came from the Hindus *and* the Muslims, as they closely watched both parties during eruptions of violence. Some of the children from areas where there was a Muslim backlash claimed they saw 'large groups of men in *lungis* [worn by Muslims] with cycle chains and knives come into their homes and Hindu families had to flee through the back door.' Others saw their Aghadi mothers 'forcibly entering the Muslim homes and tearing the *burqas* off the women.' Still others saw 'groups of Hindu police-men open fire, hitting some Muslims in their legs and hips.'

The children's 'visions' of the riots seemed to be partially informed by the media and the incessant rumour-mongering of the women. When the riots first broke out, the children were taken out of school and kept in the house with their mothers and television sets. They spent their days indoors, watching broadcasts of the riots and listening to tales of gore propagated by the women. Since the television channels repeatedly played the same scenes of violence, the boys felt it had escalated even though in some areas it may have been in check.

Chimpu (14): 'There were bodies of children that were cut and thrown into the gutter.'
AS: 'Did you see it?'
C: 'I saw the riots going on on the TV, it must've happened in all the slums.'
AS: 'Did *you* see the bodies of children in the gutters, Chimpu?'
C: 'My mother did.'

Some of the children experienced the resistance offered to supposed Muslim attacks by assisting their mothers on those 'fateful nights'. During times of vigil the children helped their mothers with the cooking, fetching water and serving the men who kept awake as self-styled night-guards in the neighbour-hood. Children in some of the slums were also given the task of throwing stones at Muslims from terraces of Hindu homes.

According to the children, these experiences made them aware of the benefits of functioning as a group. This created the sense of preparedness in the boys to be on the alert for sudden assaults, because as children they felt they were the 'most vulnerable to attacks of all sorts'. Furthermore, often mentioning that Muslims were 'badly affected during the riots' and that 'they may seek revenge', the children thus 'needed to organise as well'.

AS: 'What will you do when a riot breaks out?'
Ghutlu: 'If my mother says …'

AS: 'If she says "Yes", then?'

G: 'Then! We'll seal off all the entry and exit routes, some of us will lie on our chests on the terraces bordering the slums with sticks and stones, some of us will quickly boil hot oil and smash glasses.... Finally we have to keep some medication ready. When the riots break out, the doctors don't want to practise openly. We won't let anyone harm our homes.'

There was a perfect understanding between the children, and the perfect allocation of responsibilities—as if it were all ready and waiting to be implemented. Furthermore, the children continued to perceive the gang as a mechanism of self-defence as well as retaliation.

G: 'The children from the squatters' colonies are always being kidnapped by Arabs and made to ride camels. How can one trust these Muslims? What if something like that happened to us? The fact that we're a Sena children's group is our shield—no one can touch us.'

Staub, discussing genocide, positive social behaviour and morality, comments: 'Comprehension may lead to forgiveness, for some it is preferable not to comprehend' (1989: 302). On one occasion some of the slum children pointed out a Muslim boy in their class who often grabbed valuable things around him. 'He's a typically greedy, thieving Muslim, even though he's a child. How does one counter them unless the children unite?' one of them asked. Another day, a local NGO worker explained that the same Muslim child had lost both his parents and his home during the Mumbai riots and since then grabbed various possessions without questioning their ownership. The NGO worker feared: 'I wonder what this Muslim child, constantly facing discrimination, will grow up to be?'

And what about the Sena children as young adults?

No leaders, no hierarchies ... yet

Whyte (1981) and Miller's (1958) classic theories on gang-ism reveal that a culture of marginality necessarily organises itself around leadership and hierarchy. Whyte, for example, argues that performance of action only stems from directives from the position of a gang leader. Alexander's (2000) more recent research on patterns in Asian gang behaviour also focuses on senior leadership structure as a defining factor for gang operations. Despite their action-oriented programmes, the Sena children's gangs were not yet marked by inter-group or intra-group rivalry for space, superiority or leadership. Some Sena boys appeared to be 'spokespersons', more articulate than the others. But if referred to as 'leaders', they would all look vague and say, 'I guess someone will have to give the command when the time comes. Right now we're all the same. It's more important to be together.' Since the gang's strength lay in numbers, children from various age groups stuck together without establishing any rigid hierarchies. If more than one children's gang operated in an area, they respected each other's spaces, interacted in a friendly manner and did not inform on each other's activities. Unlike other forms of gang behaviour, Sena child 'gang-ism' was not about inter-gang competition for space, visibility and resources, but was more about learning the art of street survival.

This ambiguity over leadership did not dilute the Sena children's understanding of their potential to be 'real' gangs. Ownby and Heidhues (1993), who have studied secret societies, consider that among very small children a feeling of intense *bonhomie* in the face of adversity was the primary basis for forming societies and thus crime became a mere sub-category. This feeling of brotherhood and compassion was especially true among the Sena children; yet they could not be described as secret societies of children because of their open display of solidarity and territoriality. Most scholars on gang behaviour identify initiation ceremonies as an important channel of induction into a gang. Keiser (1969), for example, who studied black ghetto culture and American street gangs, identified wine-drinking as the most common rite of passage. The Sena children did not have any formal initiation ceremonies and would mark the entry of a member into the 'gang' by a smile of empathy and acceptance. Usually the gangs consisted of boys who had grown up together, and a new member was simply 'introduced' by a friend. The boys would carry on playing together, stealing together and displaying what they imagined to be their collective strength. The children had not even developed punitive measures for deviant members because 'I guess being left out is enough of a bad feeling ... we want to stay together,' said Rupak (14). Leadership, however, can take many forms and there *were* some children who were more articulate or charismatic than others. But for the boys themselves, developing shared dependencies seemed more important than establishing formal age and leadership hierarchies. Hence, common sentiments of 'community and family survival' created circumstances in which the dynamics of gang processes became linked.

'No one tells us it's wrong'

With the whole exercise of operating as a 'children's army' on the street and within the party, the Sena boys seemed to be advocating a dismissal of the boundary between normality and deviance. The Sena children were growing up in an environment where the leaders, especially Thackeray, constantly took responsibility for violence. The children were exposed to Thackeray's speeches, which carried euphemistic language, creating a space for the evasion of obvious questions (like whether Hindus had any real enemies and whether the Muslims were a real physical, social, economic or religious threat and needed to be opposed). With accountability diminished, the children were happy to relinquish individual responsibility and act under authority. In what can be described as a 'reversal of morality', killing was seen as right. Hence, while at one time shoplifting and pick-pocketing by children were not looked upon as criminal behaviour at all, as more and more children were mobilised into gang culture and indulged in subversive activities, even murder was not seen as a crime any longer. 'If it's for a Hindu community cause, it's fine. No one tells us it's wrong,' said Naresh (13).

According to Marquez, 'a community reacts to gang behaviour through its agencies and spokesmen' (Marquez, 1999: 27). Marquez, who studied street children's gangs in Venezuela, commented that the state tried to 'recover' these children from the streets and then to turn them into real citizens by forcing them into various institutions. The second idea propagated by state machineries was that these children were beyond recovery and therefore 'must be gotten out of the way before they take over' (Marquez, 1999: 216). For most gangs, the police and members of correction facilities were important enemies. However, the local-level state machinery in Mumbai, which is often unabashedly pro-Sena, had discriminatory policies in favour of the children from Sena families, even if they operated as a gang, giving Sena children the notion that they occupied a hallowed position on the streets. 'The police don't look upon us as disposable marginal children. They know we're following the great Hindu tradition,' said Babul (12). So while other youth gangs were either imprisoned or ended up in pathetic rehabilitation institutions, police practices were lenient towards Sena children's gangs. In this context Sena boys perceived their gang activities to be worthy of a greater cause, which placed them above petty criminals hauled in by law-enforcement agencies.

Even though many parents disapproved of their children spending time on the streets, most of them did not seem earnestly to dissuade their children from displaying organised street violence. Kotlowitz's (1992) study of children in American ghettoes represents a certain grim reality in which mothers start saving for the funeral rites of male children when the latter enter puberty. In the Sena slums, since the parents and older siblings did not spend enough time at home, the very young in the family were encouraged to be independent and to think about their own survival at an early age. On one occasion when the children returned from stoning houses in Hoshiarpur, Aghadi mother Sharda commented: 'It's a display of their patriotism.' Savitri, another Aghadi mother, said: 'It's the process of becoming men.' Thus, most Sena families did not look upon child gang members as deviants. The gangs were carrying out 'roles' which both parents and children imagined the children would fulfil in the adult 'Sena life'. This was another grim reality.

The Sena could be described as a social architect, trying to create a uniformity of culture among the lower classes. In the slums families had undergone mutations (e.g. breakdown in joint families), which were followed by an absence of solidarity systems. There was also an absence of social promotion on the basis of educational qualifications, i.e. a child born in the slums, stayed in the slums. The Sena advocated aggressive collective action as the primary channel for resolving all forms of community uncertainties. Within the Sena-dominated slums children pushed for survival, evaluated the world in terms of 'us' and 'them', learnt to devalue their imagined enemies, and used violence to raise the self-esteem of their community. The children's views may appear to be unformed and uninformed in parts, but the children *themselves* felt old enough to take their place in the social machinery. Thus the Sena children's gangs could be described as 'micro-cultures of violence' (Bar-Tal, 1990)[9] within the Sena movement in the slums, where the neighbourhood was turning into a frontier in the battle for survival. There was also a hierarchy of motives for the formation of the gangs among the children. Being part of a violent gang was necessary because it acted as a structure of compensation, a means of protest, a means of securing justice, a channel of resistance, a liberating, solidarity-building and problem-solving mechanism. Life in a charged pro-Sena environment was also a constant reminder of experiences of violence, so forgetting the past was not a way out. Instead, being part of a team increased the children's skills to make a better, more secure future.

THE CLASSROOM: SENA BOYS AND SOURCES OF 'KNOWLEDGE'

In order to support their drive towards building a martial collectivity, children hunted for 'sources of knowledge' (*jo cheez gyan detey hain*) which would do just that. Children claimed that some of their 'inspiration' to develop a Hindu militant 'gang' identity flowed from their classroom situations (the variety of which are discussed in the opening paragraphs of this chapter). Most of the Sena boys were pleased to see that the classroom, in which religious identities had for a long time remained diffused, had become segregated after the Mumbai riots. Children from both communities displayed overt hostility,

[9] As against 'sub-cultures of violence', which are more commonly used among theorists of gang behaviour and which involve a longer and more established normative system that supports violence among children.

and schools became breeding grounds for conspiracies between Hindu children and their Hindu teachers to isolate Muslim students. To justify further
Hindu militancy the students turned to textbooks and *Saamna* editorials on
nationalism. The Sena children were excited to see that 'ideas of Hindu group
survival' shared at home and within peer groups had merged with the views
of teachers and could also be found in textbooks.

Teachers, textbooks and editorials

There is an ongoing debate on the saffronisation of education in Maharashtra.
For example, Bénéï's (2001) commentary on the reproduction of nation as
imagined community (Anderson, 1991) through education in Maharashtra
reveals how 'patriotism' represented in textbook language and songs led to
the blurring of boundaries between Indian nationalism and Marathi regional-
ism. However, the role of the teachers in the display of nationalism during
school hours remained subtle in the case of Kolhapur, where Benei conducted
her research. In the case of primary schooling in the Sena slums, the teachers
and their readings of historical texts played a central part in an intense, aggressive rearticulation of Hindu nationalism in the classroom.

   According to Sena boys, teachers overtly expressed their Hindu, nationalist credentials after the Mumbai riots were over. 'Before that, it was there,
but was far more subdued,' said an NGO worker. 'The Mumbai riots made
the teachers put across their hostility towards Muslims in a more definite
way. Teachers and the police should be non-partisan, right?' she continued.
A parallel can be drawn with the police force displaying its saffron colours
(discussed in Chapter 3), although policemen had a free rein to air their
anti-Muslim sentiments *while* the riots were raging across the city. Since the
violence kept most students at home, the boys realised that the schools had
abandoned their secular agenda only after the conflict had subsided.

   Most Hindu students openly blamed the Muslims for hindering their
progress at school. 'I had to drop out of school for three years after the Mumbai riots, because the way to the building was through a Muslim area,' claimed
Pappu (14). His resentment was shared by other children who had lost time
to prepare for examinations. Some had also failed their final tests. Returning
to school after the riots the children were thrilled to find their teachers were
sympathetic to the plight of Hindu children and were willing to strategise
with them to create enmity in class. Several Sena boys, for example, wanted
to collaborate with teachers to develop pro-Hindu disciplinary policies in
some of the local schools. In some schools the boys wanted to recite the
Saraswati Vandana (a hymn in praise of the goddess of learning) in the assembly.
Group singing would assert the primacy of the Hindu identity, inculcate a

sense of pride among Hindu children, and create a fractured student community. The teachers in turn felt Hindu prayers and hymns could not be read as an overt communal statement if the school's activities were subjected to official/government scrutiny.

AS: 'But the Muslims can't recite the *Saraswati Vandana*. If they stay out of school for a song, it will lead to illiteracy in their community....'

Dhiraj (12): 'So what? We also lost out a lot on our education during the riots. It's time for them to pay for painting our goddess of learning in the nude.[10] It's like painting my class teacher in the nude. I'd kill anyone who did that. [Pause] That's a good idea actually, if they [the Muslims] remain uneducated, they'll get less jobs ... it's a way to counter them. Gives Hindus greater chances of survival.'

To reinforce further militancy in Hindu students, the teachers in the Marathi schools (who were mostly women) reinterpreted textbooks to give a provocative narrative. Thus Muslims were projected as historical villains. Shambhu (13) said:

'Our teacher tells us about the glory of *jauhar*[11] in the face of Muslim aggression. Hindu women are so brave. We all feel so agitated when we hear stories about Muslim attacks on innocent Hindus all the time. There were taxes, rape of women, breaking of temples, reduction to second-class citizenship. We've really suffered and must not fall back into the same trap.'

In the end most teachers turned to Shivaji as the martial hero who saved the Hindu face. In 1988 the board of education in Maharashtra decided to cut down on the history of Shivaji in the secondary school course to accommodate parts of modern history. The Shiv Sena launched a massive agitation and stalled the decision. The following are examples taken from history textbooks:

Shivaji never bent his knees before the Muslims. They were foreign powers. In his battle against the alien invaders, he was supported by lakhs of soldiers. (Raja Shivchhatrapati, in Chousalkar, 1995: 76)

Modern Hindu politicians and pseudo-historians have discovered a complete assimilation between the Hindus and the Muslims after the first fury of intolerance and oppression was over. But Shivaji was in any case free from such ideas. He

10 Maqbool Fida Hussain, a famous Muslim artist, painted the Hindu goddess Saraswati in the nude, which led to a huge Sena backlash in Mumbai. The Sena burned his effigies and some of his valuable paintings, following which the artist moved to London in self-imposed exile.

11 Rajput women jumping into a pyre to save their honour.

looked upon the Muslims as oppressive rulers and the Hindus as the long-suf-fering subject people. He therefore made the heroic resolve to free the Hindus from the yoke of slavery imposed upon them by Muslims. (R.C. Mazumdar, in Ahluwalia, 1984: 14)

After the Mumbai riots several isolated cases of Hindu–Muslim student clashes were brought to public attention. Most of them were traced to grow-ing hostile conditions created partially by 'hate-teaching' in classrooms. In a controversial case a teacher encouraged a classroom discussion on the death of Meenatai Thackeray, Bal Thackeray's wife. One of the children said: 'Well, the Muslims should be very glad now', a comment which made the only Muslim girl in class burst into tears.[12] One Sena boy related how a Muslim student had suddenly attacked a Hindu teacher in class. The Sena children and teachers alike concluded that it was a sign of the child's training to assault women from other communities. However, during a counselling session, it was discovered that the child was hidden in a box during the Mumbai riots and through a crack he saw a woman abusing Muslims while supervising the killing of the child's family members. Since the woman rioter had worn a *bindi*, the child began to strike the teacher (who also wore a *bindi*) the mo-ment she began criticising Muslims. One Sena boy said: 'See, you have to fight their violence with violence.' Histories of imagined antagonisms written in textbooks can be countered by rewriting them, but oral manipulation of history creates conditions in which the lack of sympathy between the hostile communities becomes aggravated in a classroom.

Some teachers also encouraged students to read *Saamna* editorials and emphasised the educational value of the Sena mouthpiece. Many of the boys who followed this directive 'learned' that Thackeray was never punished for his speeches published in the *Saamna*. Consider the following samples from editorials published during the riots:

Which is the minority community? The Muslim traitors who partitioned the country and haven't allowed us to breathe ever since. (5 December 1992)

Muslims should draw a lesson from the demolition of the Babri Masjid, otherwise they will meet the same fate as the Masjid. Muslims who criticise the demolition are without religion, without a nation.

Pakistan need not cross the borders and attack India. Twenty crore Muslims in India will stage an armed insurrection. They form one of Pakistan's seven atomic bombs. (9 December 1992)

12 This incident was uncovered by members of an anti-communal project among children called 'Khoj', and was reported in *Communalism Combat* (1999).

Muslims of Bhendi Bazar, Null Bazar, Dongri and Pydhonie, the areas we call Mini Pakistan, must be shot dead on the spot. (8 January 1993)

A petition filed against Thackeray under sections 153 A and B of the Indian Penal Code, which warned against publications affecting the national integration of the country, was rejected in court by several judges, who claimed the content in these articles 'was not enough' to spur a communal riot. For some boys this immunity from the forces of law meant swearing against and demonising the alien community was 'just' and 'acceptable' for the greater Hindu cause.

In more recent times *Saamna* articles sharpened further the perception of an 'enemy' by sensationalising the Kargil war[13] 'victory' as a display of Hindu bravery and the release of Muslim terrorists in the air-hijacking incident as a case of Hindu cowardice.[14] 'Whenever we think about Muslims, we only think about war.... We suffer from battle fatigue after an India-Pakistan cricket match,' Hari (12) said. In the war of knowledge the boys clearly became increasingly reliant on school-teachers and various media of hate-instructions to evolve a combative Hindu identity.

'Hindu Teachers and my Hindu parents are my well-wishers'

To some of the Sena children, sources of *gyan* (knowledge) further accommodated well-wishers, guides and protectors. A survey undertaken by an anti-communalism NGO in Mumbai worked in two Hindu and Muslim dominated schools, primarily with teenagers (Standards VIII–X), to uncover myths the children had learnt about other communities. Both the schools had women teachers; the senior instructors at the Hindu-dominated Municipal School seemed particularly impatient to get rid of the NGO volunteers. Data collected has been organised in Table 1.

Historical clarifications, like kings fought for treasure and not religion, and that textbooks were manipulated for political gain, made few children doubt the 'authenticity' of what they had learnt within their own communities. Most Hindu children's perceptions of Muslims were communalised (distrust based on supposed Muslim dependence on weaponry, fanaticism and aggression), while the Muslim children saw physical markers of difference in the followers of the two religions (dress codes, methods of communication with God). The Hindu children remained confused as to how their protectors

13 The Indo-Pak border skirmishes in 1998–9.
14 An Indian aeroplane was hijacked and taken to Afghanistan. The hijackers demanded the release of Muslim terrorists and, after a period of negotiation, the terrorists were set free.

Table 1　SURVEY UNDERTAKEN BY AN ANTI-COMMUNALISM NGO

Municipal School (Hindu-dominated)	Imamwada School (Muslim-dominated)
Pictures of Gods, Goddesses and posters of *Bharat Mata (Mother India)* on the walls.	Pictures of national leaders, maps, charts about the glory of hard work on the walls.
Impression of Muslims • They wear *kurta pajamas* to hide weapons; • They wear a sharp beard because it makes them look hostile; • They eat mutton because red meat makes you sexually aggressive; • They do *namaaz*, which is actually a way for everyone to meet and conspire; • They are angry and quick-tempered; • They are fanatics and not self-controlled like Hindus; • They are intolerant; • They want to conquer India.	Impression of Hindus • They do *pooja* with so many things because they have no direct connection with their Gods; • The women wear *bindis* just to demarcate themselves from the Muslim women; • They wear the *mangalsutra* and the *tikli* for the same reason; • They speak in Marathi to demarcate themselves from Muslims; • They drink the urine of cows; • They take our money away; • They want to throw us out of India.

Who teaches you all this?
* parents
* teachers
* peer groups (who may have heard from their parents and teachers)
* party leaders
* the media
* newspapers
* textbooks
* our own tendency to imitate people who we think are our superiors
* our own tendency not to confirm anything before believing
* Thackeray

Did you know ...
* Shivaji had Muslim generals, so his war was for sovereignty and not for the Hindu religion? Answer: Unanimous 'No'.
* the Somnath temple (from where BJP Home Minister L.K. Advani started his anti-Muslim *rath yatra* or chariot parade) was razed to the ground by Mughal ruler Aurangzeb? Answer: Unanimous 'Yes'.
* an infuriated Aurangzeb broke down the temple because the priest had trapped and dishonoured a Hindu queen who was part of the ruler's contingent? Answer: Unanimous 'No'.

were being projected as villains, because the NGO team made covert references to the Sena as an opportunistic political party. One of the children in the Hindu-dominated Municipal School, flabbergasted, said: 'Give me one reason why I should trust someone other than my own people? Hindu teachers, my Hindu parents, a pro-Hindu party ... surely they would all be the well-wishers of a Hindu child.'

Some children's reasons for approaching gang-ism and violence remained completely detached from the Hindutva discourse, for example, the intimate experiences of violence integral to the life-cycles of slum children, which in the absence of parental supervision in schools could be more easily revealed. As part of their extra-curricular activities the children in the Hindu-dominated Municipal School were asked to put up a skit. They performed a short play on parents beating up their children. One of the participants, Kapil (10), when asked whether he would involve himself in violence, said with a determined tone: 'Yes, I would riot. Because I want someone else to feel the humiliation of physical abuse. No one knows that better than me because I get beaten regularly.' There may be several such individual cases of children feeling rejected by their immediate families. Kapil came from a Sena family and if he took part in collective violence it would be viewed as an act of loyalty to his family and the party ideology. But few people would question whether his faith in collective violence stemmed partially from his personal experiences of abuse at home. Kapil thus represented the world of marginalised children, which was created through braiding strands of violent experiences in the home, the streets and the classroom.

Sena boys were searching for survival strategies by redefining relations at home and developing new social relations through gang-ism in the slums. They were energised by discovering that their actions as a Hindu children's collective were sanctioned even in schools and textbooks. Lopez (1999), discussing 'discourse collisions' in Latin American schools, shows how schooling can be a frustrating experience for most marginalised children whose home language radically differs from the disciplinary and supervision-centric culture in schools. For example, some forms of behaviour (like shouting during an argument) may be typical at home but it is likely to be reprimanded in schools. Some of the Sena boys told me how teachers who came from higher economic backgrounds would treat poor children as inferior beings. After the riots Hindu teachers and students developed relationships of solidarity. So 'if a child's social belief, attitude and behaviours are reinforced in school, the child is assured that he or she is progressing in the appropriate manner' (Lopez, 1999: 60). The fusion of the language at home and at school carried ideas like 'self-protection,' 'counter violence' and 'religious loyalty'.

Before the riots poor children from both communities felt alienated from the school discourse. Over time 'Hindu nation', which remained equivalent to Marathi martiality, became a shared language which diffused the power/class relations between Hindu teachers and students, and in the process ended up isolating the Muslim children. The Hindu children, on the other hand, felt an increase in their self-esteem after all 'Hindu well-wishers' were brought on to the same platform.

'THE OUTSIDERS IN OUR AREA': SENA BOYS AND ISOLATION FROM SECULAR NGOs

Sena boys expressed their disappointment with the NGO effort to resolve the differences between Hindu and Muslim children. At a time when the boys were searching for reassurances, the NGOs for children stayed briefly in Sena-dominated areas and then withdrew, adding to the sense of instability that the boys were trying to offset. Meanwhile, 'the Sena was always there for the boys'. Furthermore, most of the boys claimed that voluntary organisations played a punitive role towards them and were exhibitionist when it came to an integrated approach to solidarity-building between children from hostile communities. The Sena children said one NGO that had come to Nirmal Nagar wanted to do a play with Hindu and Muslim children. However, they wrapped up the project, since Muslim children were not willing to take part in it. 'But we were willing, and that didn't count,' said Hari (10). When asked about the incident the group in question complained that the children openly displayed rivalries, broke into fights and had to be kept in separate rooms. Communication seemed to breed greater intolerance and the sudden outbursts of violence only confirmed mutual stereotypes. This jeopardised the aims of the project, until the project leaders decided to leave the slums.

As the offspring of the aggressors, the Sena slum children did not receive much sympathy from the NGOs. 'We won yet we were marginalised,' said Gappu. The children had keenly observed their parent's hostility towards NGOs initiating peace talks and also witnessed the diverting of riot-relief funds to the 'rival community'. They claimed they had no faith in these so-called non-biased NGOs because they were 'obviously biased towards Muslims'. 'All the workers were women and we thought they'd be loving to all the children; instead they ran after the Muslim kids,' said Hari.

Hari's grievance echoed the voices of many Sena children who resented the diverting of healing maternal attention in the direction of Muslim children. So under what they felt were discriminatory circumstances, the VHP's[15]

---

15 Vishwa Hindu Parishad (World Hindu Council).

application for NGO status from UNESCO[16] became highly significant. The whole slum region backed the effort by Hindu organisations to work for their own community. ('If Christians worked for Christians it was good, but if Hindus worked for Hindus were they fundamentalists?') Secular organisations were allegedly driven by sympathy and took no preventive action in the slums. This 'deficiency' in secular NGOs became particularly evident at the time of rakhi.[17] In an effort to create a bond between Hindu and Muslim children some NGOs approached the riot-affected slums, gathered the children in an open space and asked them to tie decorative rakhis on one another. This dry act made the children feel patronised. In the RSS camp, on the other hand, children were given time to make their own rakhis, which were then separated into three categories: for friends, for siblings and for parents. They were also asked to make cards which read:

My parents/siblings/friends,

On this auspicious day I promise to dedicate myself to my nation. I will build a strong body and mind only for that purpose. I will make you proud by being a committed national soldier.

To the Sena children, this appeared to be a creative approach and they felt the RSS organisations extended themselves constructively to Hindu children. Being addressed as contributors to Hindu nationalism helped most boys resolve confusions about children's importance within the movement.

The hostility faced by NGOs in the Sena slums had serious implications for wider reconciliatory efforts between rival communities. Boys were growing up in the riot-affected slums under the shadow of an extreme right-wing ideology; they were constantly and consciously searching for knowledge and ideas that reinforced their Hindu militant identities. NGO members, therefore, have to realise that scattered classroom lectures and random peace initiatives cannot counter the sustained effort made by teachers and families to inculcate communal values in children. But NGO employees working with children and communalism appeared relieved if within their time and monetary constraints they had carried out the designed programmes. There was little effort to assess the impact of their programmes and overcome hurdles put up by the obviously communalised children. Most NGOs seriously avoided learning from right-wing organisations working in the slums, the latter having achieved a degree of success by simply stirring the imagination of children. Like the RSS, the NGOs could have approached the children

16 United Nations Economic, Scientific and Cultural Organisation.
17 A Hindu festival during which brothers and sisters tie coloured bands on each other as a sign of mutual affection and protection.

through their hobbies. Transgressing the line between an academic and an activist, I would often stop some of the slum girls to tell them how their *churidar kameezes* or their *meenakari* (lacquer work) earrings were part of the Islamic tradition. The girls enjoyed sporting these outfits and jewellery, and were not keen to reject them as cultural impurities. But every time they wore them they were forced to think whether 'there is anything called pure Hinduism'. This exercise revealed that when living with children, developing a familiarity with them was essential for them to pay attention to your words, and that building associations between familiar bric-a-brac in their social setting and a less abstract critique of communalism can make the children partially overcome their insularities.

What the Sena children were searching for was a reinforcement of their violent, collective, Hindu identity through proximity with saffronised classroom teaching and distancing from the secular NGO movement. While teachers were encouraging the children's aggression towards Muslims, the feeling of marginalisation from women NGO workers was increasing relationships of envy and hostility among children. In neither of these contexts were the Sena children reassured by their family members. Instead, the children were allowed to believe that they were discriminated against—historically by Muslims (as told by the teachers) and in the present allotment of attention and resources (by the behaviour of NGO workers). Thus, the boys wanted to counter all these feelings of deprivation by organising collective strategies against these 'enemies'.

CONCLUSION

War does not supplant everyday life, it takes place in everyday life. (Nordstrom and Robben, 1995: xii)

The process of defining and redefining a continued existence, where one stands in relation to another in a battle for survival, is a lengthy, complex and challenging one. Are the struggles in the slums of Mumbai leading to what Postman and Asher (1994) describe as the disappearance of childhood? An understanding of children with no childhood has recently been recovered within anthropology by Schwartzman (2001) to comprehend the child at risk within societies marked by unfettered capitalism. While trying to discern a street-gang reality, Vigil (1996) comments: 'Humans are so malleable and resilient that, rather than remaining lost in this aura of marginality, confused and full of rage, they reconstitute an identity using bits and pieces of the past mixed with the present but all shaken by the forces of a difficult city reality' (1996: 34). The Shiv Sena boys, during their gang meetings, would always subject their individual identity and assumptions to scrutiny. Whether in order to woo women, or to offer their support to mothers playing a violent public role, or to view the role of martial children as a social necessity, the boys were continually investigating possibilities and trying to reconstruct their ideas of childhood, adulthood, normalcy and survival accordingly. The world of the Sena children was thus taking on a life of its own.

According to Becker (1997), the enactment of new cultural themes emerges from efforts to mediate disruption. 'Groups amend normalising ideologies to reflect their particular views and because these amended ideologies carry particular moral force for group members and buffer them from more generalised ideologies of normalcy, they facilitate agency' (1997: 111). Thus individual views of normalcy are reshaped through sharing in groups. The boys wanted to keep a sexual polarity alive and not encourage complete sameness between the sexes. They still felt women could not achieve the extent of order and justice that men could (boys making up for weaker Aghadi women), and children had to be prepared to protect themselves as well as their family. But the boys also succumbed to the allure of 'romance' to make the hardships of slum life more bearable. However, they did not abandon the value of 'terror' and at the same time created their own notions of morality (about love, family, religion, justice etc.).

Within the RSS children were made to undergo sessions of rigorous training on Hindu culture and community pride (Jaffrelot, 1996). The organisation had its own system of schooling and textbooks. It also provided special courses for adolescent children attending schools not run by the RSS (McDonald, 1999). The Sena children on the other hand tried to develop more pragmatic physical survival strategies. They used elements of Hindutva to justify their current struggle for Hindu martiality, but their concerns were rarely related to the survival of the fundamentalist ideology.

According to Scheper-Hughes (1987), unequal class relations were the basis of understanding the operatives of children and cultures of street violence. Further, Aptekar's (1988) analysis of the relationship between the lives of street children and the economically and politically dominant classes revealed that the latter viewed street children as a threat to the patriarchal family and to the social order. Placing the Sena children within the larger Sena movement we see that political leaders, the state machinery and the family do not look upon the activities of the Hindu Sena children as threatening. The acceptability of violent children within this social machinery created conditions in which the children found it beneficial to view the world in terms of certain binary opposites—Hindu and non-Hindu, Marathi and non-Marathi, victims and aggressors. They never spoke about being rich or poor as homogenous categories. Feelings of economic inferiority were countered by feelings of religious and numerical superiority; one kind of insularity was used to overcome another.

However, of great concern was the impression that many people were deemed incapable of living in a society envisioned by the Sena children. Thus their behaviour could be interpreted as being potentially genocidal. This was because the children could not strategise like their parents, primarily their mothers. While the mothers wanted the enemy and consequently the struggle kept alive, the children wanted the communal 'war' to end, the enemies to die and to have a peaceful, romantic home life. The Sena boys also believed that children were the specific targets and the easiest victims of genocidal behaviour displayed by enemy groups.

Several scholars of gang behaviour depend on a 'multiple marginality theory' as an integrated framework to comprehend aggression (cf. Vigil, 2003). To what extent were the Sena children 'marginalised'? They lived in a Hindu-dominated slum; after the Mumbai riots the Muslims had been chased away to live only along the periphery of the slum area; the children and their parents were affiliated with a violent and visible Hindu-nationalist organisation, which should have considerably reduced their feelings of vulnerability; the children did not face enormous hostility from the police. However, the children did come from poor, fragile families. So the question remains, why did the children imagine themselves to be unsuspecting targets of violence and feel the need to organise into gangs? Fanon, discussing minority complexes in majority communities, wrote, 'I can recapture my past, validate or condemn it through my successive choices' (Fanon, 1986: 228). The Sena children remembered fretfully that they had not achieved enough during their past experiences of violence, i.e. the Mumbai riots, when: they were smaller; some of them were shunted out of the slums; and even when they did help their families, their contributions went largely unnoticed. Also, 'then' they had felt afraid, and 'now' they were still afraid. So their present choices, including gang-ism, involved a quest for a state of order and fearlessness to make up for past losses.

It cannot be concluded that the experiences of the girls were the same as those of the boys. But the girls also supported their mother's association with the Aghadi. They were aware that the Aghadi managed to break the negative cultural attitude towards the education of girls, but not towards prostitution and promiscuity. So the girls acquired more freedom to work and move around, but they avoided staying out late so as not to be given 'a bad name'. Despite the fact that the pressure to run a home more often fell on the female rather than the male children, they still felt they were far better off than their counterparts in the village who worked harder tending cattle or in the field. However, they were confused about their equal status with men in situations of armed conflict (their mothers were more aggressive and it may be their opinions were submerged under the personality of a strong mother), but they *were* aware that menstruation hampered women's agility and movement in those situations. The girls had obviously given some thought to the possible future paths of women's action.

This chapter has shown how a violent political movement is reproduced through the institution of the family. Although children would appear to be more concerned with immediate gratifications, since provisions for future growth are part of the workings of an adult mind, while dealing with concepts of marriage, career, collectivity, society or safety, the outlook and actions of the children were oriented towards securing a happier future.

There is an increasing global awareness about child warriorhood. A UNICEF survey of South East Rwanda, for example, conducted after the genocidal conflict of 1994 found that almost 42 per cent of the children interviewed said they had seen children kill each other and 56 per cent said that they had seen children kill adults (UNICEF, 1995: 28). More recent studies conducted by the World Bank have shown that children were used as executioners by terrorist organisations in Liberia because adults were often reticent to carry out extreme roles involving violence (World Bank, 2003). This creation of a child with no mercy and the trend towards violence could lead to the crystallisation of a militaristic society where children are considered to be just as dangerous as adults in conflict situations.

Research for the present study has focused on children who were not formal recruits into self-styled militia, but formed armies to organise child survival. Nevertheless, some of the *Saamna* editorials sampled began with references to children. (For example: 'Every child knows all Muslims sympathise with Pakistan and Bangladesh ....') Furthermore, all the Sena children felt they were obliged to 'know' about the enemy and resist it at all costs. By the end of my research in the Sena-controlled slums there were scores of children's gangs and I left brooding over the gradual creation of child mercenaries in the streets of Mumbai. However, I cannot end this section with no hope for the 'dark' children I loved so much. During a sports meet arranged by Salokha, an NGO, in Byculla (in Mumbai), both Hindu and Muslim children were invited to take part. The sky was overcast, there was a slight wind. To start with the children avoided each other and stayed within their own groups. Over the races and relays the atmosphere grew less and less tense. But the sky grew darker. Then there was a game of musical chairs and when a foot-tapping Marathi pop song came on, suddenly all the children grabbed each other as partners and began to dance. The skies shot arrows of rain on to the ground. 'You and I have become tied in the same thread, so there are drops of rains …' the love song played on. I murmured some of my favourite lines from Tagore. 'On the shores of eternal time, the children play / Suddenly oblivious to the war of merchant ships, unaware of the cruel nets of fishermen, unconscious of the deceptions of death / On the shores of eternal life, the children pick their pebbles … '

6

WOMEN, HISTORY AND THE FUTURE
SAMAJ (SOCIETY)

This chapter attempts to grasp a 'women's logic' for aspiring to create a militaristic society in the future, in which Hindu women play a more vital role. To achieve this society the Aghadi women tried to place the past, the present and the future in a continuum so that the imagined martial society of 'a Hindu past' could be regarded as the model society of the future (though modernised in parts). Thus the present could be described as that moment in the continuum which draws inspiration from the past and is engaged in the construction of that 'ideal' future.

As discussed in Chapters 4 and 5, the Shiv Sena put a great deal of emphasis on medieval history in Maharashtra, which singularly concerns the life of Shivaji, a regional king after whom the Shiv Sena were named. The party-men in general and the women in particular were tactically obsessed with the medieval mytho-histories which developed around the role of this Hindu hero in challenging the Mughal rulers. The Aghadi felt that if women were to be involved in the conception of a Hindu militaristic society, it was imperative to recover women's agency in forming a martial society in Shivaji's times. Since the medieval past was central to Sena identity politics, constructing a prestigious martial tradition for women could also raise the self-esteem of the underprivileged Aghadi members living in urban slums.

For all the Sena women, forms of narratives—whether 'real', constructed or modified—could be furnished with authenticity through reiteration and repetition. As part of the apparatus of myth-making in the slums, sections of Sena women with oratory skills were involved in telling/circulating stories of Shivaji, specifically focusing on his relationships with various women. Some of the women narrators were former Marathi stage actresses and some were Aghadi leaders, but most were housewives with the time to 'tell stories'. Thus the Aghadi made conscious efforts to manipulate and dramatise mytho-histories about Shivaji in order to highlight women's roles in a martial past. Groups of slum women would collectively or individually narrate tales to

155

men, women, children (and an odd anthropologist) sitting around the narrator. Sometimes they were told in children's parks or in the *shakhas*. At other times they were narrated in the temple complexes where the women met regularly to sing devotional songs. Through repeated storytelling the narrators would try to show how women's militancy was integral to the tradition of Marathi Hindu militancy in general and that it was legitimised in history by Shivaji's overt support of martial queens, women warriors and his 'autonomist' mother.

From this point the Aghadi tried to develop an ideal 'Shivaji-like' martial society, though primarily on the model of a modern army. The women imagined that modern militaristic societies would engender myriad advantages for right-wing women, often allowing them to coordinate their militant identities and martial skills. According to the designs of the Sena women, the future Hindu society should be such that its members will be well-informed about all their enemies, and the exercise of visible and invisible forms of violence against these enemies will be efficiently organised. In their present attempt to carve out the 'perfect' society of the future, women began to treat the home as their points of departure; since their association with the Aghadi had already given them considerable power within the home, they exploited their 'say' in the household to project it as a breeding ground for military activities.

Scholars defend the argument that martial societies thrive on women's vulnerabilities. According to Vagts (1967), for example, militarism in society is understood as the array of customs, actions and thought associated with armies and wars, where the physical superiority of men is emphasised and 'weakness' is associated with women. Even though the Aghadi leaders and cadres envisaged an army society, the Sena women were vigorously trying to orient thought and action towards overcoming their 'weaknesses'. '*Roz ke samaj mein aurat kamzor hain, sena samaj mein nahin* [in everyday society women are weak, not in an army society],' summed up Radhika, a cadre. Imagining a battle between feminist women and 'real women', the Aghadi upheld the superiority of real women in a militaristic social setting, in which their actual desires (which they felt remained misunderstood through Western categories) could be fulfilled. The women's ideas, arguments and understanding about the past, the present and the future were scattered and incoherent, but for them a military society was one 'where every aspect of life was built and run like an army'. The Aghadi wanted to underline the role of women in the creation and regeneration of that ideal *samaj*. But can women really achieve this goal to militarise society at large? Either way, their efforts reflect the initiatives of poor slum women to create their own history, determine their present status within a male-dominated ethno-nationalist struggle, and establish a central role for women within a future social order.

THE PAST

Narration of mytho-histories: tales of Shivaji and the restoration of agency to women in martial 'history'

Shivaji, a controversial figure in Maharashtrian history, has been attributed several identities ranging from 'the liberator of the Marathi nation' (Grant Duff, 1873; Laine, 2003; Sarkar, 1992; Sen, 1977; Takakhav, 1998) to 'a common bandit' (Lane Poole, 1893). According to historians, he was born to a petty landlord (*jagirdar*) Shahaji Bhonsle and his wife Jijabai in 1630 and grew up to be a self-proclaimed king, *Chhatrapati*. He annexed the regions of several neighbouring Muslim *and* Hindu rulers to his own *jagir*, but since he carried on a prolonged struggle against the former, he was glorified as a Marathi 'Hindu' hero (Bakshi and Sharma, 2000; Bhave, 2000). He died in 1680. Excerpts from Shivaji's life were compiled in a few manuscripts and his feats kept alive—very thinly—in local ballads. He emerged as an iconic national hero in the latter half of the nineteenth century after Tilak, leader of the anti-colonial movement in Maharashtra, revived the *Chhatrapati's* 'tales of gallantry' through celebration of the Shivaji festival (Sharma, 2003). The festival was held in Bengal (under the initiative of Sarala Devi, a member of the Tagore family[1]) and in Maharashtra to celebrate heroism, masculinity and the success of a local leader in overthrowing a powerful 'foreign' empire (Sinha, 1995). Although the festival is no longer celebrated in Bengal, its popularity continues across Maharashtra. Even the national rail terminus and the international airport in Mumbai are named after Shivaji. The Shiv Sena was also inspired by this medieval ruler, their primary focus being Shivaji's attempts to carve a strong Hindu nation out of a Muslim empire. Within this primarily masculinist discourse on a hero and his heroism, the Aghadi tried to give significance to a few scattered tales where women played an influential role in Shivaji's designs to create a *Hindu padpadshahi*, a martial Hindu political and social empire.

The narrators tried to characterise Shivaji as a man who was sensitive to women and gave recognition to women's 'special' contribution to society. Shivaji's father abandoned Jijabai after his second marriage (Bakshi and Sharma, 2000; Sarkar, 1992) and the Sena women explained that the ensuing proximate relationship between Shivaji and his mother, and the absence of

[1] The Tagores were a progressive Brahma family who took part in the anti-colonial struggle.

a strong male presence allowed him to respect the strength and ideals of women. In this context the Sena women storytellers narrowed down and highlighted those 'true tales' (*sacchi kahani*) in which their icon was fair and honourable to women from various social and political backgrounds.

The Aghadi also drew careful attention to stories of Shivaji's protectionism. According to one mytho-history narrated by women, Shivaji withdrew an honour from one of his men, Raghoji, when he discovered by chance that this front rank general lusted after a soldier's widow. Another tale relates how 'the brave Rani Savitribai', queen of Bellary, was produced in Shivaji's court in chains after her kingdom was raided by an arrogant general, Sakuji, in an act of vengeance and how Shivaji apologised to the queen, chided his general for ill-treating a woman and returned the kingdom to her. Yet another story is about a beautiful Muslim girl, the daughter of a local Maulana in Kalyana, who was captured and presented to Shivaji by one of his generals. Shivaji addressed the girl as his sister and kept her in safe custody until she was sent back to her family. The last story always ended with a prolonged phase of lamentation by the Sena women that similar treatment was not meted out to Hindu women captured by Muslim soldiers. Thus the Sena women repeatedly portrayed Shivaji as a leader with 'the strength of a man, and the heart of a woman', as he was often described in the local ballads.

During the Aghadi meetings these tales were always retold by women storytellers in the form of questions and answers, which gave the narration clarity and the feeling of immediacy. Their wild gesticulations, voice modulations and exaggerated eye movements allowed the past to filter into the present so that their enactment of events that took place in a seventeenth-century court made this history not 'a history of long ago, but a history of just yesterday' (Daniel, 1997: 27). For example, in the case of Rani Savitribai, the story goes (with the words '*phir boley*' [then it was said] used as interjections):

Shivaji: 'Sakuji, you whipped the queen? If you have insulted a woman, you have insulted my mother. You are dismissed in shame.'

Turning to Savitribai: 'Mother, will you not pardon your own son?'

Savitribai, with tears in her eyes: 'Son, I am glad that you showed respect for me. It has turned me into your compatriot. I will now fight with you for the Hindu Swaraj.'

And she took her place beside Shivaji.

By narrating the stories as dialogues, *possible* royal courtroom dramas were portrayed as *actuality*. The narrators depicted the events as a series of images that the women had viewed, as if they had been present during the exchange. The women celebrated a martial queen being freed and given equal status as an independent Hindu ruler. Since Shivaji had meted out justice to Rani Savitribai, he had 'freed' all Hindu women, throughout the generations. The women's loud public cheering of Shivaji's support for women appeared (to the men at least) a contribution towards sustaining the Shivaji tradition. However, the story-telling also became the Aghadi's covert strategy for recovering agency for women in history. The front tried to show that women, like the queen of Bellary, once unchained, were promising warriors in the struggle to carve out a martial Hindu society that existed in the past. The Sena women asserted that if they were also allowed to be free and martial, then they had the capacity to mould a militaristic, Hindu-dominated society in the future. These stories, claiming that women had a place in history and were linked to a rich tradition of Hindu martiality, enhanced the self-respect of ordinary women cadres.

Another important tale recalls Shivaji outwitting the Muslim general Afzal Khan. The Khan had invited Shivaji to come unarmed to his tent to reach an amicable settlement. The general, however, had conspired to throttle the Marathi leader. Shivaji came unarmed but stuck the claws of a tiger to his fingers; and when the Khan jumped on Shivaji and grabbed his throat, Shivaji tore the general's guts out. When news of the Muslim leader's murder spread, the Khan's army retreated. This story was narrated repeatedly in all Shivaji festivals held in the pre-Independence period (Ahluwalia, 1984; Samarath, 1975). The enemy then was the British. Aimed to inspire the youth to display their cunning against colonial rulers, the story was later usurped by the right-wing movement to promote Hindu militancy (Sarkar and Butalia, 1996). In the Sena *shakhas* the story was reiterated and even re-enacted in children's plays, most of which were directed by women. Now the enemy is markedly the Muslims. Women, while narrating this story, seemed to relish the violence. The tales were rounded off with a glorification of strategic guerrilla warfare, a pre-requisite for the creation of a martial society. As mentioned in Chapter 5, several children had learned this anecdote by heart and, by acting out this skit, had also learnt the value of remaining in a state of preparedness for counter-attacks. The story of Afzal Khan's fate did not specifically involve the role of women in the past, yet its circulation highlighted the level of women's involvement in promoting an illustrious Hindu 'history'. Its enactment in plays and narratives highlighted the initiatives of women in sustaining the Shivaji tradition. Wherever there were tales of Shivaji there were women (since reading stories about Shivaji was difficult for most semi-literate slum women). The physical and vocal visibility of women in these places reflected the urgency felt by the Sena women to incorporate their presence in history and how it is told.

Another episode that women enjoyed narrating was a directive from Ji-jabai (Shivaji's mother) to her son to recapture Kondana Fort (later renamed as Singhad), where Jijabai had been imprisoned for a period. According to studies on Shivaji, capturing the fort from the Mughals was of strategic im-portance for the Marathi leader (Bhave, 2000). For the Sena women, how-ever, it was a question of revenge against the Muslims. The directive was the proof of overt militancy in a wronged Hindu mother, who could send her son to a 'just' war without fearing the possibility of his death. Jijabai's orders seemed to highlight the contribution of right-wing women in creating martial sons, well-trained for combat situations.

Jijabai said: 'My son, I have trained you to become the best warrior in the coun-try. Will you not free the fort where your mother remained captive for so long and take revenge for her humiliation?'

Shivaji said: 'O Mother, your valour runs in my blood. Your wish is my command.'

This tale depicted an ideal relationship between a Hindu mother and a good, fearless Hindu son, and it too was employed to emphasise women's position in a continuing tradition of martial motherhood. Consequently, this story of a mother instigating her son to fight for her honour was extensively circulated in the slums. Several women even claimed to have a shared womb with Jijabai ('still giving birth to many Shivajis').

Most of these women-centric mytho-histories became increasingly popu-lar as nascent rebellions against Sena men who still remained sceptical of women's strength. The tales appealed for equality within a martial order and for the sanctioning of women's 'warrior' status. 'If Shivaji, the great Maratha ruler, had allowed a woman to be his compatriot, what can our men say to oppose his ruling?' asked Nandini, who always played a primary role in the narration of these tales. Talking with the Sena men about these mytho-his-tories and the women's desire to gain visibility within the movement, two conclusions emerged. One, the men played a nominal role in developing and narrating mytho-histories. Two, most men preferred tales about Muslim women who were the objects of Shivaji's generosity even though the king had 'the right' to abuse them to avenge the Mughals. Nonetheless, they seemed curious about the Aghadi's effort to revive tales of Shivaji's 'respect' for Hin-du women. Chandan, a Sena aide, said, 'I wonder whether these women can really create a martial society.' 'At least he's beginning to wonder,' his wife, an active Aghadi member, murmured. Most men within the party referred to Thackeray's late wife, Meena Thackeray, as Matoshree, the name reverentially used by Shivaji to address his mother. Meena Thackeray was idolised as the 'good' wife and mother, who supported Thackeray through all his endeavours, but remained outside the political limelight. But Aghadi leaders, while deferential in public, categorically refused to accept Meena Thackeray as their icon. 'To be honest, she was just too passive,' they would say. The image of an inspirational and militant mother, sustained within the tales of Shivaji, was obviously far more appealing for the Sena women, and to the storytellers who hoped their vivid narratives would inspire a change in the orientation of men towards women's active involvement in social reconstruction.

Here then are pools of highly illustrative stories that were identified and narrated by women as their 'history'. It was striking that of all the Sena women I met, none had ever set foot in Singhad or Raighad (Shivaji's capital) or Shivneri (Shivaji's birthplace) to pay tribute to their great leader. Thus there was a clear demarcation between heritage and the strategic use of history. Heritage was static, unchanging, boring and of no social value to the women. History, however, could be a collection of spicy stories, imagined as reality merely through repetition: it had drama to grab the attention of listeners; it was dynamic and malleable enough to be transformed through embellishments; and it had the potential to empower a group of marginalised right-wing women to develop a valorous identity. Hence the creation of a historical narrative in which women played a visible role would justify their efforts to recreate the militaristic society designed by Shivaji.

According to Daniel, the assertions of academic history are logically future-oriented even though they may be about the past. Thus 'history is not so much about *finding* truth as it is about *making* true' (Daniel, 1997: 70). Insofar as it is future-oriented, history nurtures the hope that when a line of inquiry is pursued long enough, there will be a congregation of academics who will agree that a definite picture about the past has emerged from the enquiry. The assertions of mytho-histories, by contrast, insist that past 'actualities' are contemporaneous, that what is now is what was then and what was then is what is now (Tambiah, 1996). 'It is this collapse of time, where past becomes present enactment, that characterises myths' (Daniel, 1997: 52). In a mythic world the very same conditions and concerns that made past events possible still prevail. In the construction of mytho-histories by the Sena women, society in the past was marked by Muslim aggression, the Hindu effort to counter it, the aggressive role of women in public and the subsequent creation of a martial society. The concerns at that time were to regain physical, cultural and religious hegemony over the Muslims, reclaim land and honour taken away by them. The contingencies remained the same at present.

Daniel points out further that the history of the transformation of the Liberation Tigers of Tamil Eelam (LTTE), a Tamil rebel group in Sri Lanka, was an optic encounter for the Sinhala Buddhists (Daniel, 1997: 47). Tamil terrorism was a lived-in experience and the emergence of Tamil groups as militant organisations was a development the Sinhalese population could *see*. Hence the Sinhalese could easily identify all Tamils as their enemy. In the case of Maharashtra, there were no Islamic organisations that displayed militancy in their operations. The women were aware of Islamic fundamentalism in other parts of India, mainly through their association with the Shiv Sena and through the media, but the observation of Muslims as a dangerous, lustful enemy of Marathi Hindus, particularly women, was purely through the lens of history. Thus the relation between the past and the present as viewed by the Sena women cannot be understood in temporal terms. The way the women viewed history was neither as written chronologies nor as a linear progression of episodes. Their narrations of history were performative, ritualistic and flexible and had no relationship with unitary truths. Within the constraints of a masculinist discourse, these tales restored women to history and history to women.

While recovering their agency in the past, the Sena women inextricably linked it to their agency at present. If the past casts light on the present, current actions must also enrich the past. According to a leader, Neelamtai, 'The Marathi women have always fought for their religion and honour. We're still fighting for our religion; it would make Shivaji really proud of us.' So Shivaji was not a chapter that has been closed; he was still being written. Marathi women were continuing to satisfy his aspirations for Hindu supremacy. Neelamtai rounded off the discussion: 'Through our heroic actions we'll become the glorious past for the next generation of Marathi Hindu women.' Sena women thus saw themselves as participants in the process of history. As 'descendents' of a newly constructed martial tradition for women they wanted to emphasise their role in making history.

However, the Sena women were often hesitant of being radical in recovering women's agency. They preferred negotiation without any overt hostility towards the men and the movement. What really surprised me was the definite unpopularity among the Sena women of Rani Laxmibai of Jhansi, the warrior queen in the revolt of 1857. Laxmibai was the image of militant motherhood developed by the extremists during the anti-colonial movement. The nationalist rebel leader Subhas Bose also named the women's wing of his self-styled Indian National Army after the martial queen. The Rani had led her troops not as a legitimate ruler but as the regent of her infant son, adopted as the prospective male heir in order to justify her role as head of state. Her classic battle line when the British announced the annexation of Jhansi, 'I will not give up my Jhansi to anyone', were the first words in women's history that we studied as children. She would seem to be the ideal female icon for the Sena women: an independent female warrior; a mother who defines her political legitimacy fighting for her son; a Hindu woman with a more recent history of fighting the British in the mid-nineteenth century. However, the Sena women were at first dismissive about Laxmibai; then they claimed they were not very aware of her history. In time it became evident that the highly rebellious image of the Rani was not acceptable either to the Mahila Aghadi or to the male members of the Sena. The Aghadi cadres could be 'affiliated' with a masculine hero (like the queen of Bellary's association with Shivaji), but the women could not be identified as independent actors (as the queen of Jhansi). This became clear through meetings with the notorious Aghadi leader in Bhayander, Yogita. She compared herself to Rani Laxmibai and her female followers also referred to her by that name. Yogita, who openly carried a gun and took no orders, was severely criticised by male Sena members, and Sena women from other areas remained wary of her. Even though the Rani acted on behalf of her son, she was a sovereign queen, independent of male aides. As part of Shivaji's Sena, men would like to believe that women were 'granted' rather than asserted their freedom. Women would also like the men to believe so.

In an even greater significant deviation from the pan-Indian Hindu nationalist movement and its models for the future social order, the Sena women did not invoke 'the mythic, Hindu past of Lord Ram' ('*Ramrajya nahin chahiye*') envisioned in the Hindutva discourse as the ideal future society. During the peaceful and patriarchal reign of Lord Ram women were put 'safely' in their homes. The Aghadi instead wanted to focus on a medieval 'historical, Hindu past' (Shivaji's *Hindu padpadshahi*), where women had achieved a degree of martiality and autonomy. The Aghadi was trying to counter nostalgia for a *Ramrajya*, and promote an image of a society perpetually threatened by enemies. This 'required' men *and* women to organise themselves as an army, and women would have to carry out militaristic activities for the security of the Hindu community.

THE FUTURE

Hoping that their role as social architects would not remain restricted to the slum 'community', the Sena women preferred to use the term 'society' to describe their future designs. They wanted to create a *sena samaj* (an army society) as against a Sena *samaj* (a society dominated by the Shiv Sena, a political party).

One of the major reasons why the Aghadi had grown to believe it could exist as a parallel organisation for justice was because the country was marked by institutions (like the army and the police) that were authorised to practise absolute violence. These institutions played a conspicuous public role and deeply influenced women's imagination of the martial future. Within the slum community there was a curiosity about the armed forces as the sole agents of terror, whether for purposes of offence or defence. There were constant border skirmishes, which kept the army in the news; the selflessness in soldiers was glorified further in movies; and it was only within the army that coercive steps were always viewed as corrective steps. 'It's important to belong in the army, to be included, and humiliating to be cast out. You see films like *Border*, *Pukar*, *Gadar* etc. and you want your society be like them,' said Suparna, a cadre.[2]

Women's ideas of the *sena samaj* were also informed by their interaction and negotiation with the police, especially when the Aghadi cadres were involved in conflict situations. Parkin (1986), discussing the legitimisation of illegitimate violence, says institutions like the army or the police often encourage the public to resort to physical violence to counter criminality. In the case of the Sena women, during the riots they realised that a saffronised police force offered them unconditional support in their tirade against the Muslims. 'If the state police can support us, why can't we be a force by ourselves? There are so few of them to save us. We have to get organised to protect ourselves,' said Suparna.

Also folk wisdom in Maharashtra is replete with examples of resistance in which being part of the army of the 'good' enhanced the self respect of even the humblest foot soldier, the most glorious saga being that of Shivaji and his bringing together of a Hindu army to fight the intimidating Mughals. With historical 'evidence' came 'obviousness' about the need to be militaristically structured to guard against an enemy. Radhika, a leader, asserted: 'We [Marathi Hindus] are used to the idea of conventional and unconventional warfare and training, ideas of organising ourselves and the beneficial use of coercion.'

According to the Sena women, there were three main aims they wanted to fulfil in the utopian *sena samaj*. First, the society should have the features of a modern army, to maintain honour and coherence in the behaviour of community members. Second, if the society operated like a modern army, then women *sainaks* would have the freedom to acquire new and more subtle warfare skills (like repressive violence and invisible violence—discussed later in this section). Furthermore, they could more openly practise these alternatives to direct, confrontational violence. Third, if all forms of women's

---

[2] Movies on border skirmishes, Partition and terrorism.

violence had to be legitimised at the grass-roots level, then women would act as warrior leaders within the home, train their children as soldiers and 'transform' their homes into frontiers. This state of preparedness for war, if inculcated in the home atmosphere, would strengthen women's militancy in the future.

Sena samaj: the army as a role model for social reconstruction

Sena women felt that the army practised violence and yet maintained a stable, noble image. If society operated like an army, then violent actions would be honoured as heroism (*herogiri*) by *sena* members, and not dismissed as terrorism (*dadagiri*) by Sena members. The army had certain features, described as 'merits' by the women, which enabled the institution to organise violence. What, though, were these 'merits' and why, from among other alternatives, did the Sena women specifically desire to redesign their society on the model of an army? Aghadi members explained what the various aspects of an army society were (*ek sena samaj mein kya kya hai*) that would primarily equip women to be mobile, independent warriors and they insisted they needed to pursue this line of thinking, however underdeveloped it was at present, because not only the Aghadi, but also the society has to be tough (*sirf Aghadi nahin, samaj ko bhi tagra banna hai*).

Merits: honour and stronger bonds   Sena women workers felt that immobility and exposure to extreme poverty in the slums had over time affected the self-esteem of the labouring classes. When soldiers—often from deprived class, caste and minority backgrounds—carried out roles of defending and purifying society, it led to a surge in their self-respect. If a community operated like an army, its 'soldiers', despite their social disadvantages, could also develop a sense of honour over time. Thus the *sena samaj*, in the eyes of these women, was the highest homogenising form of social order.

Another section of the Sena women asserted that the army offered scope to establish bonds that transcended narrower forms of community. Earlier it was discussed how the breakdown of community enclaves and a permanent slum life made women feel isolated but that the formation of the Sena brought sections of poor people together. However, women feared that congregating people on the basis of mere party politics would not last. Consequently, several Sena women felt that a strong military society would not be so brittle as to collapse if people's interests in politics diminished. 'Right now many women are drawn to us by the work we do for them. But if those needs went away, there would be no Aghadi. In an army people are tied together by group loyalty, and not *only* by the facilities provided by the army. If society operates like an army, then that society has a chance to survive in the long run,' said Kalpana, a Sena leader. This train of thought has two major implications: one, it highlights the women's growing scepticism about the Aghadi's temporary successes, and their search for more stable survival tactics; two, it reveals the Aghadi's uncertainty about the future of politics and political parties. Despite being part of a strong political movement, the Aghadi was willing to look beyond the party and its activities in the slums, to see whether certain principles followed by society at large could integrate community and gender interests.

Most Aghadi leaders believed the coherence of martial societies remained unchallenged because members were taught not to jeopardise the integrity of their community. This was the pressure of group action over individual initiatives. 'In the case of subversion, since the act affected the well-being and coordination of the whole group, people wouldn't do it,' said Mamta, a leader. There were also mechanisms to counter selfishness among detractors. Some people who disobeyed collective laws had to be isolated to such an extent that they would abstain in the future. Others would receive more severe punishments in the form of physical torture or even death sentences. Thus, people were not allowed simply to quit the organisation if they began to disagree with its policies.

AS: 'What if the self-proclaimed armymen felt coerced into action?'

Aghadi leader, Kuntala: 'If they'd been threatened you'd say it's bad. If they'd been under peer pressure, it wasn't that bad, right? In an army some soldiers are motivated by fear; as long as they're motivated to act, it's enough.'

This was in keeping with the Aghadi's practice of demanding action from its members in what they understood as situations of crisis.

Several women sanctioned a *sena samaj* because martial societies could emotionally and physically equip its members to overcome feelings of helplessness in the face of social or historical forces; ordinary people could become agents of social change and resist ideas of 'fate'. Kuntala said:

'I heard people say after the riots that Muslims have *always* tortured Hindus, so there's nothing they can do to change that now. Why do people feel that way? Because the Muslims say they're organised and aggressive, right? We must also start organising ourselves as an army and it has to start right away. What the Muslims have achieved over the years, we have to achieve as soon as possible....'

Aghadi women felt it was easy to build up a rebellion amidst people affected by poverty, discrimination or conflict. One could create enemies and easily pass the blame on to them. After a while such revolts die out. But an army, even in the absence of direct war, remained a permanent institution. The women were well aware of the political situation in Islamic states like Pakistan and Afghanistan and speculated that the people in these countries had trained to be warriors for several centuries, which had turned them into a martial race. It was 'about time' that the Hindus also developed a permanent martial society, reduced their vulnerability to enemy communities, and protected their own land. However, this could be achieved only when the whole society had a long-term strategy to operate as a large and well-organised army.

When it came to their reflections on the nature of leadership, women considered a *sena samaj* would be even better than an army. The Aghadi leaders were cynical of the dispassionate guidance of army generals, who according to them 'yelled orders merely because they were trained to do so'. In the martial society of the future they wanted inspirational leaders like Thackeray, who could share their anxieties. The experiment in a military society would work successfully because in an ethnic army the leadership had to emerge from within a culture. Only leaders who were aware of the potential within the group could act out of sympathy. The women felt the membership of the Sena was such that the group would not accept any other form of leadership.

Merits: organised violence glorified   Riches, in the context of perceiving violence as a performance, argues that violent action 'was inherently liable to be contested on the question of legitimacy' (1986: 23). Sena women thought that an unquestioning acceptance of the legitimacy of organised violence could only exist in a *sena samaj*. As Rumki, a leader, put it, 'If you're an army, then you have to fight; and people always feel that it must be for the right reasons ... they never ask questions.'

Aghadi members pointed out how the Shiv Sena had already initiated the process of justifying their aggression in terms of 'army action for a good cause'. In one incident, following the death in a road accident of a notorious Shiv Sena leader from Thane (Anand Dighe, known as the 'Thackeray of Thane'), Shiv Sena men and women wreaked havoc in the hospital injuring several doctors and damaging hospital property. It could have been a case of sheer vandalism, or the Sena cadres could have been giving vent to their grief, but the party claimed their leader had been given inadequate medical treatment and that this 'bruised the honour of the Shiv Sena'. The incident was justified within the Sena realm as retaliation from 'a people's army'. So the Sena men *and* women were aware that when acts of violence invited controversy, they could be given a coat of legitimacy by declaring their action as one of retrieving 'the army's honour'.

The militant Aghadi 'social workers' felt the visibility of collective violence could not remain diffused in a military society. All the members could draw a sympathetic understanding from violent acts and images. When the Aghadi women privately threatened a Muslim man engaging in sexual harassment, only a few people surrounding his home would come over to survey the spectacle. Most of them may not have known about 'the social plague' that was being addressed, and would not offer their support to the deliverers of justice. 'Instead, if there was a long march to a Muslim man's house, shouting of slogans all the way, a symbol of unity of the self-styled army, like saffron bandanas worn by both men and women, and then the enemy was thrashed in public as a forewarning against sexual aggression—it would generate sympathy,' felt Sunita, a leader. In such an overt display of martial power there would be no misunderstanding as to who was the enemy implicated in the performance of violence; the importance of key social ideas (like sexual harassment) would be dramatised; and the organised display of the army's strength and dedication to a good cause would win over witnesses' support.

AS: 'This long-term dependency on organised violence that you're trying to create, don't you think it'll destroy any hope for peace?'

Sunita: 'Listen, those who are going to criticise our reliance on violence are women who are already well-protected. Like you. For those who have never had the power, status and privilege of being in charge of their own lives can turn to any movement, I repeat, any movement that offers them some dignity even in the slightest measures.'

Merits: 'Warriors do not get beaten at home'   Some Sena women believed a martial society would make their roles as warriors permanent, and 'warriors do not get beaten at home'. According to Overing, who studied the Piora of Venezuela, few aspiring militaristic societies are without norms stipulating how violence should be organised. They specify, for example, the sorts of weaponry that might be used against particular adversaries. She argues, 'because of kinship type constraints, objective everyday relations are free of violence, and in relations with outsiders, violence is allowed in full sway' (1985: 6). For Sena women, they were allowed to combat 'the others' physically. But violence was also part of their everyday personal experiences (for example, domestic violence and gang war which threatened their lives). However, these women had achieved a limited amount of freedom from physical abuse by developing a martial image within the Sena, and they wanted to instil vitality in this new gender dynamics. Along with contesting their enemies, envisioning a martial society was also a conscious strategy to decrease women's vulnerability to 'closer' forms of aggression. It would lead to better, safer domestic lives.

The Aghadi women had turned into self-proclaimed interpreters of 'merits' in a *sena samaj*. While the Sena men were more integrated with Hindutva's utopian vision of a future society, the women's ideas about the *sena samaj* showed their more down-to-earth, practical involvement with group survival, cohesion and women's autonomy.

Relationship with the enemy

Chandana, an Aghadi cadre: 'During the riots we make sure the other community knows we're the boss. But there has to be a system whereby after the bouts of riots the enemy still knows who's boss. We have to keep them on their toes. If we relax, they'll strike.'

Having considered the in-group qualities the women wanted to develop in the *sena samaj* and how they idealised the army as a social model, we now turn to how the Aghadi women look outwards and put forward different arguments on subjugating their enemies in the future. The women wanted to ensure that their violent acts had a lasting impact on their victims and spoke about new strategies of 'counter-violence' that could be developed further within the 'army society'.

A 'weapon-like' society to compensate for a lack of sophisticated weapons The largest section of women known to have a militant public image spoke about organising direct, destructive action like an army. Some felt it was important for the practice of violence to be so aggressive and organised that it always created an intense, lasting impression in the senses of the enemy. For example, slapping a man did not have the same effect as shooting him (without killing him). A victim could recover from a temporary sense of humiliation, but when maimed for life, the act of violence would be lodged in the body and the victim would carry it around for the rest of his or her life. Sena women realised that their display of violence did not entail the use of specialised equipment or expert knowledge, so they feared its image or memory in the mind of the victim may not be potent enough. This was a shortcoming that could be countered in the *sena samaj* by 'turning organisation itself into a form of weapon'. Thus women believed the 'other' community would be unsettled by merely seeing a society operate like an army, even without the use of weapons. According to cadre Swastika, 'Daily training, a rigorous lifestyle, a strong body language, a sense of purpose ... these are enough to distinguish a civilian lifestyle from that in an army.' Hence women considered the threat of violence and the sharp display of organisation within a militaristic lifestyle would be a strong communication of political and social opposition to a formidable enemy.

Forestall the enemy: 'Not kill them, not kill us'   Consider the following quotes:

Organisation was as important as bravery. (Hegel, 1964: 168)

'Bravery's not enough. It has to be organised to have a force.' (Chandana, a Sena cadre)

Hegel (1964) assumed that combatants fight for honour and respect. They thus have shared reasons for testing their masculinity in situations of conflict. He also argued that the combatants' ability to challenge death 'bears testimony' to their commitment to a cause and detachment from worldly life (1964: 163–4). The Sena women wanted recognition through combat, but also remained tied to 'life', especially their work, friends, families and the act of living in general. They did not want their confrontations with the enemy to be a life and death struggle. The intent of employing violence was to impair the victim, not to eliminate him (as discussed earlier). Thus, the Sena women 'combatants' were also not ready to die for their cause, but were rather demonstrating their ability to *endure* the risk of death in a combat situation, displaying the warriors' personal and political capacity for violence. 'This was enough to keep the enemy in line,' felt Chandana. According to Riches (1986), organised violence is about securing practical advantages over the opponent in the short term by forestalling his activities. He calls it 'tactical pre-emption' (1986: 7), which incapacitates the 'other', preventing them from exerting their strength. Sections of the Sena women wanted to maintain a *sena samaj* where the organisation of violence would be enough to stop the other side from deploying its capabilities.

Most men, however, still toed the party line. 'I'm ready to die for the Sena,' said Gaurav, a male cadre. Aghadi leader Surekha shook her head:

'If there's violence, deaths on our side will be accidental. We should be organised well enough to provide back-ups for each other. Unless we live in an environment like that, we can't avoid the risk of death.'

This demonstrated the men were far less tactical than the women, or at least gave the impression that they were willing to plunge into action without carefully considering the threat of injury or death. The women were more strategic and did not want to rush into things without developing survival mechanisms.

Repressive and invisible violence: system-maintaining violence   Some Sena women were more conscious than others that they operated within a system of 'external' (state) law and order. So, even while envisioning an 'army society', they realised that direct action could not be implemented at all times. Furthermore the Sena had put pressure on all its wings to maintain a moderate image during elections. However, the feeling of power, which came with suppressing the enemy, had to persist for the women. Sections of Aghadi members tried to plan out alternative forms of violence that could be practised in the *sena samaj*. The first was what they considered repressive (*dabana*) violence. For example, cutting off supplies to other groups was a denial of resources, which would make the enemy aware and afraid of the Sena's constant presence. 'We could block a few trucks that entered Hoshiarpur [bordering Nirmal Nagar] with supplies. But we have to be ready for the *mussalman pehelwans* [Muslim strongman] as well. If these strategies have to be regularised, then all the children (*bachcha baccha*) living in the slum area have to be prepared for resistance,' said Tanika, a cadre.

As part of their future programme for the *sena samaj*, the Sena women also wanted to develop a policy to perpetrate what they described as invisible (*andekhi*) violence. For example, certain kinds of actions playfully ritualised within a group could have grave consequences when inflicted by Sena members. 'During Holi, if a Hindu man is chucked into a tank of water, then it's a joke. But when a Muslim man is just sprayed with coloured water, it's violence. It may go unnoticed during the frenzy of the festival. Someone might even think it's a friendly act. In a martial society there are no vague areas about what is violence even if it's not directly visible,' felt Sujata, a cadre. Giving another example, Sujata argued that seeing perpetrators of violence walking around freely causes severe mental anguish to riot victims. This was also an act of invisible violence in the slums. If ideas of what constituted violence remained dispersed, ambiguities were likely to arise from people's inability to spot the acts of hurt, especially if they were repressive or invisible. Sujata said:

'That these are also forms of violence [repressive and invisible] can be explained a few times to the women and they feel significant at that time. But this feeling of power must be sustained. It becomes a part of you only when the women are constantly aware that they're a part of an organised, substantial army, and there's no reason to fear any real resistance from the victim....'

Therefore the Aghadi felt the need for a militaristic social setting because such a system would allow both the perpetrators and victims to reach a consensus as to what qualified as an assault, and even the most subtle forms of violence would not go unnoticed. Thus, various forms of suppressive violence could be internalised and over time crystallised into collective action. This system-maintaining violence of one group against the other could be sustained only if the superior group remained militaristically organised.

In the *sena samaj* of the future some women wanted the victims to know they were organised like an army even though women warriors did not use weaponry; some wanted to carry on practising violence, albeit in alternative forms, within the system of law and order; some did not want to eliminate the enemy, nor eradicate themselves; and almost all women wanted to monitor levels of hostility in their relationship with their enemies. These women were not merely sentimentalising a past martial, social order. They were carefully seeking out those features of an institution which practised legitimate violence, which would enable them to create an ideal martial society in the future.

Attempts to 'transform' the home into a sena parivaar (army family)

Sena women were uncertain about the domains where they, specifically as women, could contribute to the attempted transformation into a *sena samaj*. Questioned on this issue, the Aghadi women sometimes claimed the motivation to build an army society should be shared equally by men and women. 'For example, the anti-Mandal women took to the streets as citizens, not just as women,' reminded Chandrima, a cadre.[3] So in all practicality an attempt to organise militaristically had to be undertaken by both men and women, even if the ideas were matured within the Aghadi. But where to begin? The Aghadi thought women should initiate the process of militarisation by turning the home into an army barrack. 'The family as army' (*sena parivaar*) could be the first stage in developing 'society as army'. Consequently, the Sena women made practical attempts, though not always successfully, to bring external ideas of developing a *sena samaj* into intra-household relationships.

Cheapest start, malleable families   In our interactions the Aghadi members maintained they were isolated from the secular women's movement. They preferred to project themselves as a 'militaristic nationalistic movement' for women across class and caste differences, which was 'unique' in the city. Furthermore, they were aware that their allegiance to the party prevented them from procuring funds from secular agencies. Thus the Aghadi tried to assert its independence from alien organisations and peoples,[4] and the women

---

[3] In 1989 Indian Prime Minister V.P. Singh revived a 10-year-old commission report put together by parliamentarian B.P. Mandal. The report suggested that 49.5 per cent of government jobs and slots in educational institutions be reserved for lower castes. The introduction of the Mandal Bill sparked protests by the student community. Women, who were moving away from traditional domestic roles and competing in the job market, took part in the demonstrations.

[4] The Sena obtained sponsorship from various corporate organisations and also

claimed they did not need 'external' financial assistance. However, sustaining a *sena* was expensive, so the Aghadi stressed transformation of the home as it was the cheapest option to demonstrate the seriousness of its intentions to make a martial social order. All this required was the physical and emotional investment of women to preserve feelings of vulnerability to an alien invasion and thus convince their family members that the home should operate like a trench.

Women realised their proximity to the Sena had allowed them to enter a 'wartime' space and viewing their social environment from this standpoint allowed them not only to gain a new freedom as wives, mothers and workers in a situation of religious and community crisis, but also to value it. Poverty, communal tensions and the strong presence of the Aghadi had led to 'the weakening of the family system', the destabilisation of which had commenced with migration, as there was a marked break away from a subservient or dependent position of women in matters of family and finances. Further, there had been a sudden need for alertness to combat enemy invasion. As a result, the aggression of Sena members brought about changes in the previous order of everyday life. Several Sena women in Nirmal Nagar thus felt that while the home order was in a state of transition and hence malleable, they should try to 'swing things their way and turn the family into an army'. They believed only women could achieve this within the home and play a role in determining their own futures.

Advertisement and women's 'liberation'   Several stray factors were making migrant women in the urban context realise the value of their role within the family system. In their rural setting there was nothing which reflected their responsibilities as housewives as something remotely constructive. Ironically, it was the urban advertisement industry which glamorised and centralised the role of women within the (Hindu) home, and also highlighted their importance as consumers. While accepting the gender specific division of labour in which women were in charge of domestic life, the women confessed they were lured by feel-good advertising for women. Although the glitzy advertisements made them 'respect themselves as housewives' and as patrons of home products, television was probably not the best channel of communication in their rural setting and their lack of education also reduced exposure to alternative ideas of women's status within the home. However, there was a

---

thrived on forms of illegal and extortionist money transactions. These funds were appropriated by various party wings. The Aghadi women claimed they did not receive much.

committed move within the Sena to counter the influence of commercialism, especially the exploitation of women by advertising groups. Other Hindu fundamentalist groups, like the RSS, also had special strategies to challenge 'Westoxication'. Some RSS women in Mumbai, for example, held classes for women which trained them not to look at mirrors. Self-admiration could enhance a sense of beauty which in turn made women susceptible to Western products. However, the Sena women often expressed that the advertisements which projected women as the controllers of the home made them realise that 'many things could happen within a family if women wanted it to be that way'. Chakravarti (2002), analysing the assumptions of advertisements in their portrayal of Indian women, suggests they 'mislead' women to believe that any form of agency is liberating. Women are projected as agents for buying and consuming products that could even solve interpersonal relationships. Even domestic violence is resolved by buying the right kind of taps! However, for the Sena women, watching television at night and gaping at hoardings made them feel that the nature of the home could be reconstructed by women. According to the women, this exposure to advertisements reinforced their decision to change their homes into battlefronts, an initiative that uncovers a deeply complex relationship between agency, advertisement and the communalisation of lower-class families.

Exchanging ideas about home and war   As discussed earlier, the Aghadi created various spaces outside the home where women could meet and interact, including child care facilities, areas for *kirtans* to be sung, counselling centres and night schools for women. Despite differences in their approaches towards an ideal *sena samaj* and *sena parivaar*, the women liked to share their various thoughts and hence all these spaces were used as gathering grounds for women to exchange their ideas about appropriate steps to make the home more prepared for a state of war. The following are quotes selected from discussions, held during such meets, between women who were trying to militarise the home front. Some were speculations and future concerns, while others were actually implemented.

'We have to change the structure of the homes. Flat roofs mean that bombs from neighbouring areas will burst right on the flat surface. If the roofs are slanted the bombs will roll off. This is a trench and we have to guard ourselves.'

'I use strongly provocative language at home. "Fight, the Sena's right behind you," I tell them. I always tell the children you have to be strong warriors.'

'You should see how I speak at home about the indignities of living in fear of the other community. I could turn an ordinary mild person on the street into

.a strong soldier of his or her personal faith and property. Soldiers, they have to be soldiers.'

'If I leave the house, I tell those in the house always to be on alert. There could be an attack anytime.'

'I can assume the role of Mother Durga if any Muslim demon even looks at my house slyly. But I still have to hold the home together so that all the tension around us doesn't take away our daily fun.'

The Sena women sought to endow the home with military purpose, especially with the use of war terminology, and since the home revolved around women's labour, it gave visibility to the women's role in inspiring male warriors or the warriors-in-training. What women claimed to be a wartime way of life required a deeply felt commitment to the 'we shall overcome' outlook and in the creation of this the women played a significant role. Thus, they often gathered to discuss strategies through which the women-household-militarisation nexus would come to form the building-blocks of all homes.

Motherhood and child soldiers   Even while envisioning an army society, Sena women felt that motherhood remained the fundamental nature of women and that this would create no confusion at home. As discussed earlier, children were even defensive of their mother's militant public role and had developed their own coping skills in relation to the violence around them. Rohini, a widowed Aghadi cadre in Nirmal Nagar, claimed she was making a 'serious effort' to keep her children (two boys) alert and agile like soldiers. The children were made to rise early in the morning, do their daily tasks strictly on time, go to school, say their prayers and, last but not least, to perform a martial drill with sticks every night. It seemed to be a re-creation of the situation in which Shivaji and his mother, living by themselves, jointly developed survival strategies. Although this could be seen as a very weak attempt to forward the Aghadi's ideas of militarising society, many children were open to receiving these 'wartime' values and sanctioned the women's efforts to turn their homes into frontiers. Mohan—who studied in a local Catholic school and whose mother was an aggressive Aghadi member—in an attempt to represent his household drew a sketch (Fig. 1) which was a fusion of two apparent extremes: a portrait of mother Mary holding the child Jesus and the militant image of a form of the goddess Durga (*Sherawali*). Virgin Mary, on the one hand, was the ideal mother and the embodiment of humility and peace; the Hindu goddess, *Sherawali*, on the other, rode a tiger, wielded arms in all ten hands and killed demons; she was also a mother and the protector of her children.

Fig. 1   Mohan's representation of his household

Anthropologists such as Marglin (1985) and Bennet (1983), while developing a critique of the exclusive dichotomies introduced by structuralism in anthropological writing, showed how female power within the Hindu discourse represented a joining of the violent and the non-violent, the benevolent and the malevolent. In his studies on cultural perceptions, Nandy (1980b) observed the absence of contradiction between masculinity and femininity because concepts of power, malevolence and militancy were more readily associated with Hindu goddesses. Since there was no apparent clash between the mother as militant and the mother as loving, women probably did not lose their 'femininity' and social acceptability as participants in various forms of violence. So there could be a fusion of passivity and aggression in the same mother. Mohan's sketch represented the attitudes of many children who did not see any paradox in warrior women being kind mothers, like Mary. Thus, the home was a flexible space that could accommodate both war and peace.

Home, war and women in the workplace   Wartime situations often have similar repercussions on women across cultures. Ryuichi *et al.* (1998) and Koonz (1988) observed that women could not escape their second-class status in Second World War Japan and Germany respectively. However, in both parts of the world women could establish their own sphere of control in the margins of the men's world. Women sought to carve out what anthropologists call 'a women's realm'. Both scholars argue that situations of war incorporate more women into the labour market, as most men leave for the front. This leads to an explosion of problems as the visibility of working women increases considerably. Most of the problems faced by women are partially resolved with the proliferation of women's organisations who champion the cause of labour-class women. The Aghadi argued that it was playing a similar interventionist role for women in wartime society. The Sena women were fighting male resistance to women's advancement into the workforce by projecting women's economic pursuits as virtuous acts. However, women still faced several difficulties. The war situation in the slums was not an ongoing, visible, life-and-death battle. Also, the men remained within the slums discreetly to supervise or actively to restrict women's actions, often becoming competitors within the unorganised labour economy. Further, men who were away in the army gained an honour and self-respect which could not be achieved easily within harsh slum lives. 'If the society was militaristically organised, then the men, often unemployed, often criminalised and marginalised, would acquire a social worth. Their focus would be diverted from their wives. They'd begin to see women as contributors to the development of a garrison Hindu state,' said Sudha, a cadre. So the controversial theme of women in a public role could re-emerge as women workers for the Hindu nation.

Sena samaj: a fantasy or a possibility?

Some regions in South Asia have developed 'military societies', since militant groups shape the social, economic and ideological settings in these areas. These towns and villages, which are often raided by security forces, have developed what Smyth (1998) calls a 'surveillance culture', and look upon themselves as parallel armies serving and protecting the interests of their own communities. Women have been recruited into these militant organisations to serve specific functions. Manchanda (2001) has noted that women comprise one-sixth of the Liberation Tigers in Sri Lanka and one-third of the Maoists in Nepal. They are also active combatants in other militant organisations like the Shanti Bahini of the Chittagong hill tracts in Bangladesh, the National Socialist Council of Nagaland and the United Liberation Front of Assam in India. A smaller but sizeable number of women militants operate in Kashmir. According to Manchanda, women have been increasingly present in these movements to compensate for the heavy casualties sustained over years of 'war' with the state. According to Goswami (1999), the Dukhtaran-e-Milat, an Islamic women's terrorist group, use the *burqa* to hide weapons and their femininity to ward off body-searches. Also, security forces are hesitant to shoot at women guerrillas. In interviews with members of the People's War Group,[5] a Naxal underground movement in Andhra Pradesh in India,

---

5 As part of my prior research with Naxal organisations.

the men declared they recruited women for strategic purposes. Women were ordered to swallow cyanide capsules when captured, to avoid being raped by the enemy. However, to the men, protecting women's honour was a ploy to keep female prisoners from disclosing information during interrogation. In the past the militant outfit had been 'betrayed' by male militants who—after being tortured—had 'spilled the beans'.

For the Aghadi women, to what extent is this exercise of envisioning a military society a fantasy? The Sena women were certainly militant rioters and aggressive 'social workers', but they operated within the limits set upon them by the Sena, which was, after all, a political party keen on maintaining a moderate face before the electorate. The women were not even prepared to die for their cause, according to Surekha, who claimed deaths during militant operations would be accidental. Hence, it is difficult to conclude that the social environment in the slums would take a decisive turn towards militarisation, especially if a marginalised group of women were trying to implement such a radical scheme.

However, the Sena women did comprise a militant, majoritarian women's wing, encompassing a host of procedures and discourses to establish their hegemony in the slums. Even their social imaginings about their own modification and transformation into a militaristic society had caused a large degree of damage to others living close by. This threat of operating as an army, a *sena*, made minority communities live in apprehension of future turns of events and even the cultural and emotional decadence of the group marked as 'the enemy' seemed a possibility. The attempted militaristic organisation of simple household activities and the saffronisation of children were making the Muslims more ghettoised and afraid for their survival, but whether they would turn to other forms of 'fundamentalism' to counter their insecurities is merely speculation. The women's attempts to revitalise their status according to the *modus operandi* of a militaristic society were *ad hoc* and scattered in parts, but they progressed with their agenda under the patronage of senior leaders. Thus, at least until I left the field, the Aghadi remained convinced that they were moving in the 'right' direction.

CONCLUSION

The Aghadi women, in their unique way, were trying to rediscover a past (through tales of Shivaji) where they played an equal public role with men and were visible agents in the creation of social honour and a martial Hindu society. They wanted to show that their present ideas to create an ideal future would not be inconsistent with the past—because the social and political conditions and concerns remained the same. They were making women prominent in a martial past so that a conspicuous role for them in the martial future would not be seen as deviant. Thus the Aghadi was preoccupied with manipulating the past and shaping the future, so that a favourable position for Marathi Hindu women could be created in society.

As an agenda for the future, the Aghadi was trying to foresee Hindus as constantly confronting an emergency, and hence advocated the need to develop features of a defence society to counter the crisis. In the process the Aghadi was also encouraging women to construct a family life which would not crumble during war. Since the household was the microcosm of society at large, establishing women as warrior leaders within the *sena parivaar* would give women visibility as martial heroes in the *sena samaj*.

Several scholars offer compelling analyses of gender in conflict situations and uncover the links between gender relations and militarised violence that occur in the course of and, significantly, in the absence of direct conflict. Among them Ruddick comments that women need men to protect them and men need war to protect women and children.

The culture of militarisation—coercive power structures and practices, hierarchies and discipline—relies on patriarchal patterns and patriarchy in turn relies on militarisation.... War magnifies the already existing inequalities of peacetime. (Ruddick, 1998: 212)

So when a community feels it is under siege, women are pressured to embrace identity constructs that undermine their authority and autonomy. To reverse that trend and manage their survival the Sena women were attempting to place themselves in a long history of women's militancy. They were trying to construct a critical consciousness, typically using the politics of sexual assault and self-defence in a conflict situation, by developing new insight into a social framework that acknowledges the necessity of militarism, not just to protect women but also to ensure the survival of the Hindu society and religion. Thus the Aghadi cadres can be seen as agents of social transformation, with the potential to upturn gross power imbalances within a social system, which remains openly prejudicial against women. Women's experiences of everyday and extraordinary violence (extended from home to the street to the 'battlefield' riot situations) are not homogenous, and thus their coping mechanisms are also diverse. The Sena women's visions were influenced by the fact that women's expressions of support and resistance flow from their own cultural experiences of being discriminated and disempowered. If women feel that their indulgence in organised violence offers them relief from everyday moral restrictions, it is linked to their own immediate, maybe narrow, construction of women's visibility and social worth.

7

CONCLUSION

'The slums of Mumbai are unchanging. This is one of [the city's] permanent features. Yet the people inhabiting that space feel the impermanency of their existence more than anyone else.' (A friend)

Through my analysis of the relationship between gender and right-wing activism I have attempted to open a window for the reader onto multiple sites of violence in which women and children are easily implicated. This study focuses primarily on the actions and circumstances surrounding the Shiv Sena women and in this context pursues questions about the practise and legitimisation of collective violence and reflects on the use of 'war' as a survival strategy for women and children. By way of conclusion, a brief discussion follows of how this analysis raises questions within the discourse of women in/and conflict and also contests deterministic theories about violence within a fundamentalist discourse, especially in the Indian context. This discussion also highlights the importance of Indian feminists to rethink certain principles of their movement. Finally, I briefly address the issue of covert research and how future anthropologists could resolve questions of ethics and security during fieldwork among criminalised groups.

However, before an examination of some of the wider implications of this study, let me draw out the main issues around which this ethnography has been organised. The work is dependent on the oral narratives of women, old and young, and children in the urban slums. Poor slum women joined the violent Sena ethno-nationalist movement because the organisation provided shade from what they described as 'the scalding effects' (*man jalana*) of urbanisation, industrialisation and migration in Mumbai. Within the movement groups of women began to use collective violence for wresting jobs and land. After forming a women's wing and joining the Hindutva bandwagon the Sena women developed a militant image by organising themselves into task forces and street patrols. Women's participation in the Mumbai riots brought the activities of the Aghadi into the spotlight and violent actions gave women visibility, power and autonomy. Consequently, for nearly two generations of

Sena women, violence became an instrument for wresting social, economic and gender benefits in marginalised urban slums.

The women's wing wanted to expand and often resisted restrictive decrees on women's morality to retain fluidity in its mobilisational strategies. They selected certain elements of Bal Thackeray's dictates on women and formed their own 'convenient' ideology on women's role within the movement. The Aghadi maintained its unique militant image, but was not constituted solely of violent women, or women emulating their aggressive leaders. The wing developed highly flexible, accessible, 'woman-friendly' policies to attract young and old, mobile and restricted, affluent and impoverished women into its fold. But they developed their strategies without directly challenging the patriarchal structures within the party and in the slums.

The Sena children too were developing a militant identity to ensure their own survival as weaker, more vulnerable members of the Sena movement. They openly advocated the need for urban child soldiering and took various initiatives to organise themselves into street gangs, even prior to their formal recruitment into the party. They also practised more indiscreet violence and wanted to eliminate the enemy to gain a future peace. However, in this context the women and children clashed over their strategic use of violence. Indeed, the Sena women wanted the enemy to be out there for them to sustain female martiality; 'peace' meant women's complete domesticity. Furthermore, instead of returning to a life of everyday domesticity and economic struggle, the women wanted to build a militaristic society in the future, where women's militancy, mobility and martial motherhood would be permanently legitimised.

GENDER AND CONFLICT

Studies on women and conflict are marked by the assumption that in their approach to internal and external conflict situations women are more passive than men. Women are perceived to be more accepting of compromises to resolve disputes, and less likely than men to believe in the urgency and necessity of armed forces (Chenoy, 1996; Enloe, 1989; Koithara, 1999; Navlakha, 2000; Reardon, 1999; Ruddick, 1998; Sharoni, 1996, 1998; Tessler *et al.*, 1999). Contesting the centrality of men's experiences in violence, Manchanda (2001), for example, focuses on women providing alternative and non-violent ways of negotiating identities during conflict. The six chronicles presented in her work demonstrate women's capacity to emerge as agents of social transformation and highlight their perspectives on 'just' peace. Manchanda concedes, however, that conflict leads to the emergence of new forms of identity for women:

It is precisely at the time of dramatic shifts in gender roles, brought about by the societal upheaval attendant on conflict, that the impulse to promote women's social transformation and autonomy is circumscribed by the nationalist or communitarian project. This may also explain why peace is invariably conceptualised as a return to the gender status quo irrespective of the non-traditional roles taken on by women in conflict. (Manchanda, 2001: 13)

The Shiv Sena women were well aware of the possibilities of being isolated from the movement and public spaces if the communal tensions in the slums were resolved. Their experiences in the slums of Mumbai, providing day-to-day food, shelter and security, had given them myriad perspectives on what constituted their 'peace' and 'safety'. The Sena women *were* trying to be agents of social transformation. However, with their main goals being select access to areas of power and physical mobility, they imagined their futures within 'army societies'. Since this freedom could only be achieved in conflict and not during peace, it is important, within the discourse of gender and conflict, to review the ideas and circumstances of women who are more at peace when 'at war', and hence women's efforts and initiatives to retain conflict in society.

This book also contests some deterministic political theories which link violence displayed by fundamentalists to larger dynamics of national religious activism, mobilisation and votes, contributing to the growth and legitimisation of these movements. From a local point of view, the Sena women's activism for Hindutva was on *behalf* of politicised religion, not because they endorsed it. They had their own agenda, an agenda that was personalised and localised. It was associated with notions of space, professional and personal mobility, self confidence and visibility, which informed the quotidian narrower realities of their lives.

Scholars like Hansen (1999), Heuze (1995) and Patel and Masselos (2003) have analysed the aggression displayed by the Shiv Sena and linked it to anomie and globalisation processes in Mumbai. This explanatory trajectory needs to be explored further, since the dynamics within the Sena women's wing unfurls different relations between gender identity and the politics of urban violence. While the present study certainly reveals that older Sena cadres were isolated in an urban context and their experiences played a substantial role in consolidating women's militancy with the movement, the world-views of the younger generation of Aghadi members show that the use of collective violence had equipped women to contest certain patriarchal structures and considerably influence the internal gender dynamics of the slum areas. Thus the Hindutva discourse cannot be assumed as a unitary voice. It encompasses multiple positions and has degrees of discrepancy and agency built into it.

As an elementary appeal of Hindutva, van der Veer (1996) locates frustration stemming from an unfulfilled display of Hindu strength in public as the source of local violence, where the enemy is blamed for eclipsing the Hindu capacity for excitement and enjoyment. Taking this argument further, Hansen (1999) contends that 'excesses' imagined within the enemy community (Muslims are viewed as excessively lustful and violent) motivates Hindu fundamentalists to develop an ideology of self-control and discipline. Reviewing these positions from the standpoint of gender, it is argued here that the Sena women felt fortunate to enjoy far more freedom than Muslim women. Hindu women did not wear *purdah*, making each woman an individual in public. Many women claimed their religion allowed them to display unfettered violence without questioning women's morality and self-control (citing the example of the militant goddess Kali going on an unstoppable violent rampage to kill her enemies). Thus Sena women's capacity to take part in local violence partially stemmed from a 'sense of privilege' to indulge in certain excesses. These excesses were considered denied to Muslim women trapped in a more conservative religious discourse. Thus social processes leading to conflict need to be examined in greater depth to critique some essential myths about religion, violence and everyday anti-minority vigilantism.

FEMINIST STUDIES AND HINDU NATIONALISM

My research uses feminist concepts (such as 'agency' and 'empowerment') and carries elements of feminist methodology (in representing the voices of marginalised women). My informants aggressively contested traditional silencing mechanisms, and tried to transform the gender dynamics within their homes and workplaces. Even though their actions could be interpreted as an assertion of submissive, subaltern voices (cf. Spivak 1998), women taking recourse to political violence, brutal vigilantism and militant nationalism remain at the periphery of the feminist discourse. In this context, my ethnography will, perhaps, sit more comfortably within the broader ambit of 'women's studies' or 'gender studies'. In addition, my observations about women within a fundamentalist movement should add subtlety to positions in the feminist treatment of Hindu nationalism. I will highlight briefly certain contemporary interpretations of women's action within religious movements, which I will contest later.

According to several feminist scholars (Chakravarti, 1987; Sarkar, 1991, 1998; and others), women's empowerment within Hindu nationalism cannot be declared as feminism since it leads to the ultimate subordination of women's rights within an authoritarian community structure. According to

Chakravarti (1987), women's power and agency is given safe recognition
when they are 'guided' by the interests of the community at large. Thus, fore-
grounding women within the Hindu nationalist movement does not add up
to feminism. Gedalof (1999) confronts the difficulties that white Western
feminism has in balancing issues of gender with other forms of difference,
such as race, ethnicity and nation. Discussing Dietrich's approach to the impact of communalism on the women's movement, Gedalof points out that
Dietrich tries to develop a more complex model of women's identity. In her
earlier writings Dietrich (1988) argues that women cannot name their rights
as women when they remain within a social movement in India. However, she
later concedes that caste and religion have often proved to be stronger community ties for women than gender, 'at least in situations of communal strife'
(Dietrich, 1994: 44). Addressing the vexing question of whether women's
participation in Hindu fundamentalism authentically expresses the empowerment of women, Sarkar highlights its limitations. In her study of RSS women
she argues that 'self assertion through violent communalism is probably accompanied by a certain growth in self confidence that the Samiti has generated over several generations' (Sarkar and Butalia, 1996: 40). However, she
asserts that RSS women's aggression remains a middle-class phenomenon,
in which women joining the trade sector for the first time feel assured and
hardened through physical training exercises to deal with their extra-domes-
tic responsibilities.

The Aghadi women I worked with were poor, from low-caste groups, yet
they engaged with a fundamentalist discourse primarily to gain greater self-
confidence and mobility *as women*. They used the limited freedom offered to
women within a violent fundamentalist discourse to increase their freedom in
other spheres of their daily lives. For example, their overt display of violence
during a riot had given them a reputation of being a fierce band of women
soldiers. The Sena women then exploited this hallowed position as religious
warriors to name specific gender interests and accrue social benefits for slum
women. However, these women still remained underprivileged and could
not overtly battle the patriarchal structures in the ghettoes.

In many slum regions in Mumbai groups of older women have been known
to express their resistance to patriarchal domination through individualised
forms of resistance. For example, in Hoshiarpur, bordering Chaturwadi,
menopausal Muslim women are allowed to enter forbidden areas in mosques.
They are not denied entry because after a certain age, when 'breasts begin
to sag', women are no longer considered sexual beings and can be treated
as equal to men. But 'public violence' was squarely a male domain, and the
Sena women taking part in it were in their youth. Thus, perpetrating overt

and covert conflict required women's deliberate participation and the Sena slum women gave their informed consent to the Aghadi advocating collective action for women. Even women who were docile at home displayed militancy in public. For some women it was a patriarchal bargain, hoping to be rewarded with mobility for good conduct at home (Kandiyoti, 1988). For others it was a demonstration of alternative forms of women's behaviour, especially to their families. So the women joined the Aghadi knowing full well the pitfalls and possibilities of engaging with a violent movement. However, research here shows further the distinctive standpoints of these women, who, by asserting themselves in countless ways, were trying to invert some conventional gender hierarchies. While the women were projecting an image of *adapting* to certain male dominant values within a fundamentalist discourse, they were consciously trying to contest it.

The question is, has the Sena women's initiative to transform their identity from passivity to militancy lead to their 'empowerment'? If empowerment can be seen as a change in overt systems of domination, then the Sena women have certainly accrued some in their familial and social environment. If empowerment entails an awareness of the advanced capabilities of women, then the Sena women have empowered themselves through collective action. And if empowerment entails 'wresting power' (Basu, 1998: 236), then the Sena women have gained in power and visibility through their aggression. However, at stake here is the extent to which women have developed a unique consciousness of *what* constituted their own empowerment, even if it was an emotion, and it is their creative endeavours to achieve that state of mind which this study has uncovered.

The Aghadi developed its own strategies, primarily based on violent collective action, to extort social and economic benefits from the party in particular and society at large. Eckert (2003), discussing the internal dynamics of the Shiv Sena, points out how violence opens up new spaces for identity-building within the party:

Violent action has frequently been denied creative potential as it has been interpreted as not only destructive, but as resulting from the oppression or inhibition of creative action. The hesitation to include violent action in the realm of creative action possibly arises from the fact that theories which have done so (as for example, Sorek, Junger or Fanon) have idealised violence as having a *specific* potential for violence. Such an idealisation of violence has legitimised the most terrifying sort of rule. (Eckert, 2003: 269)

Even though Eckert focuses on the participatory value of 'direct action', it is women's active *and* permissive roles in violence that have 'empowered' women and transformed their submissive identities in the slums. According to Vidal *et al.* (2003) an important approach to the anthropology of violence is to study the various forms of violence practised in society and the ways in which they institute and transgress social ties. In this context Bajwa and Das (2003) discuss how the discourses of martyrdom (death to the self), and feud and vendetta (death to the other) define community in the Punjab and equip its members to ward off the hegemony of a secular state. The authors conclude that multiple discourses on violence can coexist in a single community, even though these discourses appear to be in contradiction with each other. The Sena women were careful not to eliminate themselves or their enemy, as both entities had to coexist and thrive in a hostile relationship. This hostility would enable the women to develop and sustain their militancy. If a Hindu fundamentalist group is defined by its militancy for religious sovereignty and an aggressive feminist movement is defined by its militancy for gender justice, why should we assume that the twain shall never meet? The Aghadi's strategies and operations reveal the creative potential in violence as women developed ways in which a superficial display of religious violence crossed paths with a 'real' display of violence for securing gender equality. This point of intersection in the two discourses on violence helped Sena women resist oppressive social dictates in the slums. The subordination of gender interests remained only a *pretence* to ward off complete social isolation.

I am not, through my work, endorsing women's violence. Nor am I overlooking the fact that the actions of the Sena women could be detrimental for women's 'real' empowerment in the long run. Kim (2003), studying the hostility in Hindu–Christian relations over conversions in India, seeks to reveal the arguments both *for* and *against* conversions, which remains the main appeal of his research. According to the author, it is the debate between Hindus and Christians, rather than the dialogues, that exposes contradictory views. 'Contesting philosophies can bring out crucial issues, since conflicting stances do not seek a common ground' (Kim, 2003: 9). In the debate between feminist *versus* fundamentalist women it is important to take into account the stories of the 'evil' women warriors in order to include them within a feminist discourse and not isolate them any further. Das, discussing the fallout from 9/11, comments:

Instead of a Manichean battle between good and evil, there would be greater room for a tolerable peace if it was possible to attend to the violences of everyday life, to acknowledge the fallibility and the vulnerability to which we are all subject, and to acknowledge that the conflict is over interests, and further that these need to be renegotiated. It is not over uncompromising values. (Das, 2001)

The Sena women were reformulating patriarchal structures within their own movement and also practising a flexible brand of Hinduism. They were developing different, even new ways of being Hindu women, wives and workers. Hence their values were certainly not uncompromising and were undergoing change every day. Chandhoke (2003), discussing the ways in which identities are constructed through the politics of memory and narratives of victimisation in India, argues that Hindutva's impact on everyday society could be damaging. But if such a project is to be dismantled, the 'incivilities' in social movements must be acknowledged, as they retain the capacity to limit, expand or transform the sphere of civil society. In this context, the use of language that renders forms of women's violence fanatical blocks all possibilities of understanding when and under what circumstances women can play a role in perpetrating communal violence. Instead of recasting their actions as social aberrations and negativities, it is important to recognise that conflict has the creative potential to transform gender relations. To contest that phenomenon, the voices of women who support war and violence must also be heard.

COVERT RESEARCH ON VIOLENCE: SOME IMPLICATIONS

A part of my fieldwork with the Sena women can be described as 'covert' research. Although several anthropologists working in neighbourhoods suspicious of outsiders wore a physical disguise to become part of the community, I chose not to. I appeared as a Bengali, Hindu upper-caste woman who had come from London to uncover the Aghadi's successes. I reassured the Sena women that I was not going to side with their victims (as most people did), since I wanted to study the ideas and actions of the aggressors. I also convinced the women that I had come to learn from poor women and not to preach. I showed my humility, and the women over time allowed me to be a part of their women-criminal-political nexus. Thus, as an ethnographer I oriented my speech, dress and body language towards gaining the confidence of my informants, in order to obtain more 'authentic' responses from them during my formal interviews and informal chats. Having settled in the slums, when I asked 'disturbing' questions about violence, secularism or feminism, the women assumed that my queries flowed from my class difference with them. I did not 'know'. I never told the women about my own ideological convictions. They did not ask. They were always keen to know about London, my male friends, my smoking and drinking habits—privileges enjoyed by people of my economic status.

This form of research work with criminalised groups has two major implications: first, it gives rise to several ethical issues which are difficult to resolve. It is always far easier to study people with whom one can sympathise. I have made every effort to be fair to the Sena women and their circumstances, but it was exhausting to work with women who affected my sensibilities on a daily level. I would spend several of my waking hours wondering whether I was cheating these women, especially when they would look at me for approval after thrashing a 'deviant' person in public. I chose the easiest way in. I did not tell the women that I had different convictions. But I also had the most difficult way out. When I left the field the women fondly threatened that if I ever wrote a word against them they would kill my family and me.

This brings me to the second implication of covert research. There is always a question of personal security. I was unaware that a Sena 'detective' had tailed me for days before I was finally allowed to work in the slums. The detective had informed the women that I 'drank with men in cheap pubs', I 'smoked long cigarettes', I had a rented flat in Bandra where 'boys came', I met 'secular' journalists and academics. I was grilled on all these 'issues'. I stopped going to my flat, I stopped smoking, I quit drinking and I did not keep in touch with anybody. There were often small blasts in the slums when 'country-made' bombs would explode and I became jumpy after seeing the open use of guns, knives and bombs there. These concerns consumed a lot of my mental energy and I repeatedly had to tell myself to be 'brave' and 'show courage'. I often worried that I would be arrested by the police when I was in the middle of a demonstration or that I would be injured during a confrontation. I could not disclose my credentials at the local police station, since they were also part of the nexus in the slums. While attending an all-party meet at Sena Bhavan the Sena women bundled me into a cab and asked me to lie low for a few days. I was perplexed. When I returned to the slums I was informed that I had 'caught the naughty eye' of a senior Sena leader. It is important for a researcher in the field to be emotionally or physically equipped to protect themselves at all times. On occasions I felt I had not kept that distance from the women. Although it makes my ethnography richer, it also makes me poorer as a researcher who lived partially in fear of her informants.

Through covert ethnography and its risks and revelations I have explored the worlds of poor women marked by their agency and by the generation and regeneration of violence. The Sena women's positive experiences within a fierce nationalist movement may create dilemmas but it cannot be ignored. Drawing upon observations and experiences, this study also shows the tenacity and determination of lower-class women, in however limited capacity, to demand change. My hope is that the narratives of the Sena women and their attempts to redefine narratives of community and conflict open up areas for future research on women, identity and right-wing vigilantism.

It is cold in the scriptorium, my thumb aches. I leave this manuscript, I do not know for whom; I no longer know what it is about. (Eco, 1980: 502)

BIBLIOGRAPHY

Abraham, Taisha, 2002, *Women and Politics of Violence*, New Delhi: Shakti.

Agnes, Flavia, 1996, 'Redefining the Agenda of the Women's Movement within a Secular Framework' in Tanika Sarkar and Urvashi Butalia (eds), *Women and RightWing Movements: Indian Experiences*, New Delhi: Kali for Women.

———, Neera Adarkar and Madhusree Dutta (eds), 1996, *The Nation, the State and Indian Identity*, Calcutta: Samya.

Ahluwalia, B.K. (ed.), 1984, *Shivaji and Indian Nationalism*, New Delhi: SES.

Ahmad, Aijaz, 1984, 'Tamil Nadu Conversions, Conversion Threats, and the Anti-Reservation Campaign: Some Hypotheses and Perspectives on the Communal Problem' in A.A. Engineer (ed.), *Communal Riots in Post-Independence India*, New Delhi: Sangam.

———, 1996, *Lineages of the Present: Political Essays*, New Delhi: Tulika.

Alexander, Claire E., 2000, *The Asian Gang: Ethnicity, Identity, Masculinity*, Oxford: Berg.

Anderson, Benedict, 1991, *Imagined Communities: Reflections on the Origin and Spread of Nationalism*, London: Verso.

Annan, D., 1967, 'The Ku Klux Klan' in Norman MacKenzie (ed.), *Secret Societies*, London: Aldus.

Appadurai, Arjun, 1981a, *Worship and Conflict under Colonial Rule: A South Indian Case*, Cambridge University Press.

———, 1981b, 'The Past as a Scarce Resource', *Man*, 16, 2 (June), pp. 201–19.

Aptekar, Lewis, 1988, *Street Children of Cali*, Durham, NC: Duke University Press.

Ardener, Edwin (ed.), 1971, *Social Anthropology and Language*, London: Tavistock.

Aries, Phillipe, 1962, *Centuries of Childhood: A Social History of Family Life* (transl. from the French by Robert Baldick), New York: Vintage.

Babb, Lawrence, 1970, 'Marriage and Malevolence: The Uses of Sexual Opposition in the Hindu Pantheon', *Ethnology*, 9, pp. 137–49.

191

Bacchetta, Paola, 1993, 'All Our Goddesses are Armed: Religion, Resistance and Revenge in the Life of a Militant Hindu Nationalist Woman' in Amrita Basu (ed.), 'Women and Religious Nationalism in India', special issue, *Bulletin of Concerned Asian Scholars*, 25, 4, pp. 38–41.

——, 2002, 'Hindu Nationalist Women Imagine Spatialities/Imagine Themselves: Reflections on Gender Supplemental Agency' in Paola Bacchetta and Margaret Power (eds), *Right Wing Women: From Conservatives to Extremists around the World*, London: Routledge.

Bagchi, Jashodhara, 1990, 'Representing Nationalism: Ideology of Motherhood in Colonial Bengal', *Economic and Political Weekly*, 20 October.

Bagwe, Anjali, 1996, *Of Woman Caste: The Experience of Gender in Rural India*, Calcutta: Stree.

Bajpai, Kanti, 2002, *Roots of Terrorism*, New Delhi: Penguin.

Bajwa, R. Singh and Veena Das, 2003, 'Community and Violence in Contemporary Punjab' in Denis Vidal, Gilles Tarabout and Eric Meyer (eds), *Violence, Non-violence: Some Hindu Perspectives*, New Delhi: Manohar.

Bakker, Hans, 1986, *Ayodhya: The History of Ayodhya from the 7th Century to the Middle of the 18th Century*, Groningen: E. Forsten.

Bakshi, Rajni, 1984, *The Long Haul: The Bombay Textile Workers Strike*, Bombay: BUILD Documentation Centre.

Bakshi, S.R. and Sri Kant Sharma (eds), 2000, *The Great Marathas*, New Delhi: Deep & Deep.

Balakrishnan, Radhika (ed.), 2002, *The Hidden Assembly Line: Gender Dynamics of Subcontracted Work in a Global Economy*, Bloomfield, CT: Kumarian.

Balasingham, Anton, 2000, *The Politics of Duplicity: Re-visiting the Jaffna Talks*, Mitcham, Surrey: Fairmax.

Banerjee, Ashis and Nirmal Mukherjee, 1987, *Democracy, Federalism and the Future of India's Unity*, New Delhi: Uppal.

Banerjee, Sikata, 1996, 'Hindu Nationalism and the Construction of Women', Tanika Sarkar and Urvashi Butalia (eds), *Women and the Hindu Right*, New Delhi: Kali for Women.

——, 1998, 'Why Local Riots are not Merely Local: Violence and the State in Bijnor, 1988–93' in Partha Chatterjee (ed.), *State and Politics in India*, Delhi: Oxford University Press.

——, 2000, *Warriors in Politics: Hindu Nationalism, Violence and the Shiv Sena in India*, Boulder, CO: Westview Press.

Bar-Tal, Daniel, 1990, *Group Beliefs: A Conception for Analyzing Group Structure, Processes and Behaviour*, London: Springer-Verlag.

Basu, Amrita, 1992, *Two Faces of Protest: Contrasting Modes of Women's Activism in India*, Berkeley, CA: University of California Press.

—— (ed.), 1995, *The Challenge of Local Feminisms: Women's Movements in Global Perspective*, Boulder, CO: Westview Press.

——, 1996, 'Mass Movement or Elite Conspiracy? The Puzzle of Hindu Nationalism' in David Ludden (ed.), *Making India Hindu: Religion, Community and the Politics of Democracy in India*, Delhi: Oxford University Press.

——, 1998, 'Appropriating Gender' in Patricia Jaffery and Amrita Basu (eds), *Appropriating Gender: Women's Activism and Politicised Religion in South Asia*, London: Routledge.

Basu, Kaushik and Sanjay Subrahmanyam (eds), 1996, *Unravelling the Nation: Sectarian Conflict and India's Secular Identity*, New Delhi: Penguin.

Bayly, C.A., 1998, *Origins of Nationality in South Asia: Patriotism and Ethical Government in the Making of Modern India*, Delhi: Oxford University Press.

Becker, Gay, 1997, *Disrupted Lives: How People Create Meaning in a Chaotic World*, Berkeley, CA: University of California Press.

Benedict, Ruth, 1934, *Patterns of Culture*, Boston, MA: Houghton Mifflin.

Bénéï, Véronique, 2001, 'Teaching Nationalism in Maharashtra Schools' in V. Bénéï and C.J. Fuller (eds), *The Everyday State and Society in Modern India*, London: Hurst.

Bennet, L., 1983, *Dangerous Wives, Sacred Sisters: Social and Symbolic Roles of High Caste Women in Nepal*, New York: Columbia University Press.

Berktay, Fatmagul, 1998, *Women and Religion*, Montreal, QC: Black Rose.

Bernice, Carrol, 1987, 'Feminism and Pacifism: Historical and Theoretical Connections' in Ruth Roach Pierson (ed.), *Women and Peace*, Sydney: Croom Helm.

Bhabha, Homi K. (ed.), 1990, *Nation and Narration*, London: Routledge.

Bhargava, Rajeev, 1999, 'Introducing Multiculturalism' in Rajeev Bhargava, Amiya Kumar Bagchi and R. Sudarshan (eds), *Multiculturalism, Liberalism and Social Justice*, Delhi: Oxford University Press.

Bhattacharji, Sukumari, 1990, 'Motherhood in Ancient India', *Economic and Political Weekly*, 20 October.

Bhave, Y.G., 2000, *From the Death of Shivaji to the Death of Aurangjeb: The Critical Years*, New Delhi: Northern Book Centre.

Bidwai, Praful, Harbans Mukhia and Achin Vanaik (eds), 1996, *Religion, Religiosity and Communalism*, New Delhi: Manohar.

Blee, Kathleen, 2002, 'The Gendered Organization of Hate: Women in the U.S.

Ku Klux Klan' in Paola Bacchetta and Margaret Power (eds), *RightWingWomen: From Conservatives to Extremists Around theWorld*, London: Routledge.

Bollens, Scott A., 1999, *Urban Peace-Building in Divided Societies: Belfast and Johannesburg*, Boulder, CO: Westview Press.

Borges, Jorge Luis, 1999, *The Ethnographer*, Harmondsworth: Penguin.

Bose, Sugata and Ayesha Jalal (eds), 1997, *Modern South Asia: History, Culture and Political Economy*, Delhi: Oxford University Press.

Bourdieu, Pierre (ed.), 1990, *The Logic of Practice*, Cambridge: Polity Press.

——, 1991, *Language and Symbolic Power*, transl. Gino Raymond and Matthew Adamson, Cambridge: Polity Press.

——, 1998, *Practical Reason: On the Theory of Action*, Cambridge: Polity Press.

Bowman, Glenn, 2001, 'The Violence in Identity' in Bettina Schmidt and Ingo Schroder (eds), *Anthropology ofViolence and Conflict*, London: Routledge.

Boyden, Jo, 2001, *Social Healing in War Affected and Displaced Children*, Oxford: Refugee Studies Centre.

—— and Joanna de Berry (eds), 2004, *Children andYouth on the Frontline: Ethnography, Armed Conflict and Displacement*, NewYork: Berghahn.

Brass, Paul R., 1974, *Language, Religion and Politics in India*, Cambridge University Press.

——, 1991, *Ethnicity and Nationalism:Theory and Comparison*, London: Sage.

—— (ed.), 1996, *Riots and Pogroms*, NewYork University Press.

——, 1998, *Theft of an Idol: Text and Context in the Representation of Collective Violence*, Calcutta: Seagull.

——, 2003, *The Production of Hindu–MuslimViolence in Contemporary India*, Seattle, WA: University of Washington Press.

Breman, Jan, 1996, *Footloose Labour: Working in India's Internal Economy*, Cambridge University Press.

——, 1999, 'Ghettoization and Communal Politics: The Dynamics of Inclusion and Exclusion in the Hindutva Landscape' in Ramchandra Guha and Jonathan P. Parry (eds), *Institutions and Inequalities: Essays in Honour of André Béteille*, Delhi: Oxford University Press.

Bridenthal, Renate, Claudia Koonz and Susan Stuard (eds), 1987, *BecomingVisible: Women in European History*, Boston, MA: Houghton Mifflin.

Bunch, Charlotte, 1992, *Gender Violence: A Development and Human Rights Issue*, Dublin: ZIP Pamphlet Series.

Butalia, Urvashi, 1993, 'Community, State and Gender: On Women's Agency during Partition', *Economic and PoliticalWeekly*, 24 April.

———, 1996, 'Muslims and Hindus, Men and Women: Communal Stereotypes and the Partition of India' in Tanika Sarkar and Urvashi Butalia (eds), *Women and the Hindu Right: A Collection of Essays*, New Delhi: Kali for Women.

———, 1998, *The Other Side of Silence: Voices From the Partition of India*, New Delhi: Penguin.

Butler, Judith, 1990, *Gender Trouble: Feminism and the Subversion of Identity*, London: Routledge.

———, 1993, *Bodies That Matter: On the Discursive Limits of 'Sex'*, London: Routledge.

Byrne, Sean, 1997, *Growing Up in a Divided Society: The Influence of Conflict on Belfast Schoolchildren*, London: Associated University Presses.

Canetti, Elias, 1962, *Crowds and Power*, London: Golancz.

Chakraberty, Chandra, 1949, *The Cultural History of the Hindus*, Calcutta: Vijayakrishna.

Chakravarti, Uma, 1987, *The Delhi Riots: Three Days in the Life of a Nation*, New Delhi: Lancer.

———, 1998, *Rewriting History: The Life and Times of Pandita Ramabai*, New Delhi: Kali for Women.

———, 2002, 'Dreams Unlimited: The Make-Believe World of Advertisements' in Taisha Abraham (ed.), *Women and the Politics of Violence: Articulations and Re-articulations*, New Delhi: Shakti.

Chandavarkar, Rajnarayan, 1992, *The Origins of Industrial Capitalism in India: Business Strategies and the Working Classes in Bombay, 1900–1940*, Cambridge University Press.

Chandoke, Neera, 2003, *The Conceits of Civil Society*, Delhi: Oxford University Press.

Chandra, B., 1984, *Communalism in Modern India*, New Delhi: Vikas.

Chatterjee, B.B., 1967, *History of Riots in Rourkela: A Psychological Study*, New Delhi: Popular Book Services.

Chatterjee, Partha, 1994, *The Nation and its Fragments: Colonial and Postcolonial Histories*, Delhi: Oxford University Press.

Chaudhuri, Maitreyi, 1993, *Indian Women's Movement: Reform and Revival*, New Delhi: Sangam.

Chenoy, Anuradha, 1996, *Towards a New Politics: Agenda for a Third Force*, New Delhi: New Age.

———, 2002, *Militarism and Women in South Asia*, New Delhi: Kali for Women.

Chousalkar, Ashok, 1995, 'Communalism and Text Books in Maharashtra', *Towards Secular India*, 1, 1 (January–March).

Chowdhury, Indira, 1992, 'Mother India and Mother Victoria: Motherhood and Nationalism in Nineteenth-Century Bengal', *South Asia Research*, 12, 1, pp. 20–37.

——, 1998, *The Frail Hero and Virile History: Gender and the Politics of Culture in Colonial Bengal*, Delhi: Oxford University Press.

Colette, Pamela, 1998, 'Afghan Women in the Peace Process' in Lois A. Lorentzen and Jennifer Turpin (eds), *The Women War Reader*, New York University Press.

Cornwall, Andrea and Nancy Lindisfarne (eds), 1994, *Dislocating Masculinities: Comparative Ethnographies*, London: Routledge.

Cunningham, Karla J., 2003, 'Cross-Regional Trends in Female Terrorism', *Studies in Conflict and Terrorism*, 26, 3 (May–June), pp. 171–95.

Dandekar, Hemalata C., 1986, *Men to Bombay, Women at Home: Urban Influence on Sugao Village in Maharashtra (1942–1982)*, Ann Arbor, MI: University of Michigan Press.

Daniel, Valentine E., 1997, *Charred Lullabies: Chapters in an Anthropography of Violence*, Princeton University Press.

Das, Veena (ed.), 1992, *Mirrors of Violence: Communities, Riots and Survivors in South Asia*, Delhi: Oxford University Press.

——, 1995, *Critical Events: An Anthropological Perspective on Contemporary India*, Delhi: Oxford University Press.

——, 2001, 'Violence and Translation' in *After September 11*, Social Science Research Council, available online at <http://www.ssrc.org/sept11/essays/das.htm>.

Dattar, Chhaya (ed.), 1995, *The Struggle Against Violence*, Calcutta: Stree.

——, 1999, 'Non Brahmin Renderings of Feminism in Maharashtra: Is It a More Emancipatory Force', *Economic and Political Weekly*, 9 October.

Davies, Miranda, 1994, *Women and Violence: Realities and Responses Worldwide*, London: Zed Books.

D'Monte, Darryl, 2002, *Ripping the Fabric: The Decline of Mumbai and its Mills*, Delhi: Oxford University Press.

de Alwis, Malathi, 1998, 'Moral Mothers and Stalwart Sons: Reading Binaries in a Time of War' in Lois A. Lorentzen and Jennifer Turpin (eds), *The Women and War Reader*, New York University Press.

de Certeau, Michel, 1984, *The Practice of Everyday Life*, Berkeley, CA: University of California Press.

De Grazia, Victoria, 1992, *How Fascism Ruled Women: Italy, 1922–1945*, Berkeley, CA: University of California Press.

Desai, Radhika, 1999, 'Culturalism and Contemporary Right: Indian Bourgeoisie and Political Hindutva', *Economic and Political Weekly*, 20 March.

Dietrich, Gabriele, 1987, 'Vistas of Change' in Kamakshi Bhate, Lakshmi Menon and Manisha Gupte (eds), *In Search of Our Bodies: A Feminist Look at Women, Health and Reproduction in India*, Bombay: Shakti.

———, 1988, *Women's Movement in India: Conceptual and Religious Reflections*, Bangalore: Breakthrough.

———, 1992, *Reflections on the Women's Movement in India: Religion, Ecology, Development*, New Delhi: Horizon India.

———, 1994, 'Women and Religious Identities in India after Ayodya' in K. Bhasin, N. Said Khan and R. Menon (eds), *Against All Odds: Essays on Women, Religion and Development from India and Pakistan*, New Delhi: Kali for Women.

Dube, Leela, 1997, *Women and Kinship: Comparative Perspectives on Gender in South and South-East Asia*, New Delhi: Sage.

———, 2001, *Anthropological Explorations in Gender: Intersecting Fields*, New Delhi: Sage.

Eckert, Julia M., 2003, *The Charisma of Direct Action: Power Politics and the Shiv Sena*, Delhi: Oxford University Press.

Eco, Umberto, 1980, *The Name of the Rose*, Orlando, FL: Harcourt Brace.

Elst, Koenraad, 1991, *Ayodhya and After: Issues before Hindu Society*, New Delhi: Voice of India.

Engineer, A.A., 1984a, *Bhiwandi-Bombay Riots: Analysis and Documentation*, Bombay: Institute of Islamic Studies.

——— (ed.), 1984b, *Communal Riots in Post-Independence India*, New Delhi: Sangam.

———, 1988, *Delhi-Meerut Riots: Analysis, Compilation and Documentation*, New Delhi: Ajanta.

———, 1995, *Lifting the Veil: Communal Violence and Communal Harmony in Contemporary India*, New Delhi: Sangam.

——— (ed.), 1999, *Essays in Contemporary Politics of Identity, Religion and Secularism*, New Delhi: Ajanta.

———, 2004, *Communal Riots after Independence: A Comprehensive Account*, New Delhi: Shipra.

Enloe, Cynthia, 1989, *Gender, Armed Conflict and Political Violence*, Washington, DC: The World Bank.

Erikson, Erik H., 1968, *Identity, Youth and Crisis*, London: Faber and Faber.

Fanon, Frantz, 1986, *Black Skin, White Masks*, transl. Charles Lam Markmann, London: Pluto Press.

Feldhaus, Anne (ed.), 1998, *Images of Women in Maharashtrian Society*, Albany, NY: State University of New York Press.

Feldman, Shelley, 1993, 'Contradictions of Gender Inequality: Urban Class Formation in Contemporary Bangladesh' in Alice Clark (ed.), *Gender and Political Economy: Explorations in South Asian Systems*, Delhi: Oxford University Press.

Ferber, Abby L (ed.), 2003, *Home-Grown Hate: Gender and Organized Racism*, New York: Routledge.

Frankel, Francine R. and M.S.A. Rao (eds), 1990, *Dominance and State Power in Modern India: Decline of a Social Order*, vol. II, Delhi: Oxford University Press.

Freitag, Sandra B., 1989, *Collective Action and Community: Public Arenas and the Emergence of Communalism in North India*, Berkeley, CA: University of California Press.

Foucault, Michel, 1977, *Discipline and Punish: The Birth of the Prison*, transl. Alan Sheridan, London: Allen Lane.

——, 1980, *Power/Knowledge: Selected Interviews and Other Writings 1972–1977*, ed. Colin Gordon, New York: Pantheon.

Fuglesang, Andreas and Dale Chandler, 1993, *Participation as Process — Process as Growth: What We Can Learn from Grameen Bank*, Dhaka: Grameen Trust.

Fuller, C.J. and Veronique Benei (eds), 2001, *The Everyday State and Society in Modern India*, London: Hurst.

Gandhi, Nandita, 1996, *When the Rolling Pins Hit the Streets: Women in the Anti-Price Rise Movement in Maharashtra*, New Delhi: Kali for Women.

—— and Nandita Shah, 1991, *The Issues at Stake: Theory and Practice in the Contemporary Women's Movement in India*, New Delhi: Kali for Women.

Ganesh, Kamala, 1990, 'Mother Who is Not a Mother: In Search of the Great Indian Goddess', *Economic and Political Weekly*, 20 October.

Gardezi, Fauzia, 1990, 'Islam, Feminism and the Women's Movement in Pakistan: 1981–1991', *South Asia Bulletin*, 10, 2, pp. 18–24.

Gardner, Katy, 1995, *Global Migrants, Local Lives: Travel and Transformation in Rural Bangladesh*, Oxford: Clarendon Press.

Gedalof, Irene, 1999, *Against Purity: Rethinking Identity with Indian Feminisms*, New York: Routledge.

Ghadially, Rehana, 1988, *Women in Indian Society: A Reader*, New Delhi: Sage.

Ghosh, Anjan, 1996a, 'Symbolic Speech: Towards an Anthropology of Gossip', *Journal of the Indian Anthropological Society*, 31, 3, pp. 251–6.

——, 1996b, *The Stricture of Structure*, Calcutta: Centre for Studies in Social Sciences.

Ghosh, Partha S., 1999, *BJP and the Evolution of Hindu Nationalism: From Periphery to Centre*, New Delhi: Manohar.

Ghosh, S.K., 1986, *Communal Riots in India*, New Delhi: Ashish Publishing House.

Giddens, Anthony, 1977, *Studies in Social and Political Theory*, London: Hutchinson.

——, 1985, *A Contemporary Critique of Historical Materialism*, vol. II: *The Nation-State and Violence*, London: Polity Press.

——, 1994, *Beyond Left and Right: The Future of Radical Politics*, Cambridge: Polity Press.

—— and David Held, 1982, *Classes, Power and Conflict: Classical and Contemporary Debates*, Basingstoke: Macmillan.

Giles, Wenona and Jennifer Hyndman, 2004, *Sites of Violence: Gender and Conflict Zones*, Berkeley, CA: University of California Press.

Ginsburg, Faye, 1993, 'The Case of Mistaken Identity: Problems in Representing Women on the Right' in Caroline Brettell (ed.), *When They Read What We Write: The Politics of Ethnography*, Westport, CT: Bergin & Garvey.

Girard, Rene, 1977, *Violence and the Sacred*, Baltimore, MD: Johns Hopkins University Press.

Goetz, Anne Marie and Rina Sengupta, 1996, 'Who Takes Credit? Gender, Power and Control over Loan Use in Rural Credit Programmes in Bangladesh, *World Development*, 24, 1, pp. 45–53.

Gokhale, Balkrishna Govind, 1998, *The Fiery Quill: Nationalism and Literature in Maharashtra*, Bombay: Popular Prakashan.

Gokhale, Jayshree, 1993, *From Concessions to Confrontation: The Politics of an Indian Untouchable Community*, Bombay: Popular Prakashan.

Gopal, S., 1991, *Anatomy of a Confrontation: The Babri Masjid–Ram Janmabhumi Issue*, New Delhi: Penguin.

Goswami, Roshmi, 1999, 'Reinforcing Subordination: An Analysis of Women in Armed Conflict Situations', *Women in Action*, 3, 1999.

Gothoskar, Sujata, 1997, *Struggles of Women at Work*, New Delhi: Vikas.

Gottman, Jean, 1973, *The Significance of Territory*, Charlottesville, VA: University Press of Virginia.

Gough, Kathleen, 1955, 'Female Initiation Rites on the Malabar Coast', *Journal of the Royal Anthropological Institute*, 85, pp. 45–80.

Graburn N., 1987, 'Severe Child Abuse among the Canadian Inuit' in Nancy Scheper-Hughes (ed.), *Child Survival: Anthropological Perspectives on the Treatment and Maltreatment of Children*, Dordrecht: D. Reidel.

Grant Duff, James, 1873, *History of the Marathas*, Bombay: Times of India Press.

Greenhouse, Carol J., Elizabeth Mertz and Kay B. Warren (eds), 2002, *Ethnography in Unstable Places: Everyday Lives in Contexts of Dramatic Political Change*, Durham, NC: Duke University Press.

Grossmann, Atina, 1983, 'The New Woman: The New Family and the Rationalization of Sexuality', unpublished PhD diss., Rutgers University, New Brunswick, NJ.

Gupta, Dipankar, 1982, *Nativism in a Metropolis: The Shiv Sena in Bombay*, New Delhi: Manohar.

——, 1996, *The Context of Ethnicity: Sikh Identity in a Comparative Perspective*, Delhi: Oxford University Press.

Hansen, Thomas Blom, 1995, *Democratisation, Mass Politics and Hindu Identity: The Communalisation of Bombay*, Bordeaux: ECPR.

——, 1999, *The Saffron Wave: Democracy and Hindu Nationalism in Modern India*, Princeton University Press.

——, 2001, *Wages of Violence: Identity in Post Colonial Bombay*, Princeton University Press.

—— and Christophe Jaffrelot, 1998, *The BJP and the Compulsions of Politics in India*, Delhi: Oxford University Press.

Hasan, Zoya (ed.), 1994, *Forging Identities: Gender, Communities and the State*, New Delhi: Kali for Women.

Hegel, 1964, *Hegel's Political Writings*, transl. T.M. Knox, Oxford: Clarendon Press.

Helie-Lucas, Marie-Aimee, 1994, 'The Preferential Symbol for Islamic Identity: Women in Muslim Personal Laws' in Valentine M. Moghadam (ed.), *Identity Politics and Women: Cultural Reassertions and Feminisms in International Perspective*, Boulder, CO: Westview Press.

Hellmann-Rajanayagam, Dagmar, 1994, *The Tamil Tigers: Armed Struggle for Identity*, Stuttgart: F. Steiner.

Heuze, Gerard, 1995, 'Cultural Populism: The Appeal of the Shiv Sena' in Sujata Patel and Alive Thorner (eds), *Bombay: Metaphor for Modern India*, Bombay: Oxford University Press.

Hockney, Jenny and Allison James, 1993, *Growing Up and Growing Old: Ageing and Dependency in the Life Course*, London: Sage.

Hoefnagels, Marjo (ed.), 1977, *Repression and Repressive Violence*, Amsterdam: Swets and Zeitlinger.

Hoffman, Piotr, 1986, *Doubt, Time, Violence*, University of Chicago Press.

——, 1989, *Violence in Modern Philosophy*, University of Chicago Press.

Ismail, Qadri, 2000, 'Constituting the Nation, Contesting Nationalism: The Southern Tamil (Woman) and Separatist Tamil Nationalism in Sri Lanka' in Partha Chatterjee and Pradeep Jeganathan (eds), *Community, Gender and Violence*, New York: Columbia University Press.

Jaffrelot, Christophe, 1993, 'Hindu Nationalism: Strategic Syncretism in Ideology Building', *Economic and Political Weekly*, 20 March.

——, 1996, *The Hindu Nationalist Movement and Indian Politics, 1925–1990s*, London: Hurst.

Jain, Ranjana, 1992, *Family Violence in India*, New Delhi: Radiant.

James, E.O., 1959, *The Cult of the Mother Goddess: An Archaeological and Documentary Study*, London: Thames and Hudson.

Jayawardena, Kumari and Malathi de Alwis, 1996, *Embodied Violence: Communalising Women's Sexuality in South Asia*, New Delhi: Kali for Women.

Jeffery, Patricia and Amrita Basu (eds), 1998, *Appropriating Gender: Women's Activism and Politicized Religion in South Asia*, London: Routledge.

Jeffery, Roger and Patricia Jeffery, 1997, *Population, Gender and Politics: Demographic Change in Rural North India*, Cambridge University Press.

——, 1998, 'Gender, Community and the Local State in Bijnor, India' in Jeffery, Patricia and Amrita Basu (eds), 1998, *Appropriating Gender: Women's Activism and Politicized Religion in South Asia*, London: Routledge.

Jeganathan, Pradeep, 2000, 'A Space for Violence: Anthropology, Politics and the Location of a Sinhala Practice of Masculinity' in Partha Chatterjee and Pradeep Jeganathan (eds), *Community, Gender and Violence*, New York: Columbia University Press.

Jenkins, R., 1997, *Rethinking Ethnicity: Arguments and Explorations*, London: Sage.

Jenks, Chris (ed.), 1992, *The Sociology of Childhood: Essential Readings*, Aldershot: Gregg Revivals.

Jha, S.S., 1986, *Structure of Urban Poverty: The Case of Bombay Slums*, London: Sangam.

Joshi, Ram, 1995, 'Politics in Maharashtra: An Overview' in Usha Thakkar and Mangesh Kulkarni (eds), *Politics in Maharashtra*, New Delhi: Himalaya.

Kabeer, Naila, 1994, *Reversed Realities: Gender Hierarchies in Development Thought*, London: Verso.

——, 1998, 'Money Can't Buy Me Love? Re-evaluating Gender, Credit and Empowerment in Rural Bangladesh', *IDS Discussion Paper*, no. 363, Brighton: University of Sussex, Institute of Development Studies.

———, 2001, *Bangladeshi Women Workers and Labour Market Decisions: The Power to Choose*, New Delhi: Vistaar.

Kakar, Sudhir, 1978, *The Inner World: A Psychoanalytic Study of Childhood and Society in India*, Delhi: Oxford University Press.

———, 1996, *The Colours of Violence: Cultural Identities, Religion and Conflict*, Delhi: Oxford University Press.

Kandiyoti, Deniz, 1988, 'Bargaining With Patriarchy', *Gender and Society*, vol. 2, 3, pp. 274–90.

———, 1991a, 'Gender, Power and Contestation: "Bargaining with Patriarchy" Revisited' in C. Jackson and R. Pearson (eds), *Divided We Stand: Gender Analysis of Development*, London: Routledge.

———, 1991b, 'Identity and its Discontents: Women and the Nation', *American Journal of Political Science*, 34.

Kapur, Ratna, 1992, 'Feminism, Fundamentalism and Rights Rhetoric in India', *Women Against Fundamentalisms*, 4 (1992–3), pp. 38–9.

Karve, Irawati, 1990, *Kinship Organization in India*, New Delhi: Munshiram, 3rd edn.

Katzenstein, Mary Fainsod, 1979, *Ethnicity and Equality: The Shiv Sena Party and Preferential Policies in Bombay*, Ithaca, NY: Cornell University Press.

———, Uday Mehta and Usha Thakkar, 1998, 'The Rebirth of the Shiv Sena in Maharashtra: The Symbiosis of Discursive and Institutional Power' in Amrita Basu and Atul Kohli (eds), *Community Conflicts and the State in India*, Delhi: Oxford University Press.

Keiser, Lincoln, 1969, *The Vice Lords: Warriors of the Streets*, London: Holt, Rinehart and Winston.

Kim, Anne, 1991, *Face to Face: The Street Children of Bukit Ho Swee*, Singapore: Landmark Books.

Kim, Sebastian, 2003, *In Search of Identity: Debates on Religious Conversion in India*, Delhi: Oxford University Press.

Kishwar, Madhu, 1984, 'Gangster Rule', *Manushi*, 27.

———, 1990, 'In Defence of Our Dharma' *Manushi*, 60.

———, 1998, *Religion at the Service of Nationalism and Other Essays*, Delhi: Oxford University Press.

———, 1999, *Off the Beaten Track: Rethinking Gender Justice for Indian Women*, Delhi: Oxford University Press.

——— and Vanita, Ruth (eds), 1984, *In Search of Answers: Indian Women's Voices From Manushi*, London: Zed Books.

Kleinman, Arthur, Veena Das and Margaret Lock, 1997, *Social Suffering*, Berkeley, CA: University of California Press.

Koithara, Verghese, 1999, *Society, State and Security: The Indian Experience*, New Delhi: Sage.

Kolenda, Pauline, 1982, 'Pox and the Terror of Childlessness: Images and Ideas of the Smallpox Goddess in a North Indian Village' in James Preston (ed.), *Mother Worship: Themes and Variations*, Chapel Hill, NC: University of North Carolina Press.

Komarovsky, Mirra, 1971, *The Unemployed Man and His Family*, New York: Arno Press.

Kondo, Dorienne K., 1990, *Crafting Selves: Power, Gender and Discourses of Identity in a Japanese Workplace*, University of Chicago Press.

Kondos, Vivienne, 1986, 'Images of the Fierce Goddess and Portrayals of Hindu Women', *Contributions to Indian Sociology*, 20, 2, pp. 173–88.

Koonz, Claudia, 1988, *Mothers in the Fatherland: Women, the Family and Nazi Politics*, Reading: Cox & Wyman.

Korbin, J.E., 2003, 'Children, Childhoods and Violence', *Annual Review of Anthropology*, 32, pp. 431–46.

Kosambi, Meera, 1986, *Bombay in Transition: The Growth and Social Ecology of a Colonial City, 1880–1980*, Stockholm: Almqvist & Wiksell.

—— (ed.), 2000, *Intersections: Socio-Cultural Trends in Maharashtra*, London: Sangam.

Kotlowitz, Alex, 1992, *There are No Children Here: The Story of Two Boys Growing Up in the Other America*, New York: Anchor Books.

Kumar, Radha, 1993, *The History of Doing: An Illustrated Account of Movements for Women's Rights and Feminism in India, 1800–1990*, New Delhi: Kali for Women.

Kumari, Jayawardena, 1986, *Feminism and Nationalism in the Third World*, London: Zed Books.

Kurtz, S.N., 1992, *All the Mothers are One: Hindu India and the Cultural Reshaping of Psychoanalysis*, New York: Columbia University Press.

Laclau, Ernesto, 1990, *New Reflections on the Revolution of Our Time*, London: Verso.

Laine, James W., 2001, *The Epic of Shivaji: Kavindra Paramananda's 'Sivabharata'*, New Delhi: Orient Longman.

——, 2003, *Shivaji: Hindu King in Islamic India*, New York: Oxford University Press.

Lakshmi, C.S., 1990, 'Mother, Mother-Community and Mother-Politics in Tamil Nadu', *Economic and Political Weekly*, 20 October.

Lama-Rewal, Stephanie Tawa, 2001, 'Fluctuating, Ambivalent Legitimacy of Gender as a Political Category', *Economic and PoliticalWeekly*, 28 April.

Lane-Poole, Stanley, 1893, *Aurangzib*, Oxford: Clarendon Press.

Laslett, Peter (ed.), 1972, *Household and Family In Past Time: Comparative Studies in the Size and Structure of the Domestic Group over the Last Three Centuries in England, France, Serbia, Japan and Colonial North America, with further Materials fromWestern Europe*, London: Cambridge University Press.

Lele, Jayant, 1981, *Elite Pluralism and Class Rule: Political Development in Maharashtra*, University of Toronto Press.

———, 1995, 'Saffronisation of the Shiv Sena' in Sujata Patel and Alive Thorner (eds), *Bombay: Metaphor for Modern India*, Bombay: Oxford University Press.

Leslie, Julia and Mary McGee (eds), 2000, *Invented Identities:The Interplay of Gender, Religion and Politics in India*, Delhi: Oxford University Press.

Llewellyn, J.S., 1993, *The Arya Samaj as a Fundamentalist Movement:A Study in Comparative Fundamentalism*, New Delhi: Manohar.

Long, Patrick Du Phuoc with Laura Ricard, 1996, *The Dream Shattered: Vietnamese Gangs in America*, Boston, MA: Northeastern University Press.

Lopez, Marianne Exum, 1999, *When Discourses Collide: An Ethnography of Migrant Children at Home and in School*, NewYork: Peter Lang.

Low, Setha, 2003, *Behind the Gates: Life, Security and Pursuit of Happiness in Fortress America*, NewYork: Routledge.

——— and Denise Lawrence-Zuniga (eds), 2003, *Anthropology of Space and Place: Locating Culture*, Malden, MA: Blackwell.

Ludden, David, 1996, *Making India Hindu: Religion, Community and the Politics of Democracy in India*, Delhi: Oxford University Press.

Mach, Z., 1993, *Symbols, Conflict and Identity: Essays in Political Anthropology*, Albany, NY: State University of NewYork Press.

Madan, T.N., 1997, *Modern Myths, Locked Minds: Secularism and Fundamentalism in India*, Delhi: Oxford University Press.

Manchanda, Rita, 2001, 'Redefining and Feminising Security: Making a Difference in Security Policies', *Economic and PoliticalWeekly*, 27 October, pp. 4100–7.

Mani, Lata, 1998, *Contentious Traditions:The Debate on Sati in Colonial India*, Berkeley, CA: University of California Press.

Manshardt, Clifford (ed.), 1930, *Bombay Today and Tomorrow: Eight Lectures*, Bombay: D.B. Taraporevala.

Marglin, F.A., 1985, 'Types of Opposition in Hindu Culture' in J.B. Carman and F.A. Marglin (eds), *Purity and Auspiciousness in Indian Society*, Leiden: Brill.

Marquez, Patricia C., 1999, *The Street is My Home: Youth and Violence in Caracas*, Stanford University Press.

Mazumdar, Sucheta, 1995, 'Women on the March: Right-wing Mobilization in Contemporary India', *Feminist Review*, 49, pp.1–28.

McDonald, Ian, 1999, 'Physiological Patriots? The Politics of Physical Culture and Hindu Nationalism in India', *International Review for the Sociology of Sport*, 34, 4 (1 December).

McFeat, Tom, 1974, *Small Group Cultures*, Toronto, ON: Pergamon Press.

McGuire, John, Peter Reeves and Howard Brasted (eds), 1996, *Politics of Violence: From Ayodhya to Behrampada*, Thousand Oaks, CA: Sage.

Mead, M., 1929, *Coming of Age in Samoa: A Psychological Study of Primitive Youth for Western Civilisation*, London: Jonathan Cape.

Mehta, Sonal, 1986, 'We Know the Weapons Will Finally Turn on Us: Recurrent Anti-Muslim Riots in Ahmedabad', *Manushi*, 36.

Menon, Ritu and Kamla Bhasin, 1998, *Borders and Boundaries: Women in India's Partition*, New Delhi: Kali for Women.

—— and Nighat Said Khan (eds), 1995, *Against All Odds: Essays on Religion and Development from India and Pakistan*, New Delhi: Kali for Women.

Merleau-Ponty, Maurice, 1964, *Signs*, Evanston, IL: Northwestern University Press.

Mernissi, Fatima (ed.), 1987, *Beyond the Veil: Male-Female Dynamics in Modern Muslim Society*, Bloomington, IN: Indiana University Press.

Merry, Sally Engle, 1984, 'Rethinking Gossip and Scandal' in Donald Black (ed.), *Toward a General Theory of Social Control*, vol. I, New York: Academic Press.

Mies, Maria, 1979, *Towards a Methodology of Women's Studies*, The Hague: Institute of Social Studies.

Miller, W.B., 1958, 'Lower Class Culture as a Generating Milieu of Gang Delinquency', *Journal of Social Issues*, 14, 3, pp. 5–19.

Mitter, Sara S., 1991, *Dharma's Daughters: Contemporary Indian Women and Hindu Culture*, New Brunswick, NJ: Rutgers University Press.

Moghadam, Valentine M. (ed.), 1994, *Gender and National Identity: Women and Politics in Muslim Societies*, London: Zed Books.

Mohanty, Chandra Talpade, Ann Russo and Lourdes Torres, 1991, *Third World Women and the Politics of Feminism*, Bloomington, IN: Indiana University Press.

Montville, Joseph V. (ed.), 1991, *Conflict and Peacemaking in Multiethnic Societies*, Oxford: Maxwell Macmillan.

Moore, Henrietta L., 1988, *Feminism and Anthropology*, Cambridge: Polity Press.

Mukerji, Dhurjati Prasad, 1948, *Modern Indian Culture*, Calcutta: Hind Kitabs.

Mumtaz, Khawar, 1991, 'Khawateen Mahaz-e-Amal and the Sindhiani Tehrik: Two Responses to Political Development in Pakistan', *South Asia Bulletin*, 11, 1–2, pp. 101–9.

—— and Farida Shaheed, 1987, *Women of Pakistan: Two Steps Forward, One Step Back?*, London: Zed Books.

Murugkar, Lata, 1991, *Dalit Panther Movement in Maharashtra*, Bombay: Popular Prakashan.

Nandy, Ashis, 1980a, *At the Edge of Psychology: Essays in Politics and Culture*, Delhi: Oxford University Press.

——, 1980b, 'Woman versus Womanliness in India: An Essay in Cultural and Political Psychology' in Ashis Nandy, *At the Edge of Psychology: Essays in Politics and Culture*, Delhi: Oxford University Press.

——, 1983, *The Intimate Enemy: Loss and Recovery of the Self Under Colonialism*, Delhi: Oxford University Press.

——, 1998, *The Secret Politics of Our Desires*, New Delhi: Oxford University Press.

Narayan, Lata, 1994, 'Dynamics of Families Facing Societal Violence and Interventions' in *Family and Interventions: A Course Compendium*, Bombay: Tata Institute of Social Sciences.

Navlakha, Gautam, 2000, 'Downsizing National Security', *Economic and Political Weekly*, 13 May.

Nettl, J.P., 1967, *Political Mobilization: A Sociological Analysis of Methods and Concepts*, London: Faber.

Nicholas, Ralph W., 1982, 'The Village Mother in Bengal' in James Preston (ed.), *Mother Worship: Themes and Variations*, Chapel Hill, NC: University of North Carolina Press.

Nordstrom, Carolyn and Antonius C.G.M. Robben (eds), 1995, *Fieldwork Under Fire: Contemporary Studies of Violence and Survival*, Berkeley, CA: University of California Press.

Oberschall, 1973, *Social Conflict and Social Movements*, Englewood Cliffs, NJ: Prentice-Hall.

O'Flaherty, Wendy, 1981, *The Rig Veda: An Anthology*, London: Penguin.

O'Hanlon, Rosalind, 1994, *A Comparison Between Women and Men: Tarabai Shinde and the Critique of Gender Relations in Colonial India*, Madras: Oxford University Press.

Oliver, W., 2003, *The Violent Social World of Black Men*, San Francisco, CA: Jossey-Bass.

Olson, K. and L. Shopes, 1991, 'Crossing Boundaries, Building Bridges: Doing Oral History among Working Class Women and Men' in S.B. Gluck and D. Patai (eds), *Women's Words: The Feminist Practice of Oral History*, London: Routledge.

Omvedt, Gail, 1976, *Cultural Revolt in a Colonial Society: The Non Brahman Movement in Western India (1873 to 1930)*, Bombay: Scientific Socialist Education Trust.

——, 1980, *We Will Smash This Prison! Indian Women in Struggle*, London: Zed Books.

——, 1993, *Reinventing Revolution: New Social Movements and the Socialist Tradition in India*, New York: M.E. Sharpe.

——, 1995, *Dalit Visions: The Anti-Caste Movement and the Construction of an Indian Identity*, London: Sangam.

——, 1999, *Violence against Women: New Movements and New Theories in India*, New Delhi: Kali for Women.

Oppenheimer, A. and Norman Frohlich, 1978, *Modern Political Economy*, London: Prentice-Hall.

Overing, Joanna (ed.), 1985, *Reason and Morality*, London: Tavistock.

Ownby, David and Mary Somers Heidhues (eds), 1993, *Secret Societies Reconsidered: Perspectives on the Social History of Modern South China and Southeast Asia*, London: M.E. Sharpe.

Padgaonkar, Dileep (ed.), 1993, *When Bombay Burned: Reportage and Comments on the Riots and the Blasts from The Times of India*, New Delhi: UBSPD.

Pandey, Gyan, 1990, *The Construction of Communalism in Colonial North India*, Delhi: Oxford University Press.

—— (ed.), 1993, *Hindus and Others: The Question of Identity in India Today*, New Delhi: Viking.

——, 2000, 'In Defence of the Fragment: Writing about Hindu–Muslim Riots in India Today' in Ranajit Guha (ed.), *Subaltern Studies Reader*, New Delhi: Oxford University Press.

Pandian, Jacob, 1982, 'The Goddess Kannagi: A Dominant Symbol of South Indian Tamil Society' in James Preston (ed.), *Mother Worship: Themes and Variations*, Chapel Hill, NC: University of North Carolina Press.

Panini, M.N., 1991, *From the Female Eye: Accounts of Women Fieldworkers Studying their Own Communities*, New Delhi: Hindustan Publishing.

Panikkar, K.N., 2002, *An Agenda for Cultural Action and Other Essays*, New Delhi: Three Essays Press.

Park, Robert, 1950, *Race and Culture*, Glencoe, IL: The Free Press.

Parker, Andrew, M. Russo, D. Sommer and P. Yaeger (eds), 1992, *Nationalisms and Sexualities*, London: Routledge.

Parkin, David, 1986, 'Violence and Will' in David Riches (ed.), *The Anthropology of Violence*, Oxford: Blackwell.

Parsons, Talcott and Neil Smelser, 1956, *Economy and Society: A Study in the Integration of Economic and Social Theory*, London: Routledge and Kegan Paul.

Patai, Daphne and S.B. Gluck (eds), 1991, *Women's Words: The Feminist Practice of Oral History*, London: Routledge.

Patel, Sujata and Jim Masselos (eds), 2003, *Bombay and Mumbai: The City in Transition*, Delhi: Oxford University Press.

Pearson, Ruth, 1998, *Feminist Visions of Development Gender Analysis and Policy*, New York: Routledge.

Peto, Andrea, 1999, 'Introduction: Women in Politics' in Andrea Peto and Bela Rasky (eds), *Construction and Reconstruction: Women, Family and Politics in Central Europe 1945–1998*, Budapest: CEU, The Program on Gender and Culture, Austrian Science and Research Liaison Office, pp. 7–19.

Phadke, Y.D., 1975, *Social Reformers of Maharashtra*, New Delhi: Maharashtra Information Centre.

——, 1979, *Politics and Language*, Bombay: Himalaya.

——, 1990, *Social Movements in Maharashtra*, Bombay: Himalaya.

Pinto, Rochelle and Naresh Fernandes (eds), 1996, *Murder of the Mills: An Enquiry into Bombay's Cotton Textile Industry and its Workers*, a report by an independent fact-finding body, Mumbai: Lokshahi Hakk Sanghatana.

Poole, Ross, 1999, *Nation and Identity*, London: Routledge.

Poonacha, Veena, 1999, 'Exploring Differences: An Analysis of the Complexity and Diversity of the Contemporary Indian Women's Movement', *Australian Feminist Studies*, 14, 29.

Postman, Neil and Marty Asher (eds), 1994, *The Disappearance of Childhood*, New York: Vintage.

Preston, James, 1980, *Cult of the Goddess: Social and Religious Change in a Hindu Temple*, New Delhi: Vikas.

——, 1982, 'The Goddess Chandi as an Agent of Change' in James Preston (ed.), *Mother Worship: Themes and Variations*, Chapel Hill, NC: University of North Carolina Press.

Purandare, Vaibhav, 1999, *The Sena Story*, Mumbai: Business Publications.

Qadeer, Imrana and Zoya Hasan, 1987, 'Deadly Politics of the State and its Apologists', *Economic and Political Weekly*, 14 November, pp. 1946–9.

Rajan, Rajeshwari, 1993, *Real and Imagined Women: Gender, Culture and Postcolonialism*, London: Routledge.

Ram, P.R. (ed.), 1998, *Secular Challenge to Communal Politics: A Reader*, Mumbai: Vikas Adhyayan Kendra.

Ramdas, Lalita and Jaya Srivastava, 1985, 'From Day to Day: Envisioning Tomorrow', *Manushi*, 36.

Reardon, Betty, 1999, 'Women and Weapons: The Militarist Sexist Symbiosis' in Ingeborg Breines *et al.* (eds), *Towards a Women's Agenda for a Culture of Peace*, Paris: UNESCO.

Reinke, Jens, 1998, 'Does Solidarity Pay? The Case of Small Enterprise Foundation in South Africa', *Development and Change*, 29, 3, pp. 553–76.

Riches, David (ed.), 1986, *The Anthropology of Violence*, Oxford: Blackwell.

Ridd, Rosemary, 1986, *Caught Up in Conflict: Women's Responses to Political Strife*, Basingstoke: Macmillan Education in Association with the Oxford University Women's Studies Committee.

———, 1987, *Women and Political Conflict: Portraits of Struggle in Times of Crisis*, New York University Press.

Rodgers, Dennis, 2001, 'Making Danger a Calling: Anthropology, Violence and the Dilemmas of Participant Observation', *Crisis States Programme Working Paper*, no. 6, Development Research Centre, Development Studies Institute, London School of Economics.

Rouse, Shahnaz, 1986, 'Women's Movement in Pakistan: State, Class and Gender', *South Asia Bulletin*, 5, 1, pp. 30–7.

Roy, Kumkum, 1996, 'Where Women are Worshipped, There the Gods Rejoice' in Tanika Sarkar and Urvashi Butalia (eds), *Women and Right Wing Movements: Indian Experiences*, New Delhi: Kali for Women.

Ruddick, Sara, 1998, 'Women of Peace: A Feminist Construction' in Lois A. Lorentzen and Jennifer Turpin (eds), *The Women War Reader*, New York University Press.

Rude, George, 1980, *Ideology and Popular Protest*, New York: Pantheon.

Rushdie, Salman, 1991, *Imaginary Homelands: Essays and Criticisms, 1981–1991*, London: Granta.

Ryuichi, Narita, Yasushi Yamanouchi and J. Victor Koschmann, 1998, *Total War and 'Modernization'*, Ithaca, NY: Cornell University East Asia Series.

Saksena, N.K., 1990, *Communal Riots in India: 1919–1990*, Noida: Trishul Publications.

Samarath, Anil, 1975, *Shivaji and the Indian Movement: Saga of a Living Legend*, Bombay: Somaiya.

Sangari, Kumkum, 1996, 'Consent, Agency and the Rhetorics of Incitement' in T. V. Sathyamurthy (ed.), *Region, Religion, Caste, Gender and Culture in Contemporary India*, Delhi: Oxford University Press.

———, 2002, *Politics of the Possible: Essays on Gender, History, Narrative and Colonial English*, London: Anthem.

——— and Uma Chakravarti (eds), 1999, *From Myths to Markets: Essays on Gender*, New Delhi: Manohar.

——— and Suresh Vaid (eds), 1990, *Recasting History: Essays in Indian Colonial History*, New Brunswick, NJ: Rutgers University Press.

Sardesai, Rajdeep, 1995, 'The Shiv Sena's New Avatar: Marathi Chauvinism and Hindu Communalism' in Usha Thakkar and Mangesh Kulkarni (eds), *Politics in Maharashtra*, New Delhi: Himalaya.

Sarkar, Jadunath, 1992, *Shivaji and His Times*, London: Sangam.

Sarkar, Tanika, 1987, 'Nationalist Iconography: Image of Women in 19th Century Bengali Literature', *Economic and Political Weekly*, 21 November.

———, 1991, 'The Woman as Communal Subject: The Rashtrasevika Samiti and the Ramjanmabhoomi Movement', *Economic and Political Weekly*, 31 August.

———, 1996, 'Heroic Women, Mother Goddesses: Family and Organisation in Hindutva Politics' in Tanika Sarkar and Butalia, Urvashi (eds), *Women and the Hindu Right: A Collection of Essays*, Delhi: Kali for Women.

———, 1998, 'Orthodoxy, Cultural Nationalism and the Hindu Right' in Ruth Roach Pearson and Nupur Chaudhuri (eds), *Nation, Empire, Colony: Historicising Gender and Race*, Bloomington, IN: Indiana University Press.

———, 1999, 'The Gender Predicament of the Hindu Right' in K.N. Panikkar (ed.), *The Concerned Indian's Guide to Communalism*, New Delhi: Penguin.

———, 2001, *Hindu Wife and Hindu Nation: Gender, Religion and the Prehistory of Indian Nationalism*, London: Hurst.

———, Tapan Basu, Pradip Dutta and Sumit Sarkar, 1993, *Khaki Shorts, Saffron Flags: A Critique of the Hindu Right*, New Delhi: Orient Longman.

Sarkar, Tanika and Urvashi Butalia (eds), 1996, *Women and the Hindu Right: A Collection of Essays*, New Delhi: Kali for Women.

Sartre, Jean Paul, 1969, 'On Freedom', *New Left Review*.

Sassoon, Siegfried, 1945, *Siegfried's Journey*, London: Faber & Faber.

Savarkar, Vinayak Damodar, 1985, *Six Glorious Epochs of Indian History*, Bombay: Veer Savarkar Prakashan.

———, 1987, *Hindutva: Who is a Hindu?*, New Delhi: Bharti Sahitya Sadan.

Saxena, N.C., 1984, 'Nature and Origin of Communal Riots in India' in A.A. Engineer (ed.), *Communal Riots in Post-Independence India*, New Delhi: Sangam.

Scheper-Hughes, Nancy (ed.), 1987, *Child Survival: Anthropological Perspectives on the Treatment and Maltreatment of Children*, Dordrecht: D. Reidel.

—— and Peter Bourgois (eds), 2004, *Violence in War and Peace: An Anthology*, Oxford: Blackwell.

Schmidt, Bettina and Ingo Schroeder (eds), 2001, *Anthropology of Violence and Conflict*, London: Routledge.

Schuler, Margaret (ed.), 1992, *Freedom from Violence: Women's Strategies from around the World*, New York: DEF International.

Schwartzman, Helen, 2001, *Children and Anthropology*, Westport, CT: Bergin and Garvey.

Scott, David, 2000, 'Toleration and Historical Traditions of Difference' in Partha Chatterjee and Pradeep Jeganathan (eds), *Community, Gender and Violence*, New York: Columbia University Press.

Scott, James C., 1985, *Weapons of the Weak: Everyday Forms of Peasant Resistance*, London: Yale University Press.

——, 1990, *Domination and the Arts of Resistance: Hidden Transcripts*, New Haven, CT: Yale University Press.

Seabrook, Jeremy, 1987, *Life and Labour in a Bombay Slum*, London: Quartet.

Sen, Surendra Nath, 1977, *Foreign Biographies of Shivaji*, Calcutta: K.P. Bagchi.

Setalvad, Teesta, 1996, 'The Woman Shiv Sainik and Her Sister Swayamsevika' in Tanika Sarkar and Urvashi Butalia (eds), *Women and Right Wing Movements: Indian Experiences*, New Delhi: Kali for Women.

Shah, Nandita and Nandita Gandhi, 1992, *The Issues at Stake: Theory and Practice in the Contemporary Women's Movement in India*, New Delhi: Kali for Women.

Shaheed, Farida, 1994, 'Controlled or Autonomous: Identity and the Experiences of the Network of Women Living under Muslim Laws', *Signs*, 19, 4, pp. 997–1019.

—— and Khawar Mumtaz, 1990, 'The Rise of the Religious Right and its Impact on Women', *South Asia Bulletin*, 10, 2, pp. 9–17.

Sharma, Bela Rani, 1997, *Women, Marriage, Family Violence and Divorce*, Jaipur: Mangal Deep.

Sharma, Jyotirmaya, 2003, *Hindutva: Exploring the Idea of Hindu Nationalism*, New Delhi, Penguin.

Sharma, Kalpana, 1995, 'Chronicle of a Riot Foretold' in Sujata Patel and Alice Thorner (eds), *Bombay: Metaphor for Modern India*, Bombay: Oxford University Press.

Sharma, Sita Ram (ed.), 1995, *Anatomy of Communalism: Historical Perspectives on Communalism*, New Delhi: APH Publishing.

Sharoni, Simona, 1995, *Gender and the Israeli-Palestinian Accord: The Politics of Women's Resistance*, New York: Syracuse University Press.

——, 1996, 'Gender and the Israeli-Palestinian Accord: Feminist Approaches to International Politics' in Deniz Kandiyoti (ed.), *Gendering the Middle East: Emerging Perspectives*, London: I.B. Tauris, pp. 107–26.

——, 1998, 'Gendering Conflict and Peace in Israel/Palestine and the North of Ireland', *Millenium Journal of International Studies*, 27, 4, pp. 1061–89.

Shopes, Linda, 1994, *Making Sense of Oral History*, <http://historymatters.gmu.edu/mse/oral/oral.pdf>.

Simmel, Georg, 1950, 'Secrecy' in Kurt H. Wolff (ed.), *The Sociology of Georg Simmel*, New York: The Free Press.

Sinha, Mrinalini, 1995, *Colonial Masculinity: The Manly Englishman and the Effeminate Bengali in the Late Nineteenth Century*, Manchester University Press.

Smart, Josephine and Alan Smart, 1998, 'Transnational Social Networks and Negotiated Identities in Interactions between Hong Kong and China', *Comparative Urban and Community Research*, vol. VI, New Brunswick, NJ: Transaction Publishers.

——, 2004, 'Urbanization and the Global Perspective', *Annual Review of Anthropology*, 32, pp. 263–85.

Smelser, Neil, 1962, *Theory of Collective Behaviour*, London: Routledge and Kegan Paul.

Smyth, Marie, 1998, *Half the Battle: Understanding the Effects of the 'Troubles' on Children and Young People in Northern Ireland*, Londonderry: INCORE.

——, 2001, *Working with Children and Young People in Violently Divided Societies: Papers from South Africa and Northern Ireland*, Londonderry: INCORE.

Sood, Sushma, 1990, *Violence against Women*, Jaipur: Arihant.

Southall, Aidan, 2000, *The City in Time and Space*, New York: Cambridge University Press.

Spivak, Gayatri Chakravorty, 1987, 'A Literary Representation of the Subaltern: Mahasweta Devi's "Stanadayini"' in Ranajit Guha (ed.), *Subaltern Studies: Writings on South Asian History and Society*, vol. V, Delhi: Oxford University Press.

——, 1998, 'Can the Subaltern Speak?' in Cary Nelson and Larry Grossberg (eds), *Marxism and the Interpretation of Culture*, Chicago, IL: University of Illinois Press.

——, 1999, *A Critique of Postcolonial Reason: Toward a History of the Vanishing Present*, Cambridge, MA: Harvard University Press.

Staub, Ervin, 1989, *The Roots of Evil: The Origins of Genocide and Other Group Violence*, Cambridge University Press.

Stivers, Camilla, 1993, 'Reflections of the Role of Personal Narrative in Social Change', *Signs: Journal of Women in Culture and Society*, 18, 2, pp. 408–25.

Subbayya, Rajyashree, 1986, *An Ethnolinguistic Survey of Dharavi, a Slum in Bombay*, Mysore: Central Institute of Indian Languages.

Takakhav, N.S., 1998, *Life of Shivaji*, New Delhi: Rishabh.

Tambiah, Stanley J., 1996, *Levelling Crowds: Ethnonationalist Conflicts and Collective Violence in South Asia*, Berkeley, CA: University of California Press.

Tarrow, Sidney, 1994, *Power in Movement: Social Movements, Collective Action and Politics*, Cambridge University Press.

Taussig, Michael, 2002, 'Culture of Terror – Space of Death: Roger Casement's Putumayo Report and the Explanation of Torture' in Alex Hinton (ed.), *Genocide: An Anthropological Reader*, Oxford: Blackwell.

Tessler, Mark *et al.*, 1999, 'Further Tests of the Women and Peace Hypothesis: Evidence from Cross National Survey Research', *The Middle East International Centre Quarterly*, 43, pp. 519–31.

Thapan, Meenakshi, 1998, *Embodiment: Essays in Gender and Identity*, Delhi: Oxford University Press.

Thapar, Romila, 1993, *Interpreting Early India*, Delhi: Oxford University Press.

——, 2000, *History and Beyond*, Delhi: Oxford University Press.

Tharu, Susie, 1993, *Women Writing in India: 600 BC to the Present*, London: Pandora.

Tilly, Charles, 1986, *The Contentious French: Four Centuries of Popular Struggle*, Cambridge, MA: Belknap Press.

——, 2003, *Collective Violence*, Cambridge University Press.

Turner, Victor, 1974, *Dramas, Fields and Metaphors: Symbolic Action in Human Society*, Ithaca, NY: Cornell University Press.

Tuttle, William M., 1993, *Daddy's Gone to War: The Second World War in the Lives of America's Children*, New York: Oxford University Press.

Uberoi, Patricia, 1996, *Social Reform, Sexuality and the State*, New Delhi: Sage.

Vagts, A., 1967, *The Military Attaché*, Princeton University Press.

Vanaik, Achin, 1997a, *Communalism Contested: Religion, Modernity and Secularization*, New Delhi: Vistaar.

——, 1997b, *The Furies of Indian Communalism: Religion, Modernity and Seculariza-tion*, London: Verso.

van der Veer, Peter, 1994, *Religious Nationalism: Hindus and Muslims in India*, Lon-don: University of California Press.

——, 1996, 'Writing Violence' in David Ludden (ed.), *Making India Hindu: Reli-gion, Community and the Politics of Democracy in India*, Delhi: Oxford University Press.

van Wersch, Hubert W.N., 1984, *Bombay Textile Strike (1982–83)*, Bombay: Ox-ford University Press.

Verkaaik, Oskar, 2004, *Migrants and Militants: Fun, Violence and Islam in Pakistan*, Princeton University Press.

Vidal, Denis, Gilles Tarabout and Eric Meyer (eds), 2003, *Violence, Non-violence: Some Hindu Perspectives*, New Delhi: Manohar.

Vigil, J.D., 1996, 'Street Baptism: Chicano Gang Initiation', *Human Organization*, 55, pp. 149–53.

——, 2003, 'Urban Violence and Street Gangs', *Annual Review of Anthropology*, 32, pp. 225–42

Wadley, Susan, 1975, *Shakti: Power in the Conceptual Structure of Karimpur Religion*, University of Chicago Press.

—— (ed.), 1980, *The Powers of Tamil Women*, New York: Maxwell School of Citi-zenship and Public Affairs.

Weber, Max, 1968, *On Charisma and Institution Building: Selected Papers*, University of Chicago Press.

Weiner, Myron, 1978, *Sons of the Soil: Migration and Ethnic Conflict in India*, Prin-ceton University Press.

Weitz, Margaret Collins, 1995, *Sisters in the Resistance: How Women Fought to Free France (1940–1945)*, New York: J. Wiley.

Welch, Claude E., 1980, *Anatomy of a Rebellion*, Albany, NY: State University of New York Press.

West, Harry, 2004, 'Girls with Guns: Narrating the Experience of War of FRE-LIMO's "Female Detachment" ' in Jo Boyden and Joanna de Berry (eds), *Chil-dren and Youth on the Frontline: Ethnography, Armed Conflict and Displacement*, New York: Berghahn.

White, Sarah C., 1992, *Arguing with the Crocodile: Gender and Class*, Dhaka: The University Press.

Whyte, William Foote, 1981, *Street Corner Society: The Social Structure of an Italian Slum*, University of Chicago Press.

Woodward, Betty, 1977, 'Moral Reasoning and Repressive Violence' in Marjo Hoefnagels (ed.), *Repression and Repressive Violence*, Amsterdam: Swets and Zeitlinger.

Wright, Susan (ed.), 1994, *The Anthropology of Organizations*, London: Routledge.

Yuval-Davis, Nira and Floya Anthias, 1989, *Woman-Nation-State*, London: Macmillan.

———, 1992, *Racialized Boundaries: Race, Nation, Gender, Colour and Class and the Anti-Racist Struggle*, London: Routledge.

Zelliot, E., 1996, *From Untouchable to Dalit: Essays on the Ambedkar Movement*, New Delhi: Manohar.

——— and M., Berntsen, 1992, *The Experience of Hinduism: Essays on Religion in Maharashtra*, New Delhi: Sri Satguru Publications.

Zimring, Franklin E., 1998, *American Youth Violence*, New York: Oxford University Press.

Zizek, Slavoj, 1989, *The Sublime Object of Ideology*, New York: Verso.

JOURNALS AND REPORTS

Bombay Riots:The Myths and Realities, a report by the Lokshahi Hakk Sangathana and Committee for the Protection of Democratic Rights, Bombay, March 1993.

Bombay's Shame: A Report on Bombay Riots, Ekta Samiti, Bombay, 1993.

BRAC Evaluation Department Report, 1998.

Cehat (NGO) Medical Report, *The Psychological Effects of Homelessness in Children*, 2000.

'Khoj: A Report on Children Affected by the Bombay Riots', *Communalism Combat*, 1999.

Newspaper reports from *Financial Express*, *The Indian Express*, *The Hindustan Times*, *The Telegraph*, *The Times of India*, *The Deccan Herald*, *Illustrated Weekly*, *Blitz* and *Anandabazar Patrika*.

Report of the Sri Krishna Commission (vols I and II), *Appointed for Enquiry into the Riots at Mumbai during December 1992 and January 1993*, 1998.

Salokha, *A Report on Conflict: A Study of Nine Social Development Projects in Mumbai*, compiled by Kalyani Talvelkar Research Unit, Nirmala Niketan School of Social Work, 1999.

SEWA (Self Employed Women's Association) report on communal violence, *Manushi*, 33, 1986.

'The Bombay Riots', Bombay Gazette Steam Press, 1874.

'The Bombay Riots of February 1874', reprinted from *Times of India*, Times of India Printing Press, Bombay, 1893.

'The Bombay Riots of August 1893', reprinted from *Times of India*, Times of India Printing Press, Bombay, 1893.

The Police Report on the Bombay Riots of February 1929.

The People's Verdict: An Enquiry into the December 1992 and January 1993 Riots by The Indian People's Human Rights Tribunal, 1993.

UNICEF, *Annual Report in Geneva*, 1995.

Witnesses Speak: A Compilation of Evidence Produced before the Srikrishna Commission of the Enquiry into the December 1992 and January 1993 Mumbai Riots, published by Jyoti Punwani, 1998.

World Bank, *World Bank Overview of Child Soldiering*, Monograph no. 82, 2003.

INDEX

Abu Azmi, 16, 107
Afghanistan, 167
Afzal Khan, 129, 159
Ambedkar Nagar, 136
Andhra Pradesh, 9, 177
anthropology: 12, 15–18; and violence, 17–18, 187–8
anti-colonial movement, 8–9, 157
anti-price-rise movement, 6, 7
anti-rape movement, 7
Army, 135, 164
Assam, 177
Aurangabad, 36
Ayatollah Khomeini, 57
Ayodhya, 5, 25, 80

Babri Masjid, 5, 9, 13, 25, 46, 49, 83, 144
Bandra, 13
Bangladesh and Bangladeshis, 9, 34, 153, 177
Bapat, S. (police commissioner), 55–6, 61
Bengal, 157
Bharatiya Janata Party (BJP), 5, 37–8, 39
Bhayander, 83, 87, 96, 99–100, 163
Bhiwandi, 38
Bihar, 9
Bombay, *see* Mumbai
Border, 164
Bose, Subhas, 162
boys: 112–13; and their fathers, 118; and the future, 113, 121, 124–6, 128, 141, 151, 152, 153; and 'gangs', 113, 120, 133–6, 138–41, 152, 181; and girls, 120–7, 151; and Hindus/Hinduism/Hindutva, 113, 116–17, 122, 124–5, 127, 128–30, 133, 137, 140, 141–8, 148–50, 151–2; and 'knowledge', 113, 141–8; and Mahila Aghadi, 117–19,

131, 134; and marriage, 113, 122, 124–5, 153; and their mothers/grandmothers, 113, 115–20, 131–2, 134, 135, 136, 137, 151, 152, 160, 175–6; and Mumbai riots, 115–16, 136–8, 152; and Muslims, 116, 120, 125–6, 129–30, 132, 135–6, 137–8, 140, 141–8, 148–50, 152; and NGOs, 113, 145–7, 148–50; and school, 113–14, 141–8; and Shiv Sena/*shakha*, 113, 116, 121–2, 126–7, 127–32, 133–4, 139–41, 148–50, 150–2; and violence, 114, 116, 120, 124–6, 131–2, 140–1, 147–8, 150, 153, 181
Buddhists, 13, 162
Byculla, 153

castes, 4, 7, 30–1, 69–70, 172
Chaturwadi, 14, 16, 184
children: 112–14, 124, 132, 133, 150–4, 180, 181; and Mumbai riots, 115–16; and schools, 141–8; *see also* boys, girls, youths
Christians, 32, 92, 96, 97, 101, 149, 186
class, 7–8, 11, 31, 69–70, 172
communal violence: 1–3, 5, 13, 38, 49, 61, 68–73, 80–1, 115, 144; *see also* under Mahila Aghadi, Shiv Sena
communists, 4, 25, 32, 38
Congress party, 4, 27, 37

Dalit Panthers, 9
Dalits, 7
Datta, Madhusree, 93–4
Delhi, *see* New Delhi
Deshmukh (deputy police commissioner), 56 n2
Dighe, Anand, 167

217